Caprial's Desserts

Caprial's Desserts

Caprial Pence
and Melissa Carey

TEN SPEED PRESS
Berkeley • Toronto

to Heather, Jenny, Paul, and Lisa.
thank you for helping to create
such a beautiful book.
—CAPRIAL

to my Grandmother, from whom
I inherited my sweet tooth and
love of making desserts.
—MELISSA

Ten Speed Press
P.O. Box 7123
Berkeley, California 94707
www.tenspeed.com

Distributed in Australia by Simon and Schuster Australia, in Canada by Ten Speed Press Canada, in New Zealand by Southern Publishers Group, in South Africa by Real Books, in Southeast Asia by Berkeley Books, and in the United Kingdom and Europe by Airlift Book Company.

Cover and text design by Toni Tajima
Photography by Paul Yonchek
Developmental editing and writing assistance by Jennifer Morrison
Food styling by Heather Bowen, with assistance from Lisa Lanxon

The Library of Congress has cataloged the hardcover edition as follows:
Pence, Caprial.
    Caprial's Desserts/Caprial Pence and Melissa Carey.
      p.cm.
    Includes index.
    ISBN 1-58008-285-8 (alk. paper)
      1. Desserts. I. Carey, Melissa. II. Title.
TX773.P433 2001
641.8'6—dc21   2001041057

ISBN (paper): 1-58008-624-1
First printing paperback edition, 2004
Printed in Hong Kong

1 2 3 4 5 6 7 8 9 10 – 08 07 06 05 04

contents

Acknowledgments ix

Introduction 1

Cakes 13

Old-Fashioned Chocolate Cake (Master Recipe) 16
Chocolate Buttermilk Cake (Master Recipe) 17
Flourless Chocolate Cake (Master Recipe) 20
    Dark and White Chocolate–Hazelnut Cake 22
    Flourless Dried Cherry–Chocolate Cake 22
    Individual Chocolate-Raspberry Cakes 23
Yellow Butter Cake (Master Recipe) 24
    Citrus-Scented Cake 25
    Poppyseed Cake 25
Genoise (Master Recipe) 26
    Chocolate Genoise 27
    Almond Genoise 27
Angel Food Cake (Master Recipe) 30
    Coconut Angel Food Cake 31
    Hazelnut Angel Food Cake 31
    Chocolate Angel Food Cake 31
    Orange Angel Food Cake 31
Lemon Pound Cake (Master Recipe) 32
    Chocolate-Cherry Pound Cake 33
    Fresh Berry and Lemon Pound Cake 33
Gingerbread (Master Recipe) 35
    Pear-Lemon Gingerbread with Pear-Wine Syrup 36
    Gingery Pecan Gingerbread 36
Sour Cream Cheesecake (Master Recipe) 37
    Berry Cheesecake 38
    Individual Mocha-Orange Cheesecakes 39
    Chocolate Cheesecake 39
Carrot Cake (Master Recipe) 40
    Zucchini Cake 41

* * *

Whipped Cream Frosting (Master Recipe) 42
    Orange Whipped Cream Frosting 43
    Chocolate Whipped Cream Frosting 43
Chocolate Sour Cream Frosting (Master Recipe) 44
    Mocha Sour Cream Frosting 45
    Orange-Chocolate Sour Cream Frosting 45
Cream Cheese Frosting (Master Recipe) 46
    Chocolate Cream Cheese Frosting 46
Ganache 47
Italian Buttercream (Master Recipe) 48
    Almond Italian Buttercream 49
    Lemon Italian Buttercream 49
    Ginger Italian Buttercream 49
Quick Buttercream (Master Recipe) 52
    Espresso–Shaved Chocolate Buttercream 53
    Brown Sugar Buttercream 53
    Mint Buttercream 53
    White Chocolate Quick Buttercream 53
Pastry Cream (Master Recipe) 54
    Coconut Pastry Cream 55
    Chocolate Pastry Cream 55
White Chocolate Mousse Filling 56
Chocolate Mousse Filling 57
Caramel Sauce 58
Caramel-Apple Sauce 59
Chocolate Sauce 62
Berry Sauce 63
Lemon Curd (Master Recipe) 64
    Orange Curd 64

cobblers, pies, and tarts 67

Pâte Brisée 70

Chocolate Pâte Brisée 70

Nut Pâte Brisée 71

Pâte Sucrée 71

Cappy's Pie Crust 72

Shortbread Crust (Master Recipe) 74

   Graham Shortbread Crust 75

   Chocolate Shortbread Crust 75

   Orange-Pecan Shortbread Crust 75

Three-Nut Crust 76

Cornmeal Crust 76

Crumb Crust 77

Chocolate Cookie Crumb Crust 77

Streusel Topping 78

Red Wine Syrup 78

Crème Fraîche 79

✳ ✳ ✳

Berry Cobbler (Master Recipe) 82

   Cherry Cobbler 83

   Peach-Tuaca Cobbler 83

Fruit Crisp (Master Recipe) 84

   Oatmeal-Nut Crisp 85

   Individual Fruit Crisps 85

Summer Berry Pie (Master Recipe) 86

   Peach-Raspberry Pie 87

   Blueberry-Citrus Pie 87

Apple Pie (Master Recipe) 88

   Apple-Sour Cream Pie 89

   Maple-Bourbon Apple Pie 89

Pear Pie (Master Recipe) 90

   Pear-Cranberry Pie 91

   Pear–Dried Cherry Pie 91

Cranberry-Orange-Nut Pie (Master Recipe) 94

   Cranberry Pie with Dried Fruit and Hazelnuts 95

Strawberry-Rhubarb Pie (Master Recipe) 96

   Rhubarb-Raspberry Pie 98

   Rhubarb-Apple Pie 98

Banana Cream Pie (Master Recipe) 99

   Chocolate Cream Pie 101

   Coconut Cream Pie 101

Lime Curd Pie with Brown Sugar Meringue
   (Master Recipe) 103

   Lemon Curd Tart 105

   Orange-Ginger Pie with Brown Sugar Meringue 105

Fresh Fruit Tart (Master Recipe) 106

   Mascarpone Fresh Fruit Tart 107

Caramel-Pear Tart with a Graham Shortbread Crust
   (Master Recipe) 109

   Caramel-Apple-Nut Tart 111

   Strawberry-Caramel Tart 111

Italian Plum Tart (Master Recipe) 112

   Chocolate-Crusted Peach-Almond Tart 113

   Strawberry-Almond Tart 113

Caramel-Walnut Tart (Master Recipe) 114

   Fig-Hazelnut-Caramel Tart 115

   Bourbon-Pecan Tart with a Chocolate Crust 115

Lemon Cream Tart (Master Recipe) 116

   Dreamsicle Tart 117

cookies 119

Piped Butter Cookies (Master Recipe) 121

   Piped Chocolate Cookies 122

   Spiced Almond Sticks 123

Dark and White Chocolate Chunk Cookies
   (Master Recipe) 125

   Almond and White Chocolate Cookies with Lemon 126

   Oatmeal Cookies 126

Jenny's Great-Grandma's Gingersnaps (Master Recipe) 127

   Apple-Gingery Gingersnaps 128

   Gingersnap-Mascarpone Sandwiches 128

Rolled Sugar Cookies (Master Recipe) 130
  Chocolate Windowpane Cookies 131
  Orange-Spice Glazed Cookies 131
Mom's Peanut Butter Cookies (Master Recipe) 132
  Peanut Butter Everything Cookies 133
Chocolate-Hazelnut-Caramel Bars (Master Recipe) 134
  Poached Pear–Pecan Bars 135
Meringue Cookies (Master Recipe) 136
  Chocolate Meringue Cookies 137
  Almond-Coconut Meringue Cookies 137
Chocolate Brownies (Master Recipe) 138
  Double Chocolate–Cream Cheese Brownies 139
  Brownie Mousse Cake 139
Bourbon Blonde Brownies (Master Recipe) 140
  Bistro Chocolate-Bourbon Blonde Brownie Sundaes 141
  Tropical Rum Brownies 141
Vanilla Bean Shortbread Cookies (Master Recipe) 142
  Pecan-Espresso Shortbread Cookies 143
  Candied Ginger–Coconut Shortbread Cookies 143
Almond-Anise Biscotti (Master Recipe) 144
  White Chocolate–Pistachio Biscotti 145
  Orange-Hazelnut Biscotti 145

Breakfast Sweets 147

Spice Cake Doughnuts (Master Recipe) 149
  Candied Ginger–Orange Cake Doughnuts 152
  Chocolate-Espresso Doughnuts 152
Raised Doughnuts (Master Recipe) 153
  Raised Doughnuts Glazed with Ganache 155
  Lemon Doughnuts with Vanilla Sugar 155
Cinnamon Rolls (Master Recipe) 156
  Pecan Sticky Buns 157
  Dried Fruit Cinnamon Rolls 157
Hazelnut-Pear Scones (Master Recipe) 158
  Orange-Almond Scones 159

  Espresso-Chocolate Scones 159
  Summer Scones 159
  Peach-Raspberry Scones 159
Cream Cheese Pinwheels (Master Recipe) 161
  Raspberry-Almond Cream Cheese Pinwheels 162
  Apricot–Cream Cheese Pinwheels 162
Basic Muffins (Master Recipe) 163
  Blueberry Muffins 164
  Raspberry–Cream Cheese Muffins 164
  Fresh Peach Muffins 164
  Banana-Nut Muffins 164
  Lemon Muffins 164
Espresso Coffee Cake (Master Recipe) 166
  Caramel Coffee Cake 167
  Apricot-Almond Coffee Cake 168
  Fresh Fruit Coffee Cake 168
Zucchini Bread (Master Recipe) 169
  Zucchini Muffins 169
  Carrot Bread 170
Orange-Caramel Pull-Apart Bread 171
Missy's Granola 173

Puddings, Custards, and Mousses 175

Chocolate Pudding (Master Recipe) 178
  Mocha Pudding 179
  Chocolate and White Chocolate Chunk Pudding 179
Caramel Pudding (Master Recipe) 180
  Black and Tan 181
Vanilla Pudding 182
Chocolate Bread Pudding (Master Recipe) 184
  Chocolate-Raspberry Bread Pudding 185
  Chocolate and Brandied Dried Cherry
    Bread Pudding 186
  Hazelnut–White Chocolate Bread Pudding 186

Vanilla Bread Pudding (Master Recipe) 187
    Lemon-Almond Bread Pudding 188
    Apple Bread Pudding 188
    Summer Bread Pudding 188
Hard Sauce 190
Vanilla Crème Brûlée (Master Recipe) 191
    Coconut Crème Brûlée 192
    Lemon-Raspberry Crème Brûlée 192
Butterscotch Crème Brûlée 193
Crème Caramel (Master Recipe) 194
    Espresso-Spice Crème Caramel 195
    Chocolate-Orange Crème Caramel 195
Chocolate Mousse (Master Recipe) 196
    Chocolate Mousse Cake with a Three-Nut Crust 197
    Mexican Mocha Mousse 197
Grilled Rum-Soaked Pineapple with Warm White Chocolate
    Mousse (Master Recipe) 199
    Drunken Peaches with White Chocolate Mousse 201

Ice Creams, Sorbets, and Gelati 203

Chocolate Ice Cream (Master Recipe) 205
    White Chocolate Chunk–Raspberry–Chocolate
      Ice Cream 206
    Mexican Mocha Ice Cream 206
    Rocky Road Ice Cream 206
Mini-Marshmallows 207
Vanilla Bean Ice Cream (Master Recipe) 208
    Fresh Peach Ice Cream 209
    Raspberry-Lemon Ice Cream 209
    Fresh Mint Ice Cream 209
Mascarpone Ice Cream (Master Recipe) 210
    Tiramisu Ice Cream 211

    White Chocolate–Hazelnut Ice Cream 211
    Strawberry-Mascarpone Ice Cream 211
    Profiteroles 212
Espresso Coupe (Master Recipe) 214
    Caramelized Banana Coupe 214
Coconut Sorbet (Master Recipe) 215
    Tropical Ginger Sorbet 215
    Spice Ice Cream Sandwich with Coconut Sorbet 217
    Coconut-Lime-Rum Sorbet 217
Chocolate Sorbet (Master Recipe) 218
    Mocha Sorbet 219
    Chocolate-Mint Sorbet 219
Hazelnut Gelato (Master Recipe) 220
    Fresh Berry Gelato 221
    Vanilla Gelato 221
Lemon Gelato (Master Recipe) 222
    Rose Petal and Shaved White Chocolate Gelato 223
    Orange-Cinnamon Gelato 223
Griddle Cones 224

Desserts for Special Occasions 229

Chocolate Turtle Torte 231
Coconut Cream Cake 236
German Chocolate Cake 239
Chocolate Silk 241
Espresso-Orange Soufflés 243
Caramel-Apple Egg Rolls (Master Recipe) 244
    Pear-Chocolate Egg Rolls 245
Hazelnut Palmiers 246
Raspberry–Almond Praline Napoleons 250
Chocolate Toffee Mousse Cake 253

Index 256

acknowledgments

Thanks to Melissa for all her creative recipes and work on this beautiful book.

Thanks to Carl Greve for use of props, china, and glassware for the photographs. Your support and help is wonderful.

Thanks to our great staff at the Bistro for all your hard work and support.

Thanks to Traci Mandell for helping to keep things running smoothly and getting me to where I need to be.

Thanks to Toni Tajima, Aaron Wehner, Windy Ferges, and Lorena Jones at Ten Speed Press for all your hard work on the book.

Thanks to my family and friends. I love you all.

—Caprial

Thank you Cappy for the wonderful opportunity to create this book with you; Jenny for all your hard work and dedication to this project; my family for all your love and support; my friends for always being there for me; Madison for pushing me to meet my deadlines; and Paul and Heather for making our desserts look so beautiful in the photographs.

—Melissa

introduction

Whether I'm cooking at the restaurant or at home, I always seem to gravitate toward making dessert, but not just because the finished product is so alluring. I love everything about the process—the feel of dough in my hands, the aromas of melting chocolate and baking spices, and the warmth of the kitchen. The desserts I make tend to be more simple and homey, but I bake the way I cook: with bold flavors, minimal fuss, and a reflection of the season. When I first discussed writing a dessert cookbook with Lorena Jones and Aaron Wehner, my editors at Ten Speed Press, we decided that it seemed natural for the book to represent that same philosophy. My goal was to create a book with timeless recipes for foolproof desserts, a book you could really bake from and enjoy for years and years. Like the cookbooks I've written in the past, I wanted this one to be user-friendly and approachable, with something for everyone who has an interest in baking, regardless of their experience level. With the premise of the book decided, and since in no way, shape, or form do I consider myself a pastry chef, I asked Melissa Carey, our pastry chef at Caprial's Bistro, to join me in co-authoring the book.

Melissa has been with us since 1997. Before she joined the staff, the Bistro was a small operation. Along with our chef, Mark Dowers, my husband, John, and I handled everything from cooking to waiting tables. Since we didn't have the luxury of hiring wait staff, we certainly didn't bother to bring on a pastry chef. Instead, we followed what we called the "desserts by the seat of your pants" method of pastry preparation, which meant that when one of us had a little extra time, we would turn our attention to dessert and make a batch of crème brûlée or whip up a cheesecake. Although we wanted to serve desserts that were fairly simple, they also had to be so enticing that our customers couldn't resist them. No matter how crazy it got in the kitchen, somehow we managed to pull it off.

After a couple of years, business at the Bistro got busier and busier, and it became harder to keep up with the demand for desserts. When we set our sights on expanding the restaurant, we knew the time had come to bring a pastry chef on board. Mark suggested Melissa, his good friend from culinary school, and when we narrowed the candidates down to two people, she was one of them. John and I decided that a "bake-off" would help us make the final decision, so we asked each person to prepare a single, definitive dessert . . . but Melissa's didn't come out the way she intended. A very determined Melissa wanted to make sure she won us over, so she asked Mark if there was anything special she could bake for us. John and I absolutely love German chocolate cake, and Melissa's ten-pound, four-layer magnum opus of coconut, pecans, and chocolate did the trick. (If you need to win someone over, her recipe is on page 239 in the Desserts for Special Occasions chapter.)

Four years later, we are still thrilled with what Melissa turns out in the kitchen, and our customers are as happy as ever with the lush, appealing, delicious desserts. Melissa's take on pastry matches the philosophy we've maintained at the Bistro from the beginning: to steer clear of froufrou, overwrought creations that look beautiful but that lack flavor and substance. In other words, we would go for a piece of piping hot apple pie topped with a scoop of homemade vanilla ice cream over a mousse-filled chocolate sculpture any day, and experience shows that our customers would too.

I love to experiment in the kitchen, whether I am inventing a pasta dish for a family dinner or fine-tuning a recipe for hazelnut genoise to teach in a cooking class, and Melissa bakes the same way. Inspired by special ingredients we might happen to get at the Bistro, by a cookbook or an article in a food magazine, or simply by a flavor combination that might cross our minds on a whim, we will take a basic recipe and then finesse it. Improvising and modifying, we'll end up creating something completely new. Like all classically trained chefs, in culinary school we learned fundamental recipes and how to use them as a creative springboard for developing completely new recipes with unique personalities. For example, I might serve a sweet sabayon—a fluffy sauce made from egg yolks, sugar, and liquor—as a dessert on its own, or I can fold whipped cream and chocolate into it, add a shot of espresso, and create a mocha chocolate mousse.

Our approach is really no different than when a home cook creates a new dish out of necessity. We've all been there, maybe while making a batch of our favorite cookies: The recipe calls for nuts, but finding the cupboard bare in the nut department, we toss in some dried cranberries instead. The cookies are a hit, and the old favorite cookie has a new lease on life.

We followed the same idea in coming up with the recipes for this book. First, we developed 67 master recipes that are divided among the seven chapters: Cakes; Pies, Tarts, and Cobblers; Cookies; Breakfast Sweets; Custards, Puddings, and Mousses; Ice Creams, Sorbets, and Gelati; and Desserts for Special Occasions. Some of the master recipes are for classic desserts, like chocolate brownies and vanilla ice cream, while others are a bit more elaborate, such as the Grilled Rum-Soaked Pineapple with Warm White Chocolate Mousse. Then, for each master recipe, we came up with variations that take the original dessert in a different direction or to another level. As you try the master recipes and our suggested variations, you'll see how simple it is to use them as a starting point for creating your own unique desserts.

Faced with baking a pie or making an angel food cake, many perfectly capable cooks succumb to "pastry phobia" and delegate the job to a frozen crust or the local bakery. I hate to think of anyone missing out on the fun of making desserts because their grandmother never taught them how to roll out a pie crust or because they panic at the thought of beating egg whites. To explain some of the basic pastry-making techniques called for in this book, we've included step-by-step photographs with instructions and tips for success. If certain techniques have eluded you, or if you are simply new to baking, these illustrated instructions should give you plenty of confidence. On the other hand, if you are an experienced baker, you can refer to them to clarify a process or to brush up on a particular technique.

Once you are comfortable making these recipes, you'll have the tools to move on to preparing even the most intricate desserts. But after you've mastered them, I hope you find yourself turning to this book for years to come, whenever something as simple as a spice-infused, flaky apple pie or a satisfying caramel pudding lures you into the kitchen.

We designed these recipes to be very simple to prepare in a home kitchen. However, we do suggest that you

equip yourself with the following basic tools and quality ingredients, many of which you probably already have.

Baking Equipment

The following list of kitchen equipment includes essential baking tools—such as a sheet pan and rolling pin—plus extras that can help make many tasks much easier. You can get by without having absolutely everything on the list, but plan to gradually stock your kitchen over time if you find yourself making more and more desserts and getting adventurous with your baking.

BENCH OR DOUGH SCRAPER

A bench scraper—a square piece of slightly flexible metal attached to a plastic or wooden handle—is almost as valuable as a chef's knife in a kitchen. I use mine when kneading dough; to lift sticky doughs off the board; to help finish folding delicate, tender doughs, such as scone dough; and to portion dough for individual loaves or rolls. A bench scraper is also great for cleaning leftover dough and flour from your counter.

FOOD PROCESSOR

The truly well-equipped kitchen has a food processor, which makes fast work of everything from grinding nuts to making bread dough. I prefer to make cheesecake batter in a food processor instead of a mixer because the resulting texture is so smooth. When it comes to making bread and cheesecake, more is always better—so be sure to purchase the largest-capacity food processor you can afford.

PALETTE KNIFE

This flat, rounded-tip spatula with a wooden handle is a necessity for filling and frosting cakes. It is also useful for lifting smaller items off sheet pans and for freeing the edges of cakes from their pans. Palette knives come in many sizes; I suggest keeping a smaller and larger one on hand.

PARCHMENT PAPER

We go through a lot of parchment paper at the Bistro, where we use it for just about everything we bake. Use parchment paper to line sheet pans to keep baked goods from sticking without the use of oils or sprays. You can also use it to make a simple pastry bag (page 60). (At home I also line sheet pans with a Silpat, a reusable silicone baking sheet that can withstand extremely high temperatures. This fairly new product also comes in handy for covering counters or cutting boards when rolling out dough or working with sticky items.)

PASTRY BAG

A pastry bag is a cone-shaped bag usually made out of nylon or plastic-lined cotton or canvas. Pastry bags come in many different sizes and can be fitted with a variety of tips for piping out whipped cream, pastry (such as pâte à choux), and decorations and borders on cakes. For small jobs and for piping fine details, you can make a simple pastry bag out of parchment paper (page 60).

PASTRY BRUSH

I like the durability of natural-bristle pastry brushes with wooden handles. A 1/2- to 1-inch-wide brush is a good all-purpose size that's just right for applying everything from egg washes and glazes to melted butter and chocolate. Be sure to keep your dessert pastry brushes separate from the brushes you use for savory items like barbecue sauce.

PIE PLATE

I use glass pie plates at the Bistro and at home. Although both metal and ceramic pie plates also work fine, pies baked in glass have a browner bottom crust; glass also gives you a good view of the crust while it's baking.

PROPANE TORCH

You really need a propane torch to perfectly finish crème brûlée. Unlike a broiler, which can heat unevenly and also warm up the nicely chilled custards, a propane torch quickly and evenly caramelizes the sugar on top. It also gives the same great results when browning meringue on top of pies. Go to your local hardware store to buy a good-quality torch—they are much less expensive than the ones you'll find in kitchen stores.

ROLLING PIN

This simple kitchen tool comes in several different styles. If you haven't used a rolling pin before, you'll find that the French version is a great one to start with. A solid cylinder of wood without handles, it gives you lots of control and a real feel for all types of dough. The baker's rolling pin, probably the most familiar type of pin, has a handle secured through the middle with a steel rod, allowing the pin to roll freely while you grip the handles. When buying a baker's-style pin, get the heaviest one you can find; it will come in very handy for rolling out yeast doughs and other heavier doughs. To help you roll out perfect circles of dough for pie and tart crusts, try a tapered rolling pin. As the name suggests, it is widest in the middle and tapers down at each end.

SHEET PAN

When I call for a sheet pan in a recipe, it is what most home cooks refer to as a jelly roll pan—a flat metal pan with a shallow rim on all sides. I use this type of pan for baking cookies, breads, and other baked goods. For even baking and browning, use a heavy-gauge sheet pan, since lighter ones will warp at high temperatures. When shopping for a sheet pan, skip both the expensive cooking stores and your local market. You can find reasonably priced, good-quality sheet pans at any restaurant supply store.

STAND MIXER

Every serious baker needs a stand mixer, which is the type we used to test the recipes in this book. With so much more power than a hand-held mixer, a stand mixer is ideal for mixing heavy bread dough, creaming butter and sugar to a super-light consistency (one of the secrets to Melissa's fabulous cakes), and beating batters that require longer mixing times. I suggest you get as powerful a stand mixer as you can afford, with at least a 4- to 5-quart bowl and paddle, dough hook, and whisk attachments.

TART PAN

Tarts are shallower than pies, so a pie plate won't take the place of a good tart pan. If you don't have one, add a 10-inch flan or tart pan with a removable bottom to your kitchen equipment; you can also use it for quiches and other savory tarts.

WHISK

A whisk, also known as a whip, is a kitchen tool made of stainless steel loops secured into a wooden or stainless steel handle. Whisks come in various shapes and sizes and are useful for incorporating air into ingredients and for blending ingredients to a smooth consistency. A cylindrical whisk is a good tool for mixing things like batters; a balloon whisk, with a larger rounded end, makes easy work of whipping air into ingredients that need volume, such as egg whites and cream.

ZESTER

A zester removes the outer peel of citrus fruit, leaving the bitter pith behind. To remove longer strips of zest for garnishes, a traditional zester works well. Most of the recipes in this book call for finely grated zest, so if you use a traditional zester, be sure to chop the zest with a chef's knife. (The very smallest hole of a grater will also work.) I use a brand of zester called Microplane, which gives a very fine cut; you can find it at some cooking stores.

Ingredients

When I teach cooking classes, I always talk about the ingredients in the recipes, in addition to demonstrating techniques. As I tell my students, the more you know about the ingredients you use, the easier it is to understand how a recipe works—and the better the results will be. And as with everything you cook, use the freshest, best ingredients you can afford.

ALMOND PASTE

We use almond paste—a mixture of blanched almonds, sugar, glycerin, and sometimes almond extract—in fillings, cookies, and cakes to add texture and to enhance the almond flavor. Marzipan, which is finer and sweeter than almond paste, is a combination of almond paste, sugar, and unbeaten egg whites. You can form it into shapes to use as garnishes. Keep both almond paste and marzipan in an airtight container at room temperature; if it is a bit stiff when you are ready to use it, just pop it in the microwave for a few seconds to soften it.

BAKING SODA AND BAKING POWDER

These leaveners work by producing carbon dioxide gas bubbles that cause cakes or pastries to rise. Baking soda, also known as bicarbonate of soda or sodium bicarbonate, must be combined with an acidic ingredient, such as buttermilk or yogurt, in order to work. Baking powder, made from baking soda and an acid (usually cream of tartar), reacts when exposed to any liquid. Double-acting baking powder, which is what most people have in their cupboards, reacts some when exposed to moisture and some when exposed to heat. If you are out of baking powder, substitute 1 part baking soda with 2 parts cream of tartar. Keep baking powder no more than 6 months.

BUTTER

The butter we used to test the recipes—and the butter we use at the Bistro—is a locally made unsalted European-style butter, which means it has a higher butterfat content and lower moisture than domestic-style butter. For baking (and for all of your cooking), use only unsalted butter, so that you can control the amount of salt. Unsalted butter has a much shorter shelf life than salted butter, so keep it in the freezer and bring out only the amount you need. With the exception of some of our pie crust recipes, which call for shortening, we use only real butter in our recipes.

BUTTERMILK

Traditionally, buttermilk is the liquid that is left after the process of making butter, but the kind you find in the grocery store has different origins. These days, buttermilk is made by adding a special type of bacteria to nonfat or lowfat milk, which gives the milk a tangy flavor and a thicker texture.

CHOCOLATE

Chocolate is produced from the pod of *Theobroma cacao*, the tropical cocoa bean tree. *Theobroma* means "food of the gods," and if you are a chocolate lover, you can surely understand why it was given such an appropriate name!

Unsweetened chocolate, or baking chocolate, is known technically as chocolate liquor. Made by milling cleaned roasted cocoa beans to a molten state and molding the resulting paste into cakes, it contains 53 percent cocoa butter, 47 percent cocoa solids, and no sugar. Cocoa powder, made by pressing some of the cocoa butter from chocolate liquor and then pulverizing the remaining mixture into a powder, comes in two forms: natural (or nonalkalized) and Dutch process. The latter, also known as Dutched or alkalized cocoa powder, often has a richer flavor and a deeper color. You've probably seen many recipes using cocoa powder that also call for boiling water, which can release an even more intense flavor. In this book, both the Chocolate Buttermilk Cake and the Old-Fashioned Chocolate Cake take advantage of that trick.

Semisweet and bittersweet chocolate both contain chocolate liquor, cocoa butter, sugar, vanilla, and sometimes lecithin (added to help the chocolate hold its shape). Although there really isn't a standard definition of what makes one chocolate bittersweet and another semisweet, bittersweet chocolate is usually stronger, with a higher concentration of chocolate liquor and less sugar. The two chocolates can be used interchangeably in all of the recipes in this book, but I usually prefer baking with bittersweet—namely my four favorites: Valrhona (from France), Lindt (from Switzerland), Callebaut (from Belgium), and Scharffen Berger (from the United States). Chocolate chips are made to retain their shape at a high temperature and then stay soft after baking, so don't use them in any recipes that call for chocolate to be melted.

White chocolate, a combination of milk, cocoa butter, sugar, and vanilla, has a wonderful flavor, but since it contains no chocolate liquor, it technically is not chocolate. Be sure to look for one that has no other fats besides cocoa butter, because the quality and flavor is much better than those with other fats. White chocolate doesn't keep well, so buy only what you need for your dessert; it also doesn't tolerate high heat, so take special care when melting it.

To melt chocolate, coarsely chop it and place it in a metal bowl set over a pan of simmering water. Once it has melted about halfway, remove the pan from the heat (leave the bowl on the pan), and let the chocolate finish melting. If you choose to use the microwave oven instead, use a low power setting, heat the chocolate for a short duration, and stir often.

To shave chocolate, run a sharp vegetable peeler along a bar of chocolate to shave off curls. You can also use the large holes of a grater if you are going to fold the chocolate into other ingredients and not use it for garnish.

COCONUT

Most of the recipes in this book that call for coconut require the coconut to be toasted. To toast coconut, preheat the oven to 350°. Spread the shredded coconut on a sheet pan. Bake for about 5 minutes, stir, and then bake until golden brown, 5 to 7 minutes longer. Let cool completely on the pan. Keep in an airtight container for up to 5 days.

CORN SYRUP

Corn syrup, which comes in both light and dark forms, is a very sweet, thick syrup made by processing cornstarch with acids or enzymes. It is used in candy, frostings, and ganache, among other things, to keep the sugar from crystallizing, and in desserts to sweeten them and add richness.

CREAM

Cream comes in several different forms: heavy whipping cream, with 36 to 40 percent butterfat; heavy cream, which has 30 to 36 percent butterfat; and half-and-half, which is equal parts milk and cream and has 10 to 18 percent butterfat. These recipes call for heavy whipping cream, unless stated otherwise.

CREAM OF TARTAR

Cream of tartar, a fine white powder made from crystalline acid that forms naturally on the inside of wine barrels, is added to candies and frostings to make them creamier and to egg whites to give them stability when whipped.

EGGS

Eggs (essential elements in baking) emulsify ingredients, act as a leavener, and add the needed fat for rich, tender pastries. We used grade A large eggs to test the recipes for this book. Buy and use refrigerated eggs that are free of cracks. If a recipe calls for eggs that are at room temperature, bring them out of the refrigerator no more than 20 minutes before using them; any longer than that can cause problems with bacteria. You can also warm the eggs in warm water before cracking them, but be sure to use them immediately.

FLOUR

Unless otherwise noted, these recipes use all-purpose flour, which is made from a blend of high-gluten hard wheat and a low-gluten soft wheat. It is available both bleached and unbleached, but I prefer to use unbleached flour, simply because it's less processed. My favorite brand, Bob's Red Mill, is a locally made product. Some of the cake recipes call for cake flour, a fine-textured, soft wheat flour with a high starch content. Always sift cake flour before measuring it.

GINGER

When buying fresh ginger, look for a root that has a smooth skin and is not dried out and wrinkled. Most grocery stores carry mature ginger, which has a strong flavor and a brown, paper-thin skin that gets thicker with age. Unless I'm steeping it in a liquid, I like to peel this type of ginger before using it in desserts. Spring ginger (also known as young ginger) has a milder flavor and a very pink outer skin that does not require peeling.

Candied ginger—ginger slices that have been boiled in sugar syrup and then rolled in sugar—still has the peppery flavor of fresh ginger, yet it is sweet and chewy. I like to add diced candied ginger to muffins, cakes, and everything in between. I prefer to use candied ginger that is soft and pliable. The older it is, the more brittle it becomes, so buy the freshest candied ginger you can find.

MASCARPONE CHEESE

Mascarpone, a triple-cream cheese made from cow's milk, originates from the Lombardy region of Italy. If I can't find a good-quality mascarpone at the grocery store, and if I have the time, I'll make my own. Here's how:

Combine 2 cups heavy whipping cream with 1 teaspoon tartaric acid in a saucepan over medium heat, and bring just to a boil. Place the mixture in a strainer lined with several layers of cheesecloth, set the strainer over a bowl, and let it sit in the refrigerator overnight. The next day, remove the chilled mascarpone from the cheesecloth, discarding the liquid in the bowl. The mascarpone will keep, refrigerated, for one week. (Don't substitute cream of tartar for tartaric acid. Tartaric acid is available at winemaking supply shops for about $2 per 2-ounce package.)

MILK

We used whole milk in testing these recipes. With 3 1/2 percent butterfat, it is just as it came out of the cow. If you use lowfat or nonfat milk in the recipes, the results may be slightly different.

MOLASSES

The sugar content and color of molasses, a by-product of the process of refining cane sugar syrup, varies depending on the number of times the sugar has been extracted from the syrup. Unsulfured molasses, from the first stage of the sugar extraction process, is light and very sweet. Sulfured molasses comes from the second extraction and is darker and less sweet. Blackstrap molasses, from the third and final extraction, is dark, very strong, and not very sweet. We use unsulfured molasses at the Bistro; it gives desserts just enough molasses flavor without being overpowering.

NUTS

Always use the freshest nuts you can buy in all of your baking. You can store untoasted nuts in an airtight container in the freezer for up to 6 months. To toast nuts, place them on a sheet pan and bake at 350° until golden brown, 10 to 20 minutes.

PEACHES AND APRICOTS

Several of the recipes in this book call for peaches or apricots, which should be peeled before using for baking. To peel peaches or apricots, bring 6 cups of water to a rolling boil in a large pan. Place 4 cups of water in a large bowl, add 4 cups of ice cubes, and set aside.

Score the bottom of each peach or apricot with an X, place in the boiling water for about 30 seconds, and then transfer to the ice water with a slotted spoon. Slip the skin off the peach or apricot.

SPICES

Many people mistakenly believe that spices keep forever, but they are actually quite perishable and are best when fresh. Store spices in a cool, dark place for no longer than 6 months to a year. Whole spices lose their flavor more slowly than ground spices, so I'll often buy whole spices and grind just the right amount for a recipe. To round out and intensify the flavor of both ground and whole spices, you can dry-roast them in a hot sauté pan for a minute or two until fragrant.

SUGAR

Sugar is an essential ingredient in just about every dessert. Besides the obvious—adding sweetness—it also acts as a tenderizer and a flavor enhancer.

White granulated sugar, the most commonly available type, is 99.9 percent pure dried sugar crystals that have been completely refined; it has no vitamins or minerals. Regular granulated sugar will work just fine for the recipes in this book and for most of your baking at home, but for sprinkling on top of crème brûlée, superfine white sugar is our preference. In fact, we use superfine white sugar for everything at the Bistro because it incorporates into other ingredients more quickly than regular granulated sugar. If you can't find superfine sugar at the market, make your own by processing regular sugar for several seconds in a food processor.

The two other common types of sugar are made from a granulated sugar base. Powdered sugar is finely milled white sugar with 3 percent cornstarch added to prevent lumping. Light or dark brown sugar is granulated sugar combined with molasses. I bake with dark brown sugar, since I like its more assertive flavor, but light brown sugar will do in a pinch. Either type will work well in these recipes.

VANILLA

The recipes in this book call for either vanilla beans or pure vanilla extract. No matter how subtle a presence in a recipe, the vanilla you use should always be the best quality you can afford. For the most part, we use vanilla beans—which are the pods of a beautiful orchid—to infuse flavor into things like pastry cream, crème brûlée, and ice cream. We usually split them in half lengthwise before simmering them with the liquid, and then scrape out the seedy insides and discard the pod. The best vanilla beans come from Tahiti and Madagascar; they can be rather expensive but are worth it. Purchase plump, supple vanilla beans, and keep them in an airtight container so they won't dry out and lose their flavor. We never use imitation vanilla in anything we bake because its flavor is just that—imitation and very unpleasant, with none of the nuances of true vanilla. Since you never want to add something with an off flavor to anything you bake or cook, be sure to use only the finest pure vanilla extract.

VANILLA SUGAR

Combine 5 pounds sugar and 1 whole vanilla bean in a large airtight container, and let sit for 1 week before using. The vanilla sugar will keep for up to 6 months (leave the vanilla bean in the sugar).

ZEST

Zest—the colored outer rind of citrus fruit, but not the bitter white pith—contains aromatic oils that add a bright citrus flavor to your recipes. (You can use a zester to remove zest in strips.)

Yellow Butter Cake (page 24)

cakes

The first time I tasted cake was on my first birthday. Of course, I have no memory of that big event, but it must have made quite an impression on me, because for as long as I can remember, I've been in awe of towering layer cakes. There's just something so intriguing about a tall cake glistening with frosting, that classic symbol of a celebration, because you know that slicing through the frosting will reveal all those layers of cake, filling, and even more frosting.

I must confess that until a few years ago, I rarely tried my hand at baking a true American-style layer cake. I loved to bake cakes when I was young, graduating from my Easy Bake Oven to making cakes the "real way"—which, as for many people growing in the 1960s and '70s, meant from a boxed mix. Back then, cakes made from scratch were

practically unheard of, unless you had a grandmother who passed down her family recipe to your mother, and she shared the tradition with you. The only way I could make my cakes special was in the decorating, and I'd go after that with gusto, with plenty of food coloring, frosting, and sprinkles helping me along. Bake sales were a popular fund-raising event at my elementary school. (This was before food safety rules made them obsolete.) I learned early on that if I iced my cupcakes in purple or blue frosting and covered them with big silver dragées, they would sell out before the more subdued ones.

But still, despite my enterprise and knack for cooking, as the years went by, a successful layer cake from scratch seemed to elude me. Once I got into high school and started to get more serious about cooking, I abandoned layer cakes for soufflés and other more challenging recipes. In culinary school, I learned how to prepare European-style cakes, like dacquoise, but not American-style butter layer cakes. And when I became a chef, there was a pastry chef at every place I worked. While I'd make a cake on the job from time to time, I'd usually opt for something like a flourless torte or a genoise.

A couple of years after we opened the Bistro, my mom asked me to bake her a special cake for her birthday, an old-fashioned chocolate layer cake with sour cream frosting. She handed me the recipe, clipped from a magazine, I made it and it was a disaster. Bland and cardboardy, the only good thing about it was the frosting. So what began merely as a series of obstacles transformed into full-fledged cake phobia. I didn't want to put all that effort into baking a cake only to have it turn out mediocre, so I avoided them altogether. I stuck with cupcakes for a long time after that, but even those presented a problem when I baked some for a party in my son's first-grade class. All kids love chocolate, right? So I made rich, dense chocolate cupcakes frosted with chocolate ganache, and they turned out beautifully. The kids wouldn't touch them, though. They wanted super-sweet cupcakes with sprinkles and neon frosting, not the grownup treats I brought in. (Fortunately, the teachers loved them, so my pride didn't suffer too much.)

Finally, Melissa—the Queen of Cakes—came to work for us at the Bistro, and I've learned a lot since then. She is one of the lucky ones who learned early on what a real cake should be—and how to bake one—thanks to her grandmother's awe-inspiring chocolate–sour cream cake iced with chocolate buttercream. Melissa *can't* bake a short layer cake, because she loves them tall, the baked layers split into even more layers and filled with anything from English toffee to coconut pastry cream. As beautiful as they are delicious, her cakes certainly aren't for the faint of heart. We almost always have one on the dessert menu, and whenever a server brings a piece to a table, you can almost hear a collective sigh in the dining room and watch the eyes of all the customers following along.

With Melissa's help and guidance, I'm happy to report that I now know how to bake layer cakes. As I watched her at work and as we talked about baking, I discovered that her advice holds true for making just about any other kind of cake, too. Here's what we suggest:

- Give yourself plenty of time. Unless the cake is supposed to be served warm, you will need to let it cool completely before frosting it. If you have the time and can plan in advance, bake it the night before.

- Have all of your ingredients poised and ready. And, unless we note otherwise (such as when we call for boiling water or cold, diced butter), have all ingredients at room temperature, so they blend together smoothly. Remember that eggs should sit out of the refrigerator for no more than 20 minutes; you can warm them in a cup of warm water for a few minutes to take the chill off. If your milk is ice-cold, just microwave it for a few seconds.

- If a recipe calls for cake flour, sift it before measuring it (don't worry about digging out your fancy sifter; a fine-mesh sieve or strainer works just as well), and then add the other dry ingredients to it.

- Take the time to alternate the dry ingredients and the wet ingredients when blending them into the creamed butter and sugar. If you try to hurry this step along, you'll end up with a lumpy cake.

- Use a stand mixer if you have one. Although you can cream butter and sugar for a cake with a hand-held mixer, your arm is bound to get tired long before the job is done to Melissa's specifications. The creamed mixture should be totally smooth and very light and fluffy, with no bits of butter that will melt and form little craters in the cake. This takes about 10 minutes of beating, with occasional stops of the mixer to scrape down the sides of the bowl and make sure everything is blended in.

- To prepare the cake pans, grease them with cooking spray, but don't bother to flour them. No matter how hard you knock the flour out, you're always left with clumps. Instead, line the bottoms of the pans with a piece of parchment paper cut to fit.

- Bake the cakes on the middle rack in the center of the oven, so they'll cook evenly.

- Never overbake cake! Slightly undercooked but moist is much more appealing than overdone and dry. A sure-fire way to tell whether a cake is done is to touch it lightly in the center. If it slowly springs back, there's just the right amount of moisture left in it, and it's perfectly baked. If it springs back very quickly, chances are it has baked a bit too long and it will be on the dry side.

In this chapter you'll find recipes for classic layer cakes, including Melissa's instructions for how to split the layers and fill and frost the cakes. Although we offer suggestions for specific fillings and frostings, you should also check out all of the other recipes and come up with your own combinations. We haven't forgotten our other favorite kinds of cakes, either—we've included master recipes for gingerbread, angel food cake, genoise, cheese-cake, flourless chocolate cake, and a simple carrot cake. (See the Desserts for Special Occasions chapter for more-involved recipes.) As you can see, I've overcome my cake phobia and have learned to enjoy baking all kinds of cakes. And if I can do it, anyone can.

(master recipe)

old-fashioned chocolate cake

We just couldn't decide which of the following two chocolate cake recipes to include—they're both that good. Rich, moist, and foolproof, either cake deserves to become your favorite standby. Even though this cake does not have a variation, I still consider it a master recipe since it's a great springboard. Try pairing it with fresh fruit, fillings, or just about any frosting you can dream up. Melissa was given this recipe by her friend Sandra Gilbert.

Serves 14

1/2 cup unsalted butter, at room temperature

2 1/4 cups lightly packed brown sugar

2 teaspoons pure vanilla extract

3 eggs

3 ounces unsweetened chocolate, melted (page 8)

2 1/4 cups sifted cake flour

2 teaspoons baking soda

1/2 teaspoon salt

1 cup sour cream

1 cup boiling water

Preheat the oven to 350°. Grease two 9-inch round cake pans and line the bottoms with parchment paper; set aside.

Place the butter, sugar, and vanilla extract in the bowl of a mixer fitted with the paddle attachment and beat on high speed, scraping down the sides of the bowl often, until well blended, about 3 minutes. With the mixer on low speed, add the eggs, one at a time, scraping down the sides of the bowl and mixing well after each addition. Continue to beat for 5 minutes, until light and fluffy. Stop the mixer, add the chocolate, and mix well. Combine the flour, baking soda, and salt. Add about half of the dry ingredients to the batter, beat on low speed until well blended, and then add about half of the sour cream and beat well. Add the remaining dry ingredients followed by the remaining sour cream, scraping down the sides of the bowl and beating well after each addition. Add the boiling water and beat until smooth.

Divide the batter between the prepared pans and bake until the cake springs back when touched lightly in the center, 30 to 35 minutes. Let cool for about 10 minutes, then remove the cakes from the pans and let cool completely.

See page 19 for instructions on splitting, filling, and frosting the cake.

chocolate Buttermilk cake

This cake is famous. A creation of pastry chef Michelle Dennis, a dear friend of Melissa's, it has made its way around Portland restaurants and is now a favorite at the Bistro. Somewhere along the way, the buttermilk in the name has been shortened to "butt"–but that truly does refer to the buttermilk. You'll notice that the order in which the ingredients are combined is the reverse of the way a butter cake is made–you start by blending the dry ingredients in the mixer. Without any butter, the batter is thin, but the finished cake is incredibly moist and tender. Like the Old-Fashioned Chocolate Cake, this cake is a canvas waiting for you to fill and frost with your personal touch.

Serves 14

3 cups flour

2 1/2 cups sugar

1 1/2 tablespoons baking soda

1/2 teaspoon salt

1 cup unsweetened cocoa powder

1 1/3 cups vegetable oil

1 1/2 cups buttermilk

3 eggs

1 1/2 cups freshly brewed hot coffee

1 tablespoon pure vanilla extract

Preheat the oven to 350°. Grease two 9-inch round cake pans and line the bottoms with parchment paper; set aside.

Place the flour, sugar, baking soda, salt, and cocoa powder in the bowl of a mixer fitted with a paddle attachment, and mix on low speed to combine (don't mix on high speed or you will be wearing the dry ingredients). Add the oil and buttermilk and mix on medium speed until well blended. Scrape down the sides of the bowl. With the mixer on low speed, add the eggs, one at a time, scraping down the sides of the bowl and mixing well after each addition. Add the hot coffee and vanilla extract, and mix on low speed (so the batter won't splash) until smooth.

Divide the batter between the prepared pans and bake until the cake springs back when touched lightly in the center, 30 to 35 minutes. Let cool for about 10 minutes, then remove from the pans and let cool completely.

See page 19 for instructions on splitting, filling, and frosting the cake.

1

2

3

4

5

6

7

8

9

Splitting, Filling, and Frosting a Cake

Follow these steps and you'll have a beautiful cake, even for an everyday occasion.

1. Cool the cake completely. If the cake is domed, even the top with a slicing knife or a long serrated knife.

2. Split each layer in half with a long slicing knife to form 4 layers.

3. Place one layer, cut side up, on a cardboard round.

4. Using a palette knife, spread about 1/2 cup of frosting or filling over the layer, taking it to the edge of the cake.

5. Continue with the next 2 layers of the cake.

6. Set the final layer, cut side down, on top of the cake. Spread 1/2 cup of frosting over the top of the cake, again taking it to the edge of the cake.

7. Using a palette knife, generously spread frosting over the edge and sides of the cake.

8. Starting at one edge of the top of the cake, smooth the frosting toward the center.

9. Smooth out any blemishes in the frosting.

Flourless Chocolate Cake

This cake is like a super-moist fallen chocolate soufflé with a delicately crisp crust. It puffs up a lot while it bakes and then falls as it cools—so don't panic. Be sure to give it at least 20 minutes to cool before serving; if it's too warm, it will be tasty but much too difficult to cut.

Serves 12

5 eggs

1 cup granulated sugar

1/3 cup coffee liqueur

1 cup unsalted butter, at room temperature

6 ounces bittersweet chocolate, melted (page 8)

1 teaspoon pure vanilla extract

Powdered sugar, for dusting

1 1/2 cups whipped cream, as accompaniment

Organic rose petals, for garnish

Preheat the oven to 350°. Grease a 10-inch springform pan and wrap the outside with foil to prevent leaking; set aside.

Place the eggs and sugar in the bowl of a mixer fitted with a whip attachment, and whip on high speed, occasionally scraping down the sides of the bowl, until very thick and fluffy, about 10 minutes. (Yes, it really takes that long; if you mix it for a shorter length of time, the cake will be only 1/4 inch tall.) Add the liqueur and mix well.

With the mixer on medium speed, add the butter, a few pieces at a time, and beat until well blended. (The batter may look "broken," or separated, at this point, but the chocolate will bind with the butter and fix that.) With the mixer on low speed, add the chocolate and vanilla extract, and mix until smooth. Pour the batter into the prepared pan and bake until the cake moves as one mass when you gently jiggle the pan, about 30 minutes. (It's much better to underbake this cake than to overbake it; it will be a bit gooey, but I've never seen anyone turn up their nose at that.) Let cool for 10 to 20 minutes, remove the outer ring of the pan and the foil, then let cool about 30 minutes longer before serving.

Serve at room temperature, topped with a dusting of powdered sugar and softly whipped cream. Garnish with rose petals.

Variations

Flourless Chocolate Cake

DARK AND WHITE CHOCOLATE-HAZELNUT CAKE

Be sure to use chopped bar chocolate, not chocolate chips in this recipe; the lecithin in chips helps them keep their shape, but in this cake you want really gooey chunks of melted chocolate instead.

Follow the Flourless Chocolate Cake master recipe, folding 1 cup ground toasted hazelnuts, 1 1/2 cups chopped white chocolate, and 1/4 cup hazelnut liqueur into the finished batter. Bake as directed in the master recipe.

Serve warm, topped with Chocolate Sauce (page 62) and softly whipped cream.

Serves 12

FLOURLESS DRIED CHERRY-CHOCOLATE CAKE

Dried cherries have a deep, concentrated flavor that intensifies the rich taste of the master recipe. Be sure to use sour cherries, which provide the perfect contrasting tang of acidity.

Combine 1 cup dried sour cherries and 2 cups port in a saucepan over medium heat. Cook until the cherries are plump and most of the liquid is absorbed, 6 to 8 minutes. (Don't let the port completely cook away, or the cherries will burn.) Remove from the heat and let cool completely. Coarsely chop the cherries and set aside.

Follow the Flourless Chocolate Cake master recipe, folding the reserved cherries and 3/4 cup chopped bittersweet chocolate into the finished batter. Bake as directed in the master recipe.

Serve warm, topped with Chocolate Sauce (page 62), softly whipped cream, and more port-soaked cherries, if you like.

Serves 12

INDIVIDUAL CHOCOLATE-RASPBERRY CAKES

Like the individual cheesecakes later in this chapter, these make a good excuse for enjoying a delectably warm version of the master recipe. Any fresh berries work well in this recipe, and you can also experiment with different liqueurs. In winter, try poached pears and pear brandy instead. For a really special dessert, top each cake with Lemon Gelato (page 222).

Preheat the oven to 350°. Grease eight 8-ounce ramekins; set aside.

Prepare the batter as directed in the Flourless Chocolate Cake master recipe, adding 1/4 cup raspberry liqueur along with the vanilla extract. Distribute 4 cups fresh raspberries among the ramekins, and then pour the batter over the raspberries. Set the ramekins in a shallow roasting pan, and fill the pan with enough hot water to reach about halfway up the sides of the ramekins. Carefully set the pan in the oven and bake just until set, 20 to 30 minutes. Remove the ramekins from the water bath. Let cool 10 to 15 minutes. Serve the cakes warm (in the ramekins, because they're too gooey to unmold), topped with softly whipped cream and Berry Sauce (page 63) made with raspberries.

Serves 8

(master recipe)

Yellow Butter cake

You might find versions of this cake on Melissa's summer dessert menus. Buttery and fairly dense, the cake pairs well with strawberries, raspberries, blackberries, peaches, or blueberries, as well as with lighter frostings. For a memorable summer dessert, fill with macerated strawberries, using about 1 cup for each layer, then frost the cake with a vanilla buttercream.

Serves 14

1 cup unsalted butter, at room temperature

2 cups sugar

4 eggs

2 teaspoons pure vanilla extract

3/4 teaspoon salt

1 tablespoon baking powder

3 cups sifted cake flour

1 cup half-and-half

Preheat the oven to 350°. Grease two 9-inch round cake pans and line the bottoms with parchment paper; set aside.

Place the butter and sugar in the bowl of a mixer fitted with the paddle attachment and beat on high speed, scraping down the sides of the bowl often, until light and fluffy, about 5 minutes. With the mixer on low speed, add the eggs, one at a time, scraping down the sides of the bowl and mixing well after each addition. Add the vanilla extract and mix well, again scraping down the sides of the bowl.

Combine the salt and baking powder with the flour. Add about one-third of the dry ingredients to the batter, beat on low speed until well blended, and then add about one-third of the half-and-half, and beat well. Continue adding the remaining dry ingredients and half-and-half alternately, beating well after each addition.

Divide the batter between the prepared pans and bake until the cake springs back when touched lightly in the center, 25 to 30 minutes. Let cool for about 10 minutes, then remove the cakes from the pans and let cool completely.

See page 19 for instructions on splitting, filling, and frosting the cake.

pictured on page 12

Variations

Yellow Butter Cake

CITRUS-SCENTED CAKE

The generous amount of orange or lemon adds a refreshing element to this rich cake.

Follow the Yellow Butter Cake master recipe, adding the finely grated zest and juice of either 1 orange or 2 lemons to the butter and sugar. Beat on high speed until light and fluffy, and proceed as directed in the master recipe.

Split the cake layers. Fill, using about 1/2 cup Lemon or Orange Curd (page 64) and 1 cup diced ripe mango for each layer. Frost the sides and top of the cake with White Chocolate Quick Buttercream (page 53). See page 19 for instructions on splitting, filling, and frosting the cake.

Serves 14

POPPYSEED CAKE

Unlike most recipes for poppyseed cake, this one contains no almond extract, which lets the distinct flavor of the poppyseeds shine through.

Follow the Yellow Butter Cake master recipe, adding 3 tablespoons poppyseeds, 1 tablespoon finely grated orange zest, and 1 tablespoon finely grated lemon zest to the butter and sugar. Beat on high speed until light and fluffy, and proceed as directed in the master recipe.

Split the cake layers. Fill, using about 1/2 cup raspberry jam and about 1 cup Lemon Italian Buttercream (page 49) for each layer. Frost the top and the sides with the remaining buttercream. See page 19 for instructions on splitting, filling, and frosting the cake.

Serves 14

(master recipe)

Genoise

Genoise is a traditional French cake with a light, airy texture. As with angel food cake, the key to preparing genoise is to be very gentle when folding the ingredients together at the end. After whipping the egg whites to the perfect consistency, you don't want to cause yourself heartache by overmixing the batter and baking a flat cake!

Serves 14

8 eggs, separated

1 1/2 cups sugar

1 teaspoon pure vanilla extract

Pinch of salt

Pinch of cream of tartar

1 1/3 cups flour, sifted

Preheat the oven to 350°. Grease two 9-inch round cake pans and line the bottoms with parchment paper; set aside.

Place the egg yolks, 3/4 cup of the sugar, and the vanilla extract in the bowl of a mixer fitted with the whip attachment, and whip until the mixture is a light lemon color and very thick, scraping down the sides of the bowl occasionally, about 10 minutes. Transfer to a large bowl and set aside.

Wash and dry the bowl of the mixer and the whip attachment. Place the egg whites, salt, and cream of tartar in the bowl and whip on high speed until frothy. While beating, add the remaining 3/4 cup sugar, about 1 tablespoon at a time, and beat until the whites hold stiff peaks. (Be sure to add the sugar slowly so it has time to dissolve; otherwise the egg whites will lose volume and be too soupy.)

Using a large plastic spatula, gently fold about a third of the whipped egg whites into the egg yolk mixture, then fold in about a third of the flour. Continue adding the egg whites and flour alternately, folding very gently. (If you mix the batter too much, the cakes will lose their light, fluffy texture and will rise very little during baking.) Divide the batter between the prepared pans. Bake until the cake is golden brown and springs back when touched lightly in the center, 20 to 25 minutes. Let cool for about 10 minutes, then remove the cakes from the pans and let cool completely.

Split the cake layers. Fill, using about 1/2 cup Lemon Curd (page 64), 1 cup Whipped Cream Frosting (page 42), and 1 1/2 cups berries, sliced strawberries, diced mango, sliced poached pears (page 36), or other fruit for each layer. See page 19 for instructions on splitting and filling the cake.

Variations

Genoise

CHOCOLATE GENOISE

Melissa listed this on the dessert menu as PMS cake—a name our male servers didn't appreciate. Cocoa powder is heavier than flour and can weigh down the egg whites, so take extra care when folding in the dry ingredients.

Follow the Genoise master recipe, decreasing the flour to 1 cup and folding in 1/3 cup sifted cocoa powder along with the flour. Proceed to mix, bake, and cool the cakes as directed in the master recipe.

Split the cake layers. Fill, using about 1 cup Whipped Cream Frosting (page 42), 1 sliced banana, and 1/2 cup chopped toasted pecans for each layer. Drizzle the cake with a generous 1/2 cup warm Ganache (page 47). See page 19 for instructions on splitting and filling the cake.

Serves 14

ALMOND GENOISE

Almond extract gives the depth and intensity of the nut, but too much of it is overbearing; be sure to use a light touch.

Follow the Genoise master recipe, substituting almond extract for the vanilla extract, decreasing the flour to 1 cup, and folding in 1 cup finely ground toasted almonds along with the flour. Proceed to mix, bake, and cool the cakes as directed in the master recipe.

Split the cake layers. Fill, using 1/2 cup Almond Italian Buttercream (page 49) and 1 cup thinly sliced poached pears (page 36) for each layer. Frost the top and sides of the cake with the remaining buttercream. See page 19 for instructions on splitting, filling, and frosting the cake.

Serves 14

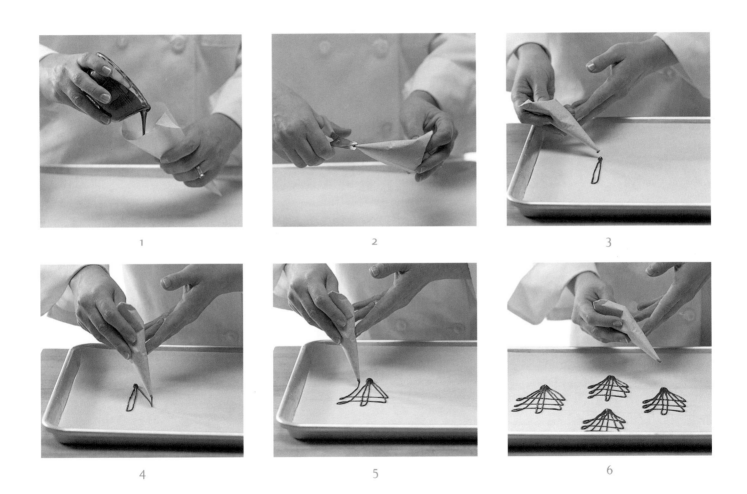

1

2

3

4

5

6

Making Chocolate Garnish

I like to melt good-quality bittersweet chocolate and pipe it into various shapes to use as garnishes for just about any dessert—from cakes to a simple dish of ice cream. This classic pattern is one that every student in culinary school learns.

1. Line a sheet pan with parchment paper; set aside. Pour warm melted chocolate into a prepared parchment pastry bag, filling the bag about halfway full.

2. Cut a very small hole in the tip of the pastry bag.

3. Pipe a 2-inch-long by 1/2-inch-wide loop of chocolate onto the prepared sheet pan.

4. Starting at the base of the loop, pipe a line out at about a 45-degree angle, stopping about 1/8 inch below the level of the top of the loop. Continue piping the line across the loop to mirror the opposite side. Make a small loop and then bring the line down to form a triangle.

5. Repeat the pattern 2 more times, spacing the top of each triangle about 1/4 inch below the previous one.

6. Refrigerate until set, and then use as a garnish.

(master recipe)

Angel Food Cake

When baking this classic dessert, be sure to use a clean, dry mixing bowl and whip attachment and take care when folding in the flour, using a bigger bowl than you think you need. Don't let the number of egg whites scare you off; you can freeze the yolks to use later in those recipes that call for them, such as Pastry Cream, Crème Brûlée, and Lemon Curd.

Serves 12

1 cup flour

1 1/2 cups powdered sugar

12 egg whites

1 1/2 teaspoons cream of tartar

1/4 teaspoon salt

1 cup granulated sugar

1 tablespoon pure vanilla extract

Powdered sugar, for dusting

1 1/2 cups whipped cream, as accompaniment

Seasonal fruit, as accompaniment

Preheat the oven to 350°.

Sift together the flour and powdered sugar 3 times; set aside.

Place the egg whites, cream of tartar, and salt in the clean, dry bowl of a mixer fitted with the whip attachment, and whip on high speed until frothy. While beating, add the granulated sugar, about 1 tablespoon at a time, and whip until the egg whites are very shiny and hold a stiff peak. (Be sure to add the sugar slowly so it has time to dissolve; otherwise the egg whites will lose volume and be too soupy.) Add the vanilla extract and mix well. Remove the bowl from the mixer.

Using a large plastic spatula, gently fold in the reserved flour mixture. Pour the batter into an ungreased 8 by 3-inch angel food cake pan (if it's greased, the batter won't cling to the sides of the pan), and bake until the cake springs back when touched gently in the center, about 1 hour. Invert the cake over a small, heavy bottle, placing the neck of the bottle inside the center opening of the pan, and let cool completely. Run a knife around the bottom and sides of the pan to release the cake.

To serve, dust the cake with powdered sugar. Serve topped with softly whipped cream and seasonal fruit.

Variations

Angel Food Cake

COCONUT ANGEL FOOD CAKE

For a fun post-barbecue dessert, serve this cake with the Grilled Rum-Soaked Pineapple with Warm White Chocolate Mousse (page 199).

Follow the Angel Food Cake master recipe, gently folding 1 cup cooled toasted coconut (page 8) into the beaten egg whites, along with the flour mixture. Proceed to mix, bake and cool the cake as directed in the master recipe. Dust the cooled cake with powdered sugar.

Serves 12

HAZELNUT ANGEL FOOD CAKE

The fat in the nuts makes this cake denser than the usual angel food cake and gives it a mellow richness. You can substitute any type of nut for the hazelnuts.

Follow the Angel Food Cake master recipe, gently folding 1 cup finely ground toasted hazelnuts into the finished batter. Bake and cool as directed in the master recipe. Glaze the cooled cake with Lemon Glaze (page 32) or 2 cups warm Ganache (page 47).

Serves 12

CHOCOLATE ANGEL FOOD CAKE

To make this a Mexican chocolate cake, add 1 teaspoon ground cinnamon along with the cocoa powder.

Follow the Angel Food Cake master recipe, adding 1/2 cup unsweetened cocoa powder to the flour and powdered sugar; sift 3 times and proceed to mix, bake, and cool the cake as directed in the master recipe. Glaze the cooled cake with 2 cups warm Ganache (page 47).

Serves 12

ORANGE ANGEL FOOD CAKE

The easy addition of orange zest to the batter adds complexity to the simple flavor of the master recipe.

Follow the Angel Food Cake master recipe, gently folding the finely grated zest of 1 orange into the beaten egg whites, along with the flour mixture. Proceed to mix, bake, and cool the cake as directed in the master recipe. To make the Orange Glaze, mix together 1 cup powdered sugar, a dash of pure vanilla extract, and 2 tablespoons orange juice. Pour glaze over the cooled cake.

Serves 12

(master recipe)

Lemon Pound Cake

Delicious by itself, this simple cake is also a good vehicle for other ingredients, such as fresh fruit or berries and whipped cream. To transform it into something truly extravagant, cover a slice with warm sautéed apples and a scoop of vanilla ice cream, top with another slice, and then drizzle with warm Caramel Sauce (page 58).

Serves 12

Lemon Pound Cake

1/2 cup unsalted butter, at room temperature

1 1/2 cups sugar

Finely grated zest of 2 lemons

3 eggs

Juice of 1 lemon

3/4 cup sour cream

2 1/4 cups flour

1 teaspoon baking powder

1/4 teaspoon baking soda

1/2 teaspoon salt

Lemon Glaze

1 cup powdered sugar

3 tablespoons lemon juice

Preheat the oven to 350°. Grease a Bundt pan; set aside.

To prepare the cake, place the butter, sugar, and lemon zest in the bowl of a mixer fitted with the paddle attachment and beat on high speed, scraping down the sides of the bowl often, until light and fluffy, about 5 minutes. With the mixer on low speed, add the eggs, one at a time, scraping down the sides of the bowl and mixing well after each addition. Add the lemon juice and sour cream, and mix well. (The batter may look separated at this point, but the dry ingredients will fix that.) Combine the flour, baking powder, baking soda, and salt, add to the butter mixture, and mix until creamy. Pour the batter into the prepared pan and bake until the cake slowly springs back when pressed gently in the center, about 1 hour. Cool for 10 minutes, then remove the cake from the pan and cool completely.

To prepare the glaze, mix together the powdered sugar and lemon juice. Pour it over the cooled cake and let sit until the glaze hardens, about 10 minutes.

Variations

Lemon Pound Cake

CHOCOLATE-CHERRY POUND CAKE

This cake is pretty intense, but don't let that keep you from embellishing it! Make a sundae by topping a slice or two with chocolate or vanilla ice cream and then pouring warm cherry compote over the top.

Soak 1/2 cup dried sour cherries in 1/2 cup almond liqueur for about 30 minutes. Coarsely chop the cherries, reserving the liqueur; set aside.

Follow the Lemon Pound Cake master recipe, omitting the lemon zest and juice. After the sour cream is incorporated, add the reserved cherries and liqueur, and mix well. Add 1/2 cup unsweetened cocoa powder to the flour mixture, combine it with the butter mixture, then add 1/2 cup chopped bittersweet chocolate, and mix well. Proceed as directed in the master recipe, omitting the Lemon Glaze.

Serves 12

FRESH BERRY AND LEMON POUND CAKE

The next time you prepare a brunch, consider this variation as a yummy substitute for coffee cake. If you don't have fresh berries, thawed frozen ones will do in a pinch, but they must be drained really well—otherwise the cake will be soggy.

Follow the Lemon Pound Cake master recipe, folding 1 to 1 1/2 cups fresh blueberries, raspberries, blackberries, or peeled, diced peaches into the batter. Bake as directed in the master recipe, topping with the Lemon Glaze.

Serves 12

Gingerbread

Gingerbread's comforting aroma of spices and molasses reminds me of when my mom made it when I was young. I'll never forget the anticipation of waiting for the gingerbread to cool so I could have a piece, then topping it with a big blob of whipped cream that would melt as I relished every bite.

Serves 12

1 1/4 cups unsulfured molasses

1 teaspoon baking soda

1 3/4 cups boiling water

3/4 cup unsalted butter, at room temperature

1/4 cup firmly packed brown sugar

2 eggs

1/2 teaspoon salt

1 tablespoon ground ginger

2 teaspoons ground cinnamon

1/4 teaspoon ground cloves

3 1/2 cups flour

1 tablespoon plus 3/4 teaspoon baking powder

Lemon Curd (page 64), as accompaniment

1 1/2 cups whipped cream, as accompaniment

Preheat the oven to 350°. Grease a 9 by 13-inch baking pan; set aside.

Place the molasses and baking soda in a bowl, add the boiling water, and let cool to room temperature.

Place the butter and brown sugar in the bowl of a mixer fitted with the paddle attachment and beat on high speed, scraping down the sides of the bowl often, until light and fluffy, about 5 minutes. With the mixer on low speed, add the eggs, one at a time, scraping down the sides of the bowl and mixing well after each addition. Sift together the salt, spices, flour, and baking powder. Add about a third of the dry ingredients to the batter, beat on low speed until well blended, then add about half of the cooled molasses mixture and beat well. Continue adding the dry and wet ingredients alternately, scraping down the sides of the bowl and beating well after each addition. Pour the batter into the prepared pan and bake until a knife inserted in the center comes out clean, about 40 minutes.

Serve warm or at room temperature, topped with Lemon Curd and softly whipped cream.

Variations

Gingerbread

PEAR-LEMON GINGERBREAD WITH PEAR-WINE SYRUP

Here's gingerbread that has a grown-up twist, with wine-poached pears, lemon to complement the spices, and a luscious syrup which is simply the poaching liquid reduced down until it is very thick and concentrated.

Peel and halve 3 firm seasonal pears. In a heavy saucepan over high heat, combine 3 cups white wine, 1 cup sugar, 2 cinnamon sticks, and 2 teaspoons finely chopped lemon zest. Bring to a boil, add the pears, lower the heat to medium, and poach until fork-tender, 8 to 10 minutes. Cool the pears in the liquid and refrigerate until ready to use. Remove the pears from the poaching liquid (reserve the liquid for the syrup) and cut into small dice; set aside.

Follow the Gingerbread master recipe, folding the diced pears and 1 tablespoon finely chopped lemon zest into the finished batter. Bake as directed in the master recipe.

Meanwhile, to make the syrup, place the reserved poaching liquid in a saucepan over medium heat and simmer until reduced to about 3/4 cup.

Serve the gingerbread warm, drizzled with the warm pear syrup and topped with softly whipped cream.

Serves 12

GINGERY PECAN GINGERBREAD

Candied ginger gives this cake complexity, and the pecans give it a pleasing crunchy texture.

Follow the Gingerbread master recipe, folding 1 cup chopped toasted pecans and 1/2 cup finely minced candied ginger into the finished batter. Bake as directed in the master recipe.

Serves 12

Sour Cream Cheesecake

This cheesecake makes an especially good springboard for an array of variations. Just change the crust, embellish the filling, or serve it with a different sauce, and you'll have given this classic an entirely new twist. Cheesecake seems like a simple dessert to put together, but it does have its quirks. A few tricks should help you bypass potential problems and almost guarantee a silky smooth, perfectly baked cake. If you have a food processor, use it to mix the ingredients—it quickly blends the batter to a perfect consistency. And speaking of consistency, make sure the cream cheese and sugar mixture is very smooth before you add the eggs, since it's almost impossible to get rid of any lumps of cream cheese after the eggs are incorporated. You can avoid turning out a cracked or overly brown cheesecake by baking it at a lower temperature for a longer length of time than many recipes direct. To tell when a cheesecake is done, jiggle the pan—if the entire cake moves as one solid mass, it is cooked throughout. When in doubt, remember that a creamy, underbaked cheesecake always tastes better than a sandy textured, overbaked one.

Serves 14

Crumb Crust (page 77) or Chocolate Cookie Crumb Crust (page 77)

2 pounds cream cheese, at room temperature

1 1/2 cups sugar

2 vanilla beans, split in half lengthwise

6 eggs

1 cup sour cream

1 1/2 cups whipped cream, as accompaniment

Mint sprigs, for garnish

Preheat the oven to 325°. Prepare the crumb crust of your choice and press it onto the bottom and halfway up the sides of a well-greased 10-inch springform pan; set aside.

Place the cream cheese and sugar in a food processor or in the bowl of an electric mixer fitted with the paddle attachment and blend until very smooth and there are no lumps of cream cheese, scraping down the sides often. Scrape the seeds from the inside of the vanilla beans into the mixture (discard the beans), and mix well. With the machine running, add the eggs one at a time, scraping

continued

continued from page 37

down the sides of the bowl and mixing well after each addition. Add the sour cream and blend until very smooth. Pour the filling into the crust and bake until the cheesecake moves as one mass when you gently jiggle the pan, about 1 hour and 15 minutes. Let cool for about 30 minutes, then chill for at least 2 hours before serving.

To serve, run a knife around the sides of the pan to loosen the cake, then remove the outer ring.

Serve chilled, topped with softly whipped cream and garnished with mint sprigs.

Variations

Sour Cream Cheesecake

BERRY CHEESECAKE

Here's a tasty way to take advantage of summer berries. Adding a berry liqueur, such as Chambord or framboise, will intensify the flavor of the fruit, but if you don't have any in your cupboard, try a complementary liqueur. One of my favorites is Tuaca, which has a caramel-vanilla flavor.

Follow the Sour Cream Cheesecake master recipe, adding the finely grated zest of 1 orange or lemon to the cream cheese mixture and omitting the vanilla bean. After the sour cream is incorporated, add 1/4 cup berry liqueur and mix well. Transfer the filling to a bowl, then fold in 1 1/2 to 2 cups fresh raspberries, blackberries, or blueberries. Bake, cool, and chill as directed in the master recipe.

Serve chilled, garnished with softly whipped cream and more berries and drizzled with Berry Sauce (page 63).

Serves 14

INDIVIDUAL MOCHA-ORANGE CHEESECAKES

I served these little cheesecakes fresh from the oven in a cooking class, and everyone loved them. Many people commented on how great it was to eat warm cheesecake, since it's almost always served chilled (slicing a warm cheesecake is nearly impossible). Individual cheesecakes can be easy to overbake, so note that the oven temperature in this variation is lower than in the master recipe.

Preheat the oven to 300°. Grease ten 8-ounce ramekins; set aside.

Prepare the batter as directed in the Sour Cream Cheesecake master recipe, adding 1 tablespoon finely chopped orange zest, 1/4 cup Grand Marnier, and 2 tablespoons instant espresso powder along with the sour cream. Divide the batter among the ramekins. Set the ramekins in a shallow roasting pan, then fill the pan with enough hot water to reach about halfway up the sides of the ramekins. Carefully set the pan in the oven and bake just until set, about 40 minutes. Remove the ramekins from the water bath, and let cool for about 10 minutes before serving.

Serve warm or chilled, topped with Chocolate Sauce (page 62) and softly whipped cream, and garnished with shaved chocolate (page 9) and mint sprigs.

Serves 10

CHOCOLATE CHEESECAKE

The chocolate makes this cheesecake much denser than the master recipe, but you can lighten up the texture, if you wish. Here's how: Separate 2 of the eggs, adding the yolks to the cream cheese along with the other eggs. Whip the whites just until they hold soft peaks, and then gently fold them into the finished batter before baking.

Prepare the Chocolate Cookie Crumb Crust (page 77), and press it onto the bottom and three-fourths of the way up the sides of a well-greased 10-inch springform pan; set aside.

Follow the Sour Cream Cheesecake master recipe, adding 1 pound melted bittersweet or semisweet chocolate (page 8) to the filling after the eggs are incorporated. Mix well. Add 1/4 cup crème de cacao along with the sour cream, and bake, cool, and chill as directed in the master recipe.

Serve chilled with softly whipped cream and Berry Sauce (page 63).

Serves 14

(master recipe)

carrot cake

I'm usually not a fan of carrot cake. It is often too klunky and heavy for my taste. Melissa's, however, is so delicate and light that it makes me want a huge piece! Her secret is in the whipping of the sugar, oil, and eggs. During this crucial first step, she takes the time to incorporate enough air into them so the mixture is very light and fluffy.

Serves 14

2 cups sugar

1 1/2 cups vegetable oil

4 eggs

4 cups finely shredded carrots

2 cups flour

2 teaspoons baking powder

2 teaspoons baking soda

1 teaspoon salt

1 tablespoon ground cinnamon

3/4 cup finely chopped pecans

3/4 cup shredded sweetened coconut

Preheat the oven to 350°. Grease two 9-inch round cake pans and line the bottoms with parchment paper; set aside.

Place the sugar and vegetable oil in the bowl of a mixer fitted with the paddle attachment and beat on high speed, scraping down the sides of the bowl often, until smooth and light, about 4 minutes. With the mixer on low speed, add the eggs, one at a time, scraping down the sides of the bowl and mixing well after each addition. Add the shredded carrots and mix well. Add the flour, baking powder, baking soda, salt, and cinnamon, and mix until smooth. Add the pecans and coconut, and mix well. Divide the batter between the prepared pans and bake until the cake springs back when pressed lightly in the center, 25 to 30 minutes. Let cool for about 10 minutes, then remove the cakes from the pans and let cool completely.

Split the cake layers, then fill and frost with Cream Cheese Frosting (page 46). See page 19 for instructions on splitting, filling, and frosting the cake layers.

Variation

Carrot Cake

ZUCCHINI CAKE

Here's a new way to get rid of extra zucchini in your garden without having to rely on zucchini bread or doling it out to your neighbors.

Follow the Carrot Cake master recipe, substituting shredded zucchini for the carrots and, if you like, adding 1 small (8-ounce) can crushed pineapple, drained, along with the nuts and coconut. Proceed as directed in the master recipe.

Serves 14

(master recipe)

Whipped Cream Frosting

This is the perfect frosting for lighter, more delicate summer cakes like the Genoise. Since it is made with heavy cream, serve cakes frosted in it as soon as possible. If you have any leftover cake (which I doubt), be sure to refrigerate it.

Makes enough to fill and
frost one 9-inch layer cake

5 cups heavy whipping cream

2/3 cup sugar

1 teaspoon pure vanilla extract

3 tablespoons cream of tartar

Place the cream in the bowl of a mixer fitted with the whip attachment and beat on high speed until it starts to thicken. Add the sugar, vanilla extract, and cream of tartar and beat until the cream holds a stiff peak. Use immediately. See page 19 for instructions on filling and frosting cakes.

Variations

Whipped Cream Frosting

ORANGE WHIPPED CREAM FROSTING

The orange in this variation provides a bit of contrast to the rich cream. Try it with cakes filled with summer fruits or berries.

Follow the Whipped Cream Frosting master recipe, adding the finely grated zest of 1 orange and 1/4 cup orange liqueur along with the sugar.

Makes enough to fill and frost one 9-inch layer cake

CHOCOLATE WHIPPED CREAM FROSTING

The addition of chocolate gives the frosting a more decadent flavor and texture, so go for the gusto and pair it with cakes that are a bit richer in texture and taste, such as the Chocolate Buttermilk Cake. Or, pair it with a light Genoise and get the best of both worlds.

Follow the Whipped Cream Frosting master recipe, adding 1/3 cup sifted cocoa powder along with the sugar.

Makes enough to fill and frost one 9-inch layer cake

(master recipe)

chocolate sour cream frosting

This is like the frosting that your grandmother probably made. It's very rich, with a nice touch of tang in the finish from the sour cream; I like to use it on intense chocolate cakes, but it is just as good on a simple butter cake.

Makes enough to fill and
frost one 9-inch layer cake

10 ounces unsweetened chocolate, chopped

1 pound cold unsalted butter, diced

3 1/2 cups powdered sugar, sifted

Pinch of salt

1 teaspoon pure vanilla extract

1 cup sour cream

2 tablespoons crème de cacao

Place the chocolate in a metal bowl set over a pan of simmering water. Once the chocolate has melted about halfway, remove the pan from the heat (leave the bowl in the pan) and let the chocolate finish melting. Meanwhile, place the butter in the bowl of a mixer with the paddle attachment and beat until very light and fluffy, scraping down the sides of the bowl often, about 5 minutes. With the mixer on low speed, slowly add the melted chocolate, and then stop the mixer and scrape down the bowl. Add the powdered sugar, very carefully turn the mixer back on at low speed (so you do not get covered in powdered sugar), and mix, again scraping down the sides of the bowl often, until smooth. Add the salt, vanilla extract, sour cream, and crème de cacao, and mix until the frosting is very smooth. Use as directed. See page 19 for information on filling and frosting cakes.

Variations

Chocolate Sour Cream Frosting

MOCHA SOUR CREAM FROSTING

This variation takes the master recipe over the top, with instant espresso powder for intensity and coffee liqueur for even more flavor.

Follow the Chocolate Sour Cream Frosting master recipe, adding 2 tablespoons instant espresso powder to the chocolate before melting, and substituting coffee liqueur for the crème de cacao.

Makes enough to fill and frost one 9-inch layer cake

ORANGE-CHOCOLATE SOUR CREAM FROSTING

Between the orange and the sour cream, there's plenty of delicious contrast to the chocolate flavor of this frosting. You can also add a pinch of cinnamon for a fragrant touch.

Follow the Chocolate Sour Cream Frosting master recipe, adding 2 tablespoons orange juice concentrate and 1/2 teaspoon ground cinnamon to the butter before beating, and substituting orange liqueur for the crème de cacao.

Makes enough to fill and frost one 9-inch layer cake

(master recipe)

Cream Cheese Frosting

This traditional frosting for carrot cake also makes a memorable match with chocolate cake. For a slightly different twist, you can add 1 teaspoon ground cinnamon along with the other ingredients or even substitute the vanilla extract with a liqueur such as Frangelico.

Makes enough to fill and frost one 9-inch layer cake

1 pound cream cheese, at room temperature

1/2 pound unsalted butter, at room temperature

2 pounds powdered sugar

1 tablespoon pure vanilla extract

Place the cream cheese, butter, powdered sugar, and vanilla extract in the bowl of a mixer fitted with a paddle attachment. Beat on low speed just to combine the ingredients, then beat on high speed, occasionally stopping the mixer and scraping down the sides of the bowl, until very light, fluffy, and smooth, about 7 minutes.

Variation

Cream Cheese Frosting

CHOCOLATE CREAM CHEESE FROSTING

Be sure to let the melted chocolate cool slightly before beating into the frosting. If you like, add 1 teaspoon cinnamon along with the chocolate for a Mexican chocolate frosting.

Prepare the Cream Cheese Frosting as directed in the master recipe. With the mixer on low speed, slowly add 4 ounces warm (but not hot) melted bittersweet chocolate (see page 8). Stop the mixer, scrape down the sides of the bowl, and then continue beating on low speed until well blended.

Makes enough to fill and frost one 9-inch layer cake

Ganache

When it comes to chocolate, ganache is not for the faint of heart. Melissa usually uses this rich, fudgy frosting on her mile-high chocolate cakes.

Makes enough to fill and
frost one 9-inch layer cake

1 1/2 pounds bittersweet chocolate, chopped

1/3 cup light corn syrup

2 cups heavy whipping cream

Combine the chocolate and corn syrup in a large bowl; set aside. Place the cream in a heavy saucepan over medium heat, bring just to a boil, and then pour it over the chocolate mixture. Let sit until the chocolate has melted about halfway, about 2 minutes, and then whisk until smooth. Let cool until thick (it should hold a soft peak). To speed up the process, refrigerate the frosting for about 15 minutes, and then stir; if it is still too thin, refrigerate it for about 5 minutes longer. (When you take it out of the refrigerator it will continue to thicken, so don't leave it in for too long.) Use as directed. See page 19 for instructions on filling and frosting cakes.

(master recipe)

Italian Buttercream

This classic vanilla buttercream pairs well with any of the cakes in this book. That is what's so great about buttercreams in general: they lend themselves to all flavors and textures of cakes. After frosting a cake with this buttercream, keep it refrigerated if you don't serve it right away. Let the cake sit at room temperature for about 20 minutes before serving—the flavors are much better that way.

Makes enough to fill and
frost one 9-inch layer cake

1 pound unsalted butter, at room temperature

2 teaspoons pure vanilla extract

1 1/4 cups sugar

3/4 cup water

2 tablespoons light corn syrup

6 egg whites

Place the butter in the bowl of a mixer fitted with the paddle attachment and beat on high speed, scraping down the sides of the bowl occasionally, until very light, fluffy, and almost white, at least 7 minutes. Add the vanilla extract and mix well; transfer to a bowl and set aside.

Combine the sugar, water, and corn syrup in a saucepan over high heat, bring to a boil, and cook until the mixture registers 238° on a candy thermometer or reaches the soft-ball stage. Pour it into a small, heatproof pitcher. (This will make it much easier to add it to the egg whites.)

Place the egg whites in a clean bowl of a mixer fitted with the whip attachment and whip on high speed until very fluffy, about 1 minute. With the mixer running on medium speed, slowly add the syrup in a steady stream, and then continue whipping until the egg whites cool, about 5 to 6 minutes. (Feel the bottom of the mixing bowl; if it's warm, keep beating until it's cool.) While continuing to beat, slowly add the softened butter, about 1 tablespoon at a time, occasionally scraping down the sides of the bowl, and mix until smooth. Use as directed. See page 19 for instructions on filling and frosting cakes.

Variations

Italian Buttercream

ALMOND ITALIAN BUTTERCREAM

This variation of the vanilla-scented master recipe also works well with any type of cake, but I especially like it with the Yellow Butter Cake filled with orange or lemon curd. For extra contrast, I finish the sides of the cake with a coating of ground toasted almonds.

Follow the Italian Buttercream master recipe, substituting 1 teaspoon almond extract for the vanilla extract, and adding 1/4 cup almond liqueur along with the extract.

Makes enough to fill and frost one 9-inch layer cake

LEMON ITALIAN BUTTERCREAM

The little taste of lemon adds a nice touch to the richness of the butter, but if you prefer the flavor of lime or orange, you can add the zest of either of those fruits instead. I like this frosting with a lighter cake filled with summer fruit.

Follow the Italian Buttercream master recipe, adding the finely grated zest and juice of 1 lemon to the beaten butter, along with the vanilla.

Makes enough to fill and frost one 9-inch layer cake

GINGER ITALIAN BUTTERCREAM

Follow the Italian Buttercream master recipe, adding 2 tablespoons coarsely chopped fresh ginger along with the water and sugar before boiling. When the syrup reaches 238° or the soft-ball stage, strain it through a fine-mesh sieve, and then proceed as directed in the master recipe. If you like, you can also add the finely grated zest of 1 orange, lemon, or lime to the egg white mixture, along with the softened butter.

Makes enough to fill and frost one 9-inch layer cake

1

2

3

4

5

6

7

8

Making Italian Buttercream

This classic buttercream can be varied quite easily, simply by adding fresh citrus zest, a touch of flavored liqueur or extract, or even a bit of instant espresso powder.

1. Using a paddle attachment, beat the butter on high speed until very fluffy and white, about 10 minutes.

2. Place the egg whites in a clean mixer bowl, and fit the mixer with a whip attachment. Whip the whites on high speed until they hold a soft peak.

3. Pour the sugar syrup that has reached 238° into a small pitcher.

4. While whipping the egg whites, slowly add the sugar syrup in a thin stream.

5. Continue whipping until all of the sugar syrup is incorporated and the whites hold a stiff peak and are very shiny. Continue whipping until the metal mixing bowl is cool to the touch.

6. Fit the mixer with a clean paddle attachment. While mixing on medium speed, add the butter, 1 tablespoon at a time, until it is all incorporated.

7. Add the vanilla extract and beat well.

8. Mix the buttercream until completely smooth. Use as directed in the recipe.

(master recipe)

Quick Buttercream

You make this easy, good, all-purpose frosting a bit differently than a traditional buttercream. First, you prepare a pastry cream as the base of the frosting, which you can flavor with just about anything. As with all buttercreams, store cakes frosted in this in the refrigerator, and bring them out 20 minutes before serving for the best flavor.

Makes enough to fill and
frost one 9-inch layer cake

2 cups half-and-half

1 egg yolk

3 tablespoons cornstarch

1 pound unsalted butter, at room temperature

3/4 cup sugar

1/8 teaspoon salt

2 tablespoons pure vanilla extract

Place the half-and-half, egg yolk, and cornstarch in a saucepan and whisk until smooth. Cook over medium-high heat, stirring constantly, until it comes to a boil and is very thick. (It's thick enough when you can see the bottom of the pan as you stir.) Strain the mixture into a bowl and refrigerate until cool, about 30 minutes.

Place the butter and sugar in the bowl of a mixer fitted with the paddle attachment and beat on high speed, scraping down the sides of the bowl occasionally, until very light, fluffy, and white, at least 10 minutes. Add the salt and mix well. With the mixer on low speed, slowly add the cold half-and-half mixture, scraping down the sides of the bowl, and mix until smooth. Add the vanilla extract and mix well. Use as directed. See page 19 for instructions on filling and frosting cakes.

Variations

Quick Buttercream

Makes enough to fill and frost one 9-inch layer cake (all variations)

ESPRESSO–SHAVED CHOCOLATE BUTTERCREAM

Try this on any of the chocolate layer cakes in this book. The espresso makes a nice flavor base for the shaved chocolate, which adds chocolate flavor and texture.

Follow the Quick Buttercream master recipe, adding 2 tablespoons instant espresso powder to the half-and-half before heating. Proceed as directed in the master recipe, gently folding 1/2 cup finely grated bittersweet chocolate into the finished frosting.

BROWN SUGAR BUTTERCREAM

Brown sugar gives this frosting a depth that granulated sugar just can't provide. Neither too light nor too heavy, this frosting tastes great with all types of cakes.

Follow the Quick Buttercream master recipe, substituting brown sugar for the granulated sugar.

MINT BUTTERCREAM

The flavor of mint goes well with many of the cakes in this book, from the Yellow Butter Cake to the rich Chocolate Buttermilk Cake.

Follow the Quick Buttercream master recipe, adding 1 cup chopped mint leaves to the half-and-half before heating. Strain the thickened half-and-half mixture through a fine-mesh sieve, and then proceed as directed in the master recipe.

WHITE CHOCOLATE QUICK BUTTERCREAM

This frosting seems to work well with just about every cake in the book, from the lighter Genoise to the Old-Fashioned Chocolate Cake–but my favorite pairing is with the Carrot Cake.

Follow the master recipe, adding 6 ounces chopped white chocolate to the thickened half-and-half mixture after removing it from the heat. Let sit until the white chocolate has melted, and then mix well. Proceed as directed in the master recipe.

Pastry Cream

Pastry cream is the base for many desserts, from cream pies to chocolate soufflés. You can make any flavor of pastry cream that you can dream up simply by steeping different ingredients in the cream during the first step of the recipe. For example, try steeping 2 or 3 slices of fresh ginger in the cream, or even try adding a couple of stems of fresh lavender for a pastry cream with a hint of Provence.

Makes about 3 cups

2 cups half-and-half

1 vanilla bean, split in half lengthwise

4 egg yolks

1/2 cup plus 2 tablespoons sugar

1/4 cup cornstarch

2 teaspoons pure vanilla extract

Place the half-and-half and vanilla bean in a heavy saucepan over medium heat and bring just to a boil. Meanwhile, whisk together the yolks, sugar, and cornstarch in a large bowl. Slowly whisk about half of the hot half-and-half into the egg mixture to temper it, or bring it up to the same temperature. Whisk in the remaining half-and-half, and then scrape the seeds from the inside of the vanilla bean into the mixture (discard the bean). Pour the mixture back into the saucepan, and again cook over medium heat, stirring constantly with a plastic spatula, until it just comes to a boil and is very thick. Transfer the pastry cream to a large bowl, add the vanilla extract, and mix well. Set a piece of plastic wrap or parchment paper on the surface of the pastry cream so that it doesn't form a skin, and refrigerate until well chilled before using, about 2 hours.

Variations

Pastry Cream

COCONUT PASTRY CREAM

Follow the Pastry Cream master recipe, substituting 1 cup coconut milk for 1 cup of the half-and-half. Mix 1 1/2 cups shredded sweetened coconut into the finished pastry cream. Cover and chill as directed in the master recipe.

Makes about 3 cups

CHOCOLATE PASTRY CREAM

Follow the Pastry Cream master recipe, mixing 4 ounces chopped bittersweet chocolate into the finished pastry cream just after it comes to a boil. Let sit for about 2 minutes to melt, and then stir the chocolate in completely. Cover and chill as directed in the master recipe.

Makes about 3 cups

55

White Chocolate Mousse Filling

You really need to make this ahead so that it can set up properly. You can also pour this into beautiful glasses and serve it on its own.

Makes enough to fill one 9-inch layer cake

8 egg yolks

1/2 cup sugar

1/3 cup Tuaca liqueur

1/3 cup water

1 tablespoon freshly squeezed lemon juice

12 ounces white chocolate, chopped

1 1/2 cups heavy whipping cream

Whisk together the egg yolks, sugar, Tuaca, and water in a metal bowl. Set the bowl over a pan of simmering water and cook, whisking constantly, until very thick, about 6 minutes. (To tell if it's thick enough, lift the whisk out of the egg mixture and drizzle a figure eight over the mixture; if it holds for 8 seconds, it is perfect.) Remove the bowl from the heat. Stir in the lemon juice and chocolate, and let sit until the chocolate has melted, and then mix until smooth. Set the bowl over a larger bowl of ice water, and let cool completely, stirring often, 10 to 15 minutes.

When the chocolate mixture is cool, place the cream in the bowl of a mixer fitted with the whip attachment, and whip on high speed until stiff peaks form. Using a plastic spatula, gently fold the whipped cream into the white chocolate mixture. Cover the mousse with plastic wrap and refrigerate until completely chilled. The mousse will keep, refrigerated, for up to 2 days.

Chocolate Mousse Filling

Melissa uses this silky smooth filling, which has a lighter texture than the Chocolate Mousse master recipe (page 196), in her Chocolate Toffee Mousse Cake. Don't hesitate to use it in any chocolate creation you dream up or even serve it on its own with cookies.

Makes enough to fill one 9-inch layer cake

12 ounces bittersweet chocolate, chopped

6 egg yolks

3/4 cup water

1/2 cup sugar

2 cups heavy whipping cream

1/2 cup sour cream

Place the chocolate in a metal bowl set over a pan of simmering water (make sure the bottom of the bowl does not touch the water). When the chocolate has melted about halfway, remove the pan from the heat (leave the bowl on the pan), and let stand until completely melted; stir until smooth. Set aside in a warm (but not hot) place so it will stay melted.

Place the egg yolks in the bowl of a mixer fitted with a whip attachment and beat on high speed until light in color and very thick, about 5 minutes. Meanwhile, combine the water and sugar in a saucepan over high heat and bring to a boil. With the mixer on medium speed, slowly add the hot sugar mixture to the egg yolks, then increase the speed to medium-high and beat, occasionally stopping the mixer and scraping down the sides of the bowl, until the mixture has doubled in volume, about 10 minutes. Transfer the mixture to a large bowl. Using a plastic spatula, gently fold in about one-half of the melted chocolate, and then fold in the remaining chocolate. Set aside.

In the bowl of the mixer fitted with the whip attachment, beat the cream and sour cream on high speed until soft peaks form. Gently fold the cream mixture into the chocolate mixture. Refrigerate until chilled, at least 2 hours (overnight is even better). Use as directed.

caramel Sauce

Although I think caramel sauce is best eaten by the spoonful out of the refrigerator, it is also wonderful on ice cream, cream pies, and even fresh fruit. It will thicken when chilled, so warm it a bit before serving.

Makes about 1 1/2 cups

1 cup sugar

1/4 cup water

1 cup heavy whipping cream

Place the sugar in a large sauté pan with sides or a heavy saucepan. Gently moisten the sugar with the water, being careful not to splash the water and sugar onto the sides of the pan. Cook the sugar mixture over high heat, without stirring, until you see any part of it turning brown, then swirl the pan to even out the color. Cook until golden brown, about 2 minutes longer. Carefully add the cream to the hot sugar, taking care to pour it in slowly because it will bubble up very violently. Cook, without stirring, until the caramelized sugar has liquefied again and the mixture is very smooth and a deep golden brown, 2 to 3 minutes. Remove the pan from the heat; let cool for 5 minutes before using.

Serve warm or at room temperature. The sauce will keep, refrigerated, for up to 1 week. Gently warm the chilled sauce in a heavy saucepan over low heat, or in a microwave on low power.

Caramel-Apple Sauce

This sauce can be used just like the caramel sauce. The addition of apple cider gives it depth and a wonderful, tangy finish.

Makes about 2 cups

1 1/2 cups sugar

1 cup good-quality apple cider

1 cup heavy whipping cream

1/4 cup bourbon or apple brandy

1 tablespoon unsalted butter

Place the sugar in a large sauté pan with sides or a heavy saucepan. Gently moisten the sugar with the cider, being careful not to splash the water and sugar onto the sides of the pan. Cook the sugar mixture over high heat, without stirring, until you see any part of it turning brown, then swirl the pan to even out the color. Cook until golden brown, about 2 minutes longer. Carefully add the cream to the hot sugar, taking care to pour it in slowly because it will bubble up very violently. Remove the pan from the heat and very carefully add the bourbon. Set the pan back over medium-high heat and cook, without stirring, until the caramelized sugar has liquefied again and the mixture is very smooth and a deep golden brown, about 5 minutes. Remove the pan from the heat, then add the butter and stir until melted. Let cool for 5 minutes before using.

Serve warm or at room temperature. Gently warm the chilled sauce in a heavy saucepan over low heat, or in a microwave on low power. The sauce will keep, refrigerated, for up to 1 week.

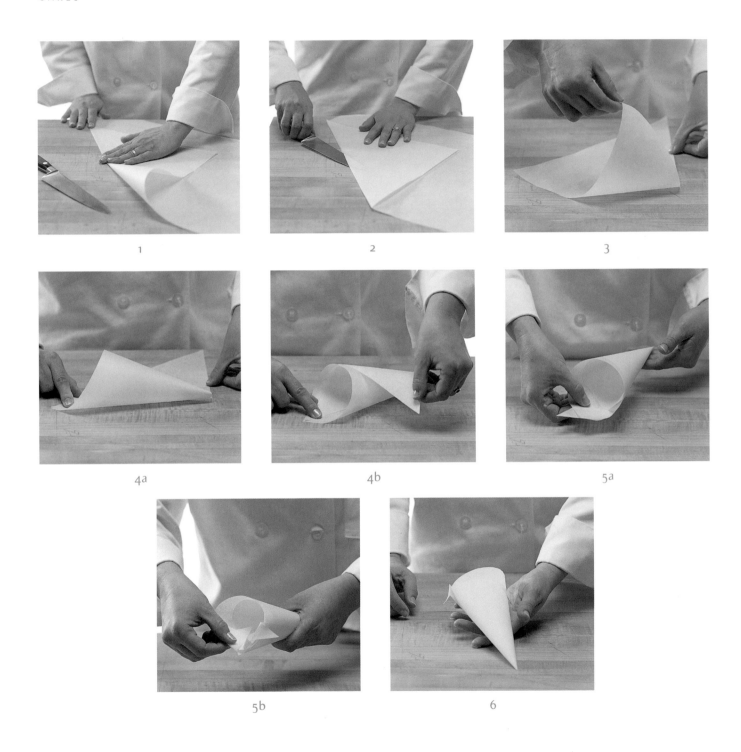

1

2

3

4a

4b

5a

5b

6

Making a Parchment Paper Pastry Bag

Parchment paper makes a versatile disposable pastry bag for small piping jobs, such as writing names on birthday cakes and making garnishes. Keep in mind that each pastry bag is good for just a single use.

1. Cut about a 19-inch-long sheet of parchment paper. Fold one corner of a sheet of parchment paper over to form a 14 by 14 by 19-inch triangle. Crease the fold well.

2. Using a very sharp knife or a pair of scissors, trim off the excess paper.

3. Bring the right-hand corner over to meet the top corner of the triangle, and hold it in place.

4. Bring the left-hand corner over and around the cone, meeting the top corner from the back.

5. Pull the top edge of the left-hand corner tight to form a fine point on the cone, and then fold all of the flaps over to secure the bag.

6. The pastry bag is ready to fill. Snip the tip and use.

Chocolate Sauce

What can I say about chocolate sauce that you don't already know? I'm sure you can think of plenty of uses for it, from drizzling over a flourless chocolate cake to topping vanilla ice cream. Every good home cook needs a recipe for a delicious chocolate sauce, and this is the one.

Makes about 2 cups

1/2 cup unsalted butter, diced

1 cup sugar

1 cup heavy whipping cream

1/3 cup unsweetened cocoa powder

Pinch of salt

1 tablespoon pure vanilla extract

Place the butter, sugar, cream, and cocoa powder in a heavy saucepan over medium heat and bring just to a boil, stirring often. Decrease the heat to low and simmer, stirring often, until the mixture is thick and coats the back of a spoon, about 7 minutes. Remove from the heat and stir in the salt and vanilla extract; let cool for 5 minutes before using. (If you like, add 2 tablespoons of your favorite liqueur along with the vanilla extract.)

Serve warm or at room temperature. The sauce will keep, refrigerated, for up to 1 week. Gently warm the chilled sauce in a heavy saucepan over low heat, or in a microwave on low power.

Berry Sauce

Make this sauce from berries at the height of the season or from frozen berries picked during the summer. At the Bistro we use raspberries, Marionberries, and blackberries, or any combination of berries.

Makes about 2 1/2 cups

6 cups fresh seasonal berries, such as raspberries, strawberries, or blackberries

1/2 cup sugar

1/4 cup berry liqueur

Purée the berries in a food processor or blender. Combine the purée, sugar, and liqueur in a saucepan over high heat, bring to a boil, and cook until the sugar has dissolved and the sauce has thickened, about 5 minutes. Strain the sauce through a fine-mesh sieve, and let cool. Refrigerate for about 2 hours before using.

Serve cold. The sauce will keep, refrigerated, for up to 1 week or frozen for up to 6 months.

(master recipe)

Lemon Curd

Whoever named this dish was really off the mark. The name curd makes you think of cottage cheese, not this rich, lemon-scented confection. Lemon curd can be used as a cake filling or poured into a tart, and your waffles will never be the same again after slathering them with it.

Makes about 2 cups

5 egg yolks

3/4 cup sugar

1/2 cup freshly squeezed lemon juice

Finely grated zest of 1 lemon

1/4 cup cold unsalted butter, diced

Whisk together the egg yolks and sugar in a metal bowl, then whisk in the lemon juice and zest. Set the bowl over a pan of simmering water (make sure the bottom of the bowl does not touch the water), and cook, stirring constantly, until very thick, 5 to 6 minutes. Remove from the heat, add the butter, let sit until melted, and stir. Strain the curd through a fine-mesh sieve. If using the curd to fill a crust, pour it into the prepared crust and refrigerate until well chilled. If using it to fill a cake, first transfer it to a clean bowl and refrigerate until completely chilled, about 2 hours.

The lemon curd will keep, refrigerated, for about 1 week.

Variation

Lemon Curd

ORANGE CURD

Here is a simple variation that is just as wonderful as its lemony counterpart.

Follow the Lemon Curd master recipe, substituting orange juice and zest for the lemon juice and zest.

Makes about 2 cups

Sugared Flowers

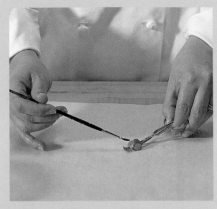

1

2

3

Sugared flowers make a beautiful garnish for everything from birthday cakes to ice cream sundaes. Only use organic edible flowers, such as violets, pansies, and roses.

1. Line a sheet pan with parchment paper; set aside. Place about 1 tablespoon of powdered egg whites (available at specialty baking stores) in a small bowl. Add just enough water to make a thin glaze, and whisk until smooth. Hold a flower at the base with a pair of large tweezers and, using a small paintbrush, gently coat it all over with the glaze.

2. Hold the glazed flower over a bowl of superfine sugar, and carefully sprinkle it with the sugar to coat.

3. Place the sugared flower on the prepared sheet pan and let dry completely, about 1 hour. Store in an air-tight container for up to 3 days.

Mascarpone Fresh Fruit Tart (page 107)

cobblers, Pies, and tarts

Cobblers, pies and tarts are rather loosely defined. In general, these culinary cousins consist of a filling surrounded by a crust, but the variations are endless. Served for dessert, as an appetizer, and everything in between, they can be sweet or savory, have a single or a double crust, or be topped with biscuits or streusel.

Pies are a very American tradition—the requisite dessert for Thanksgiving and the Fourth of July. Few desserts are so basic yet so intimidating to make. A kind of mystique surrounds the art of pie baking, perhaps because there's no middle ground with pies—they're either good or not good. To those who struggle with pies or who don't even attempt them, it seems as though some people just have that magic touch. No matter what the recipe, their pies are always perfect, with a delicate, flaky crust, expertly fluted edges, and a perfectly spiced filling, baked for just the right length of time.

Pies are to Americans as tarts are to the French. I think of tarts as more sophisticated and often prettier than pies, such as a classic French apple tart with the apple slices beautifully arranged over the crust. But when it comes right down to it, a tart is still a sweet or a savory filling in a crust.

If you've yet to bake your first pie or tart (or have been plagued by disasters), you may want to try your hand first at a cobbler or a crisp—both are nearly fail-proof. But really, the magic touch can be yours. The success of most pies and tarts hinges on how the crust is made, so if you avoid some common mistakes, you should be pleased with the results. We've included recipes for traditional pie crust, pâte brisée, pâte sucrée, shortbread crust, nut crust, and crumb crust. The methods do vary a bit, depending on the type of crust you're making.

If you're making a traditional pie crust, the most important thing is to use a gentle touch when mixing the dough. In my recipe (Cappy's Pie Crust), I use a combination of butter (for the flavor) and shortening (for the flakiness it provides), and I always use my fingertips to blend them with the flour. I like to feel what's happening with the dough so I won't overwork it, something you can't do with a pastry blender or a knife. When you combine liquid with flour and mix them together, the gluten in the flour begins to develop. For something like bread, the structure that gluten provides is desirable. Pie crust, however, should be very tender, so if you overwork the dough your crust will be tough and chewy. To avoid that, mix the water into the flour mixture just until the dough starts to come together, *not* until it becomes a smooth ball. If you are in doubt about how much water to add, remember that wetter is better: a moist dough is easier to roll out, won't crack as much, and will go into the plate more easily than a dry dough.

Next, turn the dough out onto a well-floured board (it will be crumbly) and gently form it into a disk with your hands. Let the dough rest at room temperature for at least 15 to 30 minutes (or refrigerate it for up to 2 days), so the gluten has a chance to relax. (When Melissa makes pies at the Bistro, she almost always lets the dough rest overnight and then rolls it out and makes the pies the next morning.) When the time comes to roll out the dough, use plenty of flour. You may have learned that too much flour will make a crust tough—but guess what happens if the dough sticks

to the board? You have to re-form and reroll the dough you mixed so gently, and you end up with an overworked, tough crust.

Our recipes for other types of crusts—pâte sucrée, pâte brisée, shortbread, nut crust, and crumb crusts—are made in a mixer or food processor and are, for the most part, much less temperamental than pie crust. Except for the shortbread and crumb crusts, which are pressed into the pan, roll the others out just as you would a traditional pie crust. For more instructions on mixing, rolling, and fluting crusts, see pages 73, 81, and 93.

Most of our tart recipes and many of our single-crust pie recipes call for prebaking the crust. If you have a convection oven, you should use it for this step. The circulation of the heat by the fan really helps to set the crust so that it doesn't slump. When appropriate, we've specified the temperature for both convection and standard ovens. Use the following rule of thumb to pre-bake any of the crusts (except for the Crumb Crust and the Three-Nut Crust, which do not need to pre-bake before being filled and baked) as a stepping stone for creating your own pie or tart. To prepare a par-baked crust, bake the crust in a standard or convection oven at 375° for 10 to 15 minutes. To prepare a finished crust to use for cream pies, fresh fruit tarts, or other fillings which do not require further baking, bake the crust in a standard or convection oven at 375° for about 25 minutes, or until golden brown.

Some people like to use pie weights to keep crusts nice and level while they're being prebaked, and some people don't. Either choice is fine. Melissa always lines her crusts with a piece of parchment paper and then covers the parchment with dried beans, while I opt to go without. My crusts are more lumpy and bumpy than hers, but I'm afraid to weigh them down after working so hard to make them light and flaky.

We chose to include recipes for some fairly classic fruit pies in this chapter, such as apple and strawberry-rhubarb. These were the last recipes we wrote, and I'll admit that we avoided doing so because of the challenges they posed. We bake pies by touch—telling by the feel of the fruit whether we've added enough sugar, for example—and translating that understanding into recipes with exact measurements for others to follow seemed like a puzzle. Our solution was to bake one the way we normally would, carefully keeping track of the amounts of sugar and spices we used. First, we measured and added a bit less than what we guessed the recipe needed and then we added small amounts until it felt and tasted right. We've also included recipes for pies with custard, caramel, and nut fillings, as well as beautifully arranged tarts, such as the Italian Plum Tart.

Varying the crust is the easiest way to change almost any pie or tart, and you may be surprised how different the overall flavor will be. We tried out most of the recipes with all of the different crusts. You'll see our suggestions for the combinations we really liked in each recipe. These suggestions will start you on your way to creating your own signature pie or tart, but I hope you will also try some experiments of your own.

Pâte Brisée

This crust has a finer texture than an old-fashioned one like Cappy's Pie Crust, and it is also higher in butterfat than a crust with shortening. Use it for double-crusted fruit pies or exquisite fresh fruit tarts.

Makes enough for a single-crust pie
(double this recipe for a double-crust pie)
or a 9- to 10-inch tart

1 1/2 cups flour

1/2 teaspoon salt

1/2 teaspoon sugar

3 tablespoons shortening

1/2 cup cold unsalted butter, diced

1/4 cup ice water

Place the flour, salt, and sugar in the bowl of a mixer fitted with the paddle attachment. Mix on low speed to combine. With the mixer on low speed, add the shortening and butter and mix just until the mixture resembles a coarse meal. Add the ice water and mix just until the dough starts to come together. Turn the dough out onto a well-floured board and form it into a disk with your hands. Roll the dough out and proceed as directed in the recipe, or see the instructions on page 81.

Chocolate Pâte Brisée

I use this to make crusts for both nut tarts and fresh fruit tarts. In fact, I'm not really sure if I could come up with a tart that it couldn't be used with. Like the regular Pâte Brisée, it has a fine texture and is very tender.

Makes enough for a single-crust pie
or a 9- to 10-inch tart

1 cup flour

1/2 cup unsweetened cocoa powder

1/2 cup sugar

1/2 teaspoon salt

7 tablespoons cold unsalted butter, diced

1 egg

1 teaspoon pure vanilla extract

Place the flour, cocoa powder, sugar, and salt in the bowl of a mixer fitted with the paddle attachment. Mix on low speed to combine. With the mixer on low speed, add the butter and mix just until the mixture resembles a coarse meal. Add the egg and vanilla extract and mix just until the dough starts to come together. Turn the dough out onto a well-floured board and form it into a disk with your hands. Roll the dough out and proceed as directed in the recipe, or see the instructions on page 81.

Nut Pâte Brisée

This has the fine attributes of the Pâte Brisée and the Chocolate Pâte Brisée plus the crunch and flavor of nuts.

Makes enough for a 9- to 10-inch tart
(recipe may be doubled)

1 1/2 cups flour

1/3 cup finely chopped toasted almonds, pecans, or walnuts

1/4 cup sugar

Pinch of salt

1/2 cup cold unsalted butter, diced

1 egg

1/2 teaspoon pure vanilla extract

1/2 teaspoon almond extract

Place the flour, nuts, sugar, and salt in the bowl of a mixer fitted with the paddle attachment. Mix on low speed to combine. With the mixer on low speed, add the butter and mix just until the mixture resembles a coarse meal. Add the egg, vanilla extract, and almond extract, and mix just until the dough starts to come together. Turn the dough out onto a well-floured board and form it into a disk with your hands. Roll the dough out and proceed as directed in the recipe, or see the instructions on page 81.

Pâte Sucrée

Pâte Sucrée, a classic pastry that is sweeter than both American-style pie crust and Pâte Brisée, is best used to make tarts that do not have an overly sweet filling.

Makes enough for two 10-inch tart shells
(halve the recipe to make one tart shell)

2 1/2 cups flour

1/2 cup sugar

1/2 teaspoon salt

1 cup cold unsalted butter, diced

1 egg

1 teaspoon pure vanilla extract

Place the flour, sugar, and salt in the bowl of a mixer fitted with the paddle attachment. Add the butter and mix on low speed until it resembles a coarse meal. Beat together the egg and vanilla extract in a small bowl, add it to the flour mixture, and mix on low speed just until the dough comes together. Form the dough into a disk, wrap it in plastic wrap, and refrigerate just until slightly firm, about 20 minutes. Roll the dough out and proceed as directed, or see the instructions on page 81.

The dough can be refrigerated for up to 2 days or frozen for up to 3 months.

Cappy's Pie Crust

This is the crust I use for apple pie and any of the summer pies in this book. It is a simple, traditional crust that gets its flakiness from shortening and its rich flavor from butter.

Makes enough for a single-crust pie
(double the recipe for a double-crust pie)

1 1/3 cups flour

1/4 cup cold unsalted butter, diced

1/4 cup shortening

1/2 teaspoon salt

6 tablespoons ice water

Place the flour, butter, shortening, and salt in a large bowl and, using your fingertips, blend until the mixture resembles a coarse meal. Add the water and mix with your fingertips or a large fork just until the dough comes together. Turn the dough out onto a well-floured board, form it into a disk with your hands, and let rest for 15 to 30 minutes before rolling. Roll the dough out and proceed as directed in the recipe, or see the instructions on page 81.

The dough can be refrigerated for up to 2 days or frozen for up to 3 months.

Making Pie Dough

Undermixed pie dough is always better than dough that's been overworked. During any of the stages of mixing pie dough, if you ever wonder whether you need to mix it just a bit more, the answer should always be no!

1

2

3

4

1. Place the flour, butter, shortening, and salt in a mixing bowl. Mix with your fingertips until it is well blended and resembles a coarse meal.

2. Add the cold water and mix with a large dinner fork just until the mixture begins to come together and is well moistened. (It's always better to have the dough on the wet side than too dry, because dry dough will crack and be difficult to roll out.)

3. Turn the dough out onto a well-floured board.

4. Form the dough into a disk (two if making a double-crust pie). Let it rest, uncovered, for 15 to 30 minutes, or wrap it in plastic wrap and refrigerate until ready to use.

(master recipe)

Shortbread Crust

I've been making this crust for about 12 years, ever since a woman named Zal, who I worked with at Fullers restaurant in Seattle, taught me the recipe. With a rich butter flavor and a fine texture like the Pâte Brisée and Pâte Sucrée, it goes very well with fruit, chocolate, or nut fillings.

Makes enough for one 9- to 10-inch tart

2 cups flour

1/2 cup powdered sugar

1 teaspoon pure vanilla extract

Pinch of salt

1 cup cold unsalted butter, diced

Place the flour, powdered sugar, vanilla extract, and salt in the bowl of a food processor. With the motor running, slowly add the butter and process until the dough forms a ball on top of the blade. Remove the dough from the food processor; if it's too soft to work with, refrigerate until it's easier to handle. Press the dough into a well-greased tart pan. (The easiest way to do this is to first press it into the sides of the pan, then finish with the bottom of the pan.) Refrigerate for 30 minutes before baking.

Variations

Shortbread Crust

GRAHAM SHORTBREAD CRUST

Graham flour makes this variation taste like a grown-up graham cracker.

Follow the Shortbread Crust master recipe, replacing 1/2 cup of the flour with graham flour.

Makes enough for one 9- to 10- inch tart

CHOCOLATE SHORTBREAD CRUST

Chocolate makes this pastry just a bit more delicate than the other shortbread crusts.

Follow the Shortbread Crust master recipe, replacing 1/2 cup of the flour with unsweetened cocoa powder.

Makes enough for one 9- to 10- inch tart

ORANGE-PECAN SHORTBREAD CRUST

The orange zest and toasted pecans give this crust a taste that's more like that of a great cookie than a crust.

Follow the Shortbread Crust master recipe, replacing 1/2 cup of the flour with 1/2 cup finely ground toasted pecans or other nuts (page 10) and adding the finely grated zest of 1 orange to the dry ingredients before adding the butter.

Makes enough for one 9- to 10- inch tart

three-Nut crust

This is the simplest crust in the book, since you don't have to worry about overmixing or handling it too much. The different nuts each have a distinctive taste and crunch.

Makes enough for one 9- to
10-inch tart or springform pan

3/4 cup toasted almonds (page 10)

3/4 cup toasted pecans (page 10)

3/4 cup toasted hazelnuts (page 10)

1/4 cup sugar

1/2 teaspoon ground cinnamon

1 teaspoon almond extract

6 tablespoons unsalted butter, melted

Place the nuts and sugar in the bowl of a food processor and process until the nuts are finely ground. Transfer the mixture to a large bowl, add the cinnamon and almond extract, and mix well. Add the butter and mix just until the crust holds together. Press the crust onto the bottom and sides of a well-greased tart pan or onto the bottom and halfway up the sides of a springform pan and refrigerate for about 30 minutes before using.

cornmeal crust

This crust has a tender crumb. The cornmeal provides a crisp bite and a nice touch—and against a caramel nut filling it's out of this world.

Makes enough for one 9- to
10-inch tart or springform pan

1 1/2 cups flour

1/3 cup cornmeal

1/4 cup sugar

3/4 cup cold unsalted butter, diced

1 egg, lightly beaten

Place the flour, cornmeal, and sugar in the bowl of a mixer fitted with the paddle attachment. Mix on low speed to combine. With the mixer on low speed, add the butter and mix just until the mixture resembles a coarse meal. Add the egg and mix on low speed just until the dough comes together. Turn the dough out onto a well-floured board and form it into a disk, wrap it in plastic wrap, and refrigerate until easy to handle, about 20 minutes.

crumb crust

We've all had versions of this crust on cheesecake or cream pie. Even though it has been used time and time again, it is still a favorite around the Bistro.

Makes enough for the bottom and halfway up
the sides of one 10-inch springform pan
(double the recipe if you want to press the crust
all the way up the sides of the pan)

1 1/4 cups graham cracker crumbs

2 tablespoons sugar

6 to 8 tablespoons unsalted butter, melted

In a large bowl, toss together the crumbs and sugar. Add 6 tablespoons of the butter and, using your hands, mix well. Squeeze some of the crumbs together in your fist; if they hold together, the crust is perfect, but if the mixture is too crumbly, add more butter. Press the crumbs into the bottom and sides of a well-greased 10-inch springform pan and refrigerate for about 30 minutes before using.

chocolate cookie crumb crust

Like all crumb crusts, this one takes hardly any time to put together. I use Famous Chocolate Wafers, an old-fashioned cookie that has been made since the Fifties.

Makes enough for one 9- or 10-inch tart
or springform pan (double the recipe
if you want to press the crust all the way
up the sides of the pan)

2 cups chocolate cookie crumbs (such as Famous Chocolate Wafers)

1/3 cup sugar

1 teaspoon ground cinnamon

6 tablespoons unsalted butter, melted

In a large bowl, toss the cookie crumbs with the sugar and cinnamon. Add the butter and mix just until the crust holds together. Press the crust onto the bottom and sides of a well-greased tart or springform pan and refrigerate for about 30 minutes before using.

Streusel topping

Streusel can be baked on top of a cobbler or even in place of a top crust on a pie.

Makes about 2 cups

1/3 cup brown sugar

2 tablespoons granulated sugar

1 cup old-fashioned oats

1 teaspoon ground cinnamon

1 cup flour

Pinch of salt

2 teaspoons pure vanilla extract

1/2 cup cold unsalted butter, diced

Combine the sugars, oats, cinnamon, flour, and salt in the bowl of a mixer fitted with the paddle attachment. With the mixer on low speed, add the vanilla extract and the butter, a few pieces at a time, and mix until crumbly. Use as a topping for pies, tarts, and crisps. The streusel will keep, refrigerated, for up to 1 week.

You can substitute 1/2 cup chopped toasted nuts (page 10) for 1/2 cup of the oats, if you like.

Red Wine Syrup

This might sound like a strange sauce, but it is so good with fresh berry tarts or even the Summer Berry Pie. For a beautiful presentation, first drizzle some of it onto a plate, add a drizzle of crème fraîche, and then set the slice of tart or pie off to the side.

Makes about 2 cups

1 bottle Pinot Noir or other red wine

1 1/2 cups sugar

Combine the wine and sugar in a saucepan over high heat, bring to a boil, and cook until thick and syrupy and reduced by about half, 10 to 15 minutes. Let cool for 30 minutes before using, or refrigerate until chilled, about 2 hours.

Serve warm or cold. The syrup will keep, refrigerated, for about 2 weeks.

Crème fraîche

Use crème fraîche to top a fruit crisp, to dress up a slice of pie along with the Red Wine Syrup, or to add a creamy touch to any other dessert. If you like, you can sweeten it with a couple of teaspoons of sugar and the finely grated zest of an orange.

Makes about 2 cups

2 cup heavy whipping cream

2 heaping tablespoons sour cream or buttermilk

Whisk together the cream and sour cream in a bowl. Cover with a clean dish towel and let stand at room temperature for 24 hours. Refrigerate until chilled and thickened, about 2 hours.

Serve cold. Crème fraîche will keep, refrigerated, for 1 week.

1

2

3

4

5a

5b

Rolling Dough for a Single-Crust Pie

It is actually a bit more challenging to master a single-crust pie than one with a double crust, since a double-crust pie gets a little help from the filling to weigh down the crust and help it retain its shape.

1. Place a disk of pie dough on a well-floured board. Roll it once or twice with a rolling pin to flatten it, and then lift it and turn it a quarter of a turn, dusting with a bit more flour as needed.

2. Continue rolling and turning the dough a quarter of a turn, adding more flour as needed, until it is 10 to 11 inches in diameter.

3. Gently fold the dough into fourths, transfer it to a 9-inch pie plate, and then open it back up.

4. Firmly press the dough into the pie plate, making sure that it fits snugly against the edges. Leave the excess dough hanging over the side of the plate.

5. Trim the edges of the dough to hang about 1/2 inch over the side of the pie plate. Roll the dough under to form a ridge. Using your fingers, pinch the dough to flute it. Bake as directed in the recipe.

(master recipe)

Berry Cobbler

Whenever Melissa puts individual cobblers on the menu, we go through them right away. Our customers have pretty sophisticated tastes, but a warm cobbler topped with melting ice cream really is hard to resist. There's a different interpretation of this simple, comforting dessert for every season and every fruit. Berries, apples, peaches, pears, and even cherries can be spiced with a simple touch of cinnamon or a more intense combination of diced candied ginger and orange zest and covered with a crispy streusel or a buttery biscuit topping.

Serves 8

Fruit Filling

6 cups fresh boysenberries, Marionberries, raspberries, or blueberries

1 cup cold water

1 cup sugar

2 tablespoons cornstarch

2 teaspoons ground cinnamon

2 tablespoons unsalted butter

Biscuit Topping

2 cups flour

2 tablespoons sugar

1 tablespoon baking powder

1 teaspoon salt

6 tablespoons cold unsalted butter, diced

1 cup milk

1 quart Vanilla Bean Ice Cream (page 208) or 1 1/2 cups whipped cream, as accompaniment

Mint sprigs, for garnish

Preheat the oven to 350°. Grease a 2-quart casserole dish, add the berries, and set aside.

Combine the water, sugar, and cornstarch in a heavy saucepan over medium-high heat and bring just to a boil, stirring constantly. Pour the syrup over the berries, and then sprinkle with the cinnamon and dot with the butter.

To prepare the topping, mix together the flour, sugar, baking powder, and salt in a large bowl. Add the butter and mix with your fingertips until the mixture resembles a coarse meal. Add the milk and stir just until the dough comes together. Drop the dough by spoonfuls onto the prepared fruit. Set the cobbler on a sheet pan (to save your oven in case the filling overflows) and bake until golden brown and bubbly, 45 to 50 minutes. Let cool for about 15 minutes before serving.

Serve warm, topped with vanilla ice cream or softly whipped cream and garnished with mint sprigs.

Variations

Berry Cobbler

CHERRY COBBLER

Follow the Berry Cobbler master recipe, substituting 6 cups pitted cherries for the berries and adding 1 cup chopped bittersweet chocolate to the fruit. Proceed as directed in the master recipe.

Serve warm with Vanilla Bean Ice Cream.

Serves 8

PEACH-TUACA COBBLER

Follow the Berry Cobbler master recipe, substituting 6 cups peeled, sliced peaches (page 10) for the berries and adding 1/2 teaspoon ground ginger, 1/4 teaspoon ground cloves, and 1/3 cup Tuaca liqueur along with the cinnamon. Proceed as directed in the master recipe.

Serves 8

(master recipe)

fruit crisp

I included this recipe because it's like the one John's mom made for him when he was a little boy. It comes together in a flash, so it's an ideal spur-of-the-moment dessert. The topping truly is crispy, not mushy like some fruit "crisps."

Serves 10

Classic Crisp Topping

1 cup flour

3/4 cup sugar

3/4 cup cold unsalted butter, diced

1/2 teaspoon pure vanilla extract

Pinch of salt

7 cups peeled, sliced tart apples, such as Granny Smith,
    or fresh berries

2/3 cup sugar

2 tablespoons cornstarch

1 teaspoon ground cinnamon

1/2 teaspoon ground nutmeg

1/2 teaspoon ground allspice

1/2 teaspoon ground ginger

1 teaspoon pure vanilla extract

1 quart Orange-Cinnamon Gelato (page 223) or
    1 1/2 cups whipped cream, as accompaniment

Preheat the oven to 350°. Grease a 9 by 13-inch pan; set aside.

To prepare the topping, combine the flour, sugar, butter, vanilla extract, and salt in a bowl, and mix with your fingertips until the mixture resembles a coarse meal (about the same texture as when making a pie crust); set aside.

Toss the fruit with the sugar and cornstarch in a bowl. Add the spices and vanilla, and mix well. Place the fruit mixture in the prepared pan and sprinkle with the topping. Bake until golden brown and bubbly, 45 to 50 minutes. Let cool for 10 to 15 minutes before serving.

Serve warm, topped with Orange-Cinnamon Gelato or softly whipped cream.

Variations

Fruit crisp

OATMEAL-NUT CRISP

This is my favorite way to make fruit crisp, with the addition of oatmeal to give a chewy contrast to the crispy, sugary topping.

Follow the Fruit Crisp master recipe, adding 1 cup old-fashioned oats and 2/3 cup ground toasted pecans (page 10) to the topping. Proceed as in the master recipe.

Serve warm with Vanilla Bean Ice Cream (page 208).

Serves 10

INDIVIDUAL FRUIT CRISPS

Butter eight 8-ounce ramekins; set aside.

Follow the Fruit Crisp master recipe, dividing the fruit filling among the prepared ramekins. Top with either the Classic Crisp Topping or the oatmeal-nut topping variation at left. Set the ramekins on a sheet pan (in case the filling overflows) and bake until golden brown and bubbly, 45 to 50 minutes. Let cool for 10 to 15 minutes before serving.

Serve warm with Vanilla Bean Ice Cream (page 208).

Serves 8

(master recipe)

Summer Berry Pie

For me, as for almost everyone I know who grew up in Oregon, summer and berry picking go hand in hand. Although there's nothing fancy about this pie, it is one of my favorites, and I'll even brave a hot oven at the height of summer to bake one.

Serves 8

Cappy's Pie Crust for a double-crust pie (page 72)

6 cups fresh blackberries or any other summer berries

1 cup plus 2 teaspoons sugar

1 teaspoon ground cinnamon

1/2 teaspoon ground ginger

1/2 teaspoon ground allspice

Finely grated zest of 1 lemon

Juice of 1/2 lemon

1/4 cup cornstarch

2 tablespoons unsalted butter, diced

2 tablespoons milk

1 quart Hazelnut Gelato (page 220), as accompaniment

Preheat the oven to 375°.

On a well-floured board, roll half of the dough out into a 10-inch circle. (See page 81 for instructions on working with pie dough.) Fit the dough into a 9-inch pie plate (leave the excess dough for the moment); set aside.

Toss the berries with 1 cup of the sugar and the cinnamon, ginger, and allspice in a large bowl. Add the lemon zest and juice and the cornstarch; mix well. Spoon the fruit into the crust, and dot with the butter.

Roll the remaining dough out into a 10-inch circle and fold it into quarters. Lightly wet your fingertips and run them over the edge of the bottom crust to help the top crust adhere. Set the top crust over the berries, unfold it, and trim the edges of both crusts to about 1/2 inch. Roll the edges under and flute. Dock the crust by pricking the top with a fork or cutting slits in the top with a knife. Brush the top crust with the milk and sprinkle with the remaining 2 teaspoons sugar. Bake for 15 minutes, then lower the temperature to 350° and bake until golden brown and bubbly, 35 to 40 minutes longer. Let cool for about 20 minutes before serving.

Serve warm with Hazelnut Gelato.

Variations

Summer Berry Pie

PEACH-RASPBERRY PIE

If you have super-ripe fruit, you may want to cut the sugar back by about 1/4 cup. If it's not the ripest, add 2 or 3 tablespoons of sugar, depending on the fruit.

Preheat the oven to 350°.

Prepare a single recipe of Cappy's Pie Crust (page 72). On a well-floured board, roll the dough out into a 10-inch circle. Fit the dough into a 9-inch pie plate, fold the edges under, and flute; set aside.

Follow the Summer Berry Pie master recipe, substituting 3 cups fresh raspberries and 4 peeled and sliced ripe peaches (page 10) for the blackberries, and using 1 teaspoon ground ginger and 1/2 teaspoon ground nutmeg for the spices. Top the pie with 2 cups Streusel Topping (page 78) instead of a top crust. Bake until golden brown and bubbly, about 1 hour. Let cool for about 20 minutes before serving.

Serve warm with Mascarpone Ice Cream (page 210) or softly whipped cream.

Serves 8

BLUEBERRY-CITRUS PIE

When this pie first comes out of the oven, it might be soupier than other berry pies. However, blueberries have a lot of natural pectin, so just let the pie sit for about 20 minutes, and the pectin will thicken the filling.

Follow the Summer Berry Pie master recipe, replacing Cappy's Pie Crust with a double-crust recipe of Cornmeal Crust (page 76) and the blackberries with fresh blueberries. Add the finely grated zest of 1 orange and 1 tablespoon orange juice concentrate along with the lemon zest. Proceed as directed in the master recipe.

Serve warm with Lemon Gelato (page 222).

Serves 8

(master recipe)

Apple Pie

This is a fairly traditional recipe, but the additional touch of candied ginger, with its sweet and almost peppery flavor, definitely makes it different from your grandmother's apple pie. Use firm, tart baking apples—they'll make all the difference between a pie with some nice apple texture and one that's like applesauce in a crust. I prefer Granny Smith apples, since they're readily available and always bake up perfectly.

Serves 10

7 tart baking apples, such as Granny Smith or Gravenstein,
   peeled, cored, and cut into 1/2-inch-thick slices

1 cup plus 2 tablespoons sugar, more if needed

3 tablespoons flour

2 1/2 teaspoons ground cinnamon

1/2 teaspoon ground nutmeg

1/4 cup chopped candied ginger

1 tablespoon unsalted butter, diced

Cappy's Pie Crust for a double-crust pie (page 72)

1 quart Vanilla Bean Ice Cream (page 208),
   as accompaniment

In a large bowl, toss the apples with 1 cup of the sugar, the flour, 2 teaspoons of the cinnamon, the nutmeg, and the candied ginger in a large bowl; let sit for about 15 minutes to give the apples time to get juicy.

Preheat the oven to 375°.

On a well-floured board, roll half of the dough out into a 10-inch circle. (See page 81 for instructions on working with pie dough.) Fit the dough into a 9-inch pie plate (leave the excess dough for the moment). Taste the apples, and add a bit more sugar if they're too tart; then pile them onto the crust and dot with the butter. Roll the remaining dough out into a 10-inch circle and fold it into quarters. Lightly wet your fingertips and run them over the edge of the bottom crust to help the top crust adhere. Set the top crust over the apples, unfold it, and trim the edges of both crusts to about 1/2 inch. Roll the edges under and flute. Dock the crust by pricking the top with a fork or cutting slits in the top with a knife. Combine the remaining 2 tablespoons sugar and 1/2 teaspoon cinnamon, and sprinkle over the top crust. Bake until golden brown and bubbly, about 1 hour and 15 minutes. Let cool for about 20 minutes before serving.

Serve warm with Vanilla Bean Ice Cream.

Variations

Apple Pie

APPLE–SOUR CREAM PIE

Sour cream provides a rich touch to classic apple pie. You could also use crème fraîche, which is more intense than sour cream, to raise the flavor up another notch.

Follow the Apple Pie master recipe, mixing 1/2 cup sour cream into the apple filling just before adding it to the crust. Proceed as in the master recipe.

Serve warm with Lemon Gelato (page 222).

Serves 10

MAPLE-BOURBON APPLE PIE

Here, maple syrup takes the place of the sugar in the master recipe, giving the pie another dimension. Really good bourbon has an almost vanilla-like aroma, so be sure to use a high-quality one to give the pie an intoxicating flavor! (Don't worry, the alcohol cooks off completely, so you can serve the pie to the whole family.)

Combine 3/4 cup good-quality maple syrup and 1/4 cup bourbon in a heavy saucepan over medium-high heat, and bring just to a boil. Remove the pan from the heat, stir in the cinnamon, nutmeg, and candied ginger from the Apple Pie master recipe, and let cool for about 10 minutes.

Preheat the oven and roll out the crust as directed in the master recipe. Pile the sliced, unsweetened apples into the crust, then pour the syrup over the top. Sprinkle with 1/4 cup flour and 1/2 cup chopped toasted pecans (page 10), dot with the butter, set the top crust over the apples, and proceed as in the master recipe.

Serve warm with Vanilla Bean Ice Cream (page 208) or softly whipped cream.

Serves 10

(master recipe)

Pear Pie

Pears aren't as acidic as apples, making this pie softer in texture and sweeter than apple pie, and even a bit delicate. Any type of pear will do in this recipe, as long as they are still firm and haven't ripened too much. A pear you'd want to eat out of hand would be too ripe for the pie, so there's no waiting days for pears to ripen before you can put it together.

Serves 8

7 firm pears, peeled, cored, and cut into 1/4-inch-thick slices

1 cup firmly packed brown sugar

1/4 cup flour

2 teaspoons ground cinnamon

1/2 teaspoon ground nutmeg

1/4 teaspoon ground cloves

Pâte Brisée for a single-crust pie (page 70)

3 tablespoons unsalted butter, diced

Streusel Topping (page 78)

1 quart Lemon Gelato (page 222), as accompaniment

In a large bowl, toss the pears with the brown sugar, flour, cinnamon, nutmeg, and cloves; let sit for about 15 minutes to give the pears time to get juicy.

Preheat the oven to 350°.

On a well-floured board, roll the dough out into a 10-inch circle. (See page 81 for instructions on working with pie dough.) Fit the dough into a 9-inch pie plate, fold the edges under, and flute. Pile the pears onto the crust, dot with the butter, and top with the streusel. Bake until golden brown and bubbly, about 1 hour and 15 minutes. Let cool for about 20 minutes before serving.

Serve warm with Lemon Gelato.

Variations

Pear Pie

PEAR-CRANBERRY PIE

Cranberries add a nice touch here—their acidic tang perks up the subtle flavor of the pears.

Follow the Pear Pie master recipe, decreasing the number of pears to 6 and adding 1 cup fresh cranberries to the filling. Proceed as in the master recipe.

Serve warm with Vanilla Bean Ice Cream (page 208).

Serves 8

PEAR-DRIED CHERRY PIE

In this variation, dried cherries have an effect that is almost the opposite of the cranberries in the previous variation, adding depth and richness to the mellow pear filling.

Soak 1 cup dried sour cherries and the finely grated zest of 1 orange in 1/2 cup ruby port for at least 1 hour; set aside.

Follow the Pear Pie master recipe, decreasing the number of pears to 6 and adding the reserved cherries and port to the filling. Proceed as directed in the master recipe.

Serve warm with Mascarpone Ice Cream (page 210).

Serves 8

1a

1b

2

3

4a

4b

5

6

Rolling Dough for a Double-Crust Pie

In order to be a proficient pie baker, it's important to master the technique for rolling a double crust. When you do, it will enable you to create such loved favorites as apple, strawberry-rhubarb, and blackberry pie.

1. Place one of the disks of pie dough on a well-floured board. Roll it once or twice with a rolling pin to flatten it, and then lift it and turn it a quarter of a turn, dusting with a bit more flour as needed. Continue rolling and turning the dough a quarter of a turn, adding more flour as needed, until it is 10 to 11 inches in diameter.

2. Gently fold the dough into fourths, transfer it to a 9-inch pie plate, and then open it back up.

3. Gently press the dough into the pie plate (you don't need to press it too firmly, because the filling will weigh it down), and leave the excess dough hanging over the side of the plate.

4. Add the filling to the prepared pie plate. Roll the second disk of dough into a 10-inch circle. Fold it into fourths, transfer it to the top of the filling, and unfold.

5. Trim the edges of the dough to hang about 1/2 inch over the side of the pie plate. Roll the dough under to form a ridge, and then, using your fingers, pinch the edge of the dough to flute it.

6. Cut 1-inch-long slits into the top of the dough (or prick it with a fork, also known as docking) to allow the steam to escape as the pie bakes. Bake as directed in the recipe.

(master recipe)

Cranberry-Orange-Nut Pie

When most people think of cranberries, they usually think of canned jelly and juice. But when sweetened properly, spiked with a touch of orange, and contrasted with toasted nuts, cranberries become a lovely dessert. Try this and you'll look at cranberries in a whole new light.

Serves 10

4 cups fresh cranberries

Finely grated zest and juice of 1 orange

1 cup plus 2 tablespoons sugar

2 1/2 teaspoons ground cinnamon

3 tablespoons flour

Cappy's Pie Crust for a double-crust pie (page 72)

1 cup chopped toasted walnuts or pecans (page 10)

2 tablespoons unsalted butter

1 quart Mascarpone Ice Cream (page 210)

Preheat the oven to 375°.

In a large bowl, toss the cranberries with the orange zest and juice, 1 cup of the sugar, 2 teaspoons of the cinnamon, and the flour; set aside.

On a well-floured board, roll half of the dough out into a 10-inch circle. (See page 81 for instructions on working with pie dough.) Fit the dough into a 9-inch pie plate (leave the excess dough for the moment). Pour the cranberry mixture into the crust, top with the nuts, and dot with the butter. Roll the remaining dough out into a 10-inch circle and fold it into quarters. Lightly wet your fingertips and run them over the edge of the bottom crust to help the top crust adhere. Set the top crust over the filling, unfold it, and trim the edges of both crusts to about 1/2 inch. Roll the edges under and flute. Dock the dough with a fork. Combine the remaining 2 tablespoons sugar and 1/2 teaspoon cinnamon, and sprinkle over the top crust. Bake until golden brown and bubbly, about 1 hour. Let cool for about 20 minutes before serving.

Serve warm with Mascarpone Ice Cream.

Variation

Cranberry-orange-nut Pie

CRANBERRY PIE WITH DRIED FRUIT AND HAZELNUTS

Soak 1 cup dried sour cherries and 1 cup currants in 2 cups port for at least 30 minutes. Drain the port from the fruit (reserving the fruit), and cook it in a saucepan over high heat until reduced to about 1/4 cup; set aside.

Follow the Cranberry-Orange-Nut Pie master recipe, decreasing the cranberries to 3 cups. Add the reserved fruit and the port reduction to the cranberries, and substitute chopped toasted hazelnuts for the walnuts. Proceed as directed in the master recipe.

Serve warm with Vanilla Bean Ice Cream (page 208) or softly whipped cream.

Serves 10

(master recipe)

Strawberry-Rhubarb Pie

When Melissa makes this showy pie at the Bistro, it's our first hint that spring is on its way. Soon the abundance of summer fruit will appear in our dessert menu, and apples and pears can take a rest until next winter. For a slightly different look, instead of rolling the phyllo you can crumple each sheet—as you would a piece of paper—after brushing it with the melted butter. Pile the crumpled phyllo over the filling to a height of about 4 inches, and then sprinkle with the cinnamon sugar.

Serves 10

6 cups sliced rhubarb (1/2-inch-thick slices; about 8 ribs)

2 cups fresh strawberries, hulled and quartered

3/4 cup plus 2 tablespoons sugar, more if needed

3 tablespoons flour

Finely grated zest and juice of 1 lemon

2 1/2 teaspoons ground cinnamon

1/4 teaspoon ground nutmeg

Pâte Brisée for a single-crust pie (page 70)

8 to 12 sheets phyllo dough

1/4 cup unsalted butter, melted

1 quart Mascarpone Ice Cream (page 210),
   as accompaniment

Preheat the oven to 350°.

In a large bowl, toss the rhubarb and strawberries with 3/4 cup of the sugar, the flour, lemon zest and juice, 2 teaspoons of the cinnamon, and the nutmeg; set aside.

On a well-floured board, roll the pâte brisée out into a 10-inch circle. (See page 81 for information on working with pie dough.) Fit the dough into a 9-inch pie plate, fold the edges under, and flute. Taste the filling, and add a bit more sugar if it's too tart; then pour it into the crust. Place a sheet of phyllo dough on a flat surface (keep the others rolled up and covered with a damp paper towel so they won't dry out), and lightly brush it with butter. Roll the phyllo into a loose tube about 2 inches in diameter, then place it along the outer edge of the pie, against the fluted crust. Continue with the remaining

continued on page 98

continued from page 96

sheets of phyllo, placing them end to end to form a spiral pattern that covers the entire pie. Brush the top of the phyllo spiral with the remaining butter. Combine the remaining 2 tablespoons sugar and 1/2 teaspoon cinnamon, and sprinkle it over the top. Bake until the filling is bubbly and the phyllo is golden brown, about 1 hour and 15 minutes. Let cool for 15 to 20 minutes before serving.

Serve warm with Mascarpone Ice Cream.

Variations

Strawberry-Rhubarb Pie

RHUBARB-RASPBERRY PIE

Here's another great pairing of fruit. I also like this pie topped with Streusel Topping (page 78) instead of phyllo.

Follow the Strawberry-Rhubarb Pie master recipe, substituting Chocolate Pâte Brisée (page 70) for the regular Pâte Brisée and fresh raspberries for the strawberries. Proceed as directed in the master recipe.

Serve warm with Vanilla Bean Ice Cream (page 208).

Serves 10

RHUBARB-APPLE PIE

Follow the Strawberry-Rhubarb Pie master recipe, substituting 1 peeled, diced sweet apple, such as Fuji or Gala, for the strawberries. Proceed as directed in the master recipe.

Serve warm with Mascarpone Ice Cream (page 210).

Serves 10

Banana Cream Pie

The custard in this recipe is a classic base for almost any cream pie you'd want to make. We like to use cornstarch instead of flour as a thickener in custards and pastry cream because the resulting texture is so much lighter than what you get with flour. Just be prepared to work quickly when you have the custard on the stove. Cornstarch will thicken the mixture so fast that if you don't get it off the heat, strained, and cooling right away, it can separate. To save the custard if it separates, mix in about 1/2 cup ice-cold milk, and it will come back together.

Serves 10

Custard

3 1/2 cups milk

1 egg

4 egg yolks

3/4 cup sugar

1/2 cup cornstarch

1/4 teaspoon salt

2 tablespoons cold unsalted butter, diced

2 teaspoons pure vanilla extract

Pâte Brisée for a single-crust pie (page 70)

1/2 cup warm Ganache (page 47)

2 ripe bananas, cut into 1/4-inch-thick slices

1 cup heavy whipping cream

2 teaspoons sugar

1 teaspoon pure vanilla extract

1 cup Chocolate Sauce (page 62), as accompaniment

Shaved chocolate (page 8), for garnish

Mint sprigs, for garnish

Preheat a standard oven to 400° or a convection oven to 375°.

To prepare the custard, place 3 cups of the milk in a sauce-pan over medium heat and bring just to a boil. Meanwhile, whisk together the egg, egg yolks, sugar, the remaining 1/2 cup milk, the cornstarch, and salt in a large bowl. Slowly whisk 1 to 1 1/2 cups of the hot milk into the egg mixture to temper it, or bring it up to the same temperature. Whisk in the remaining milk, pour the mixture back into the saucepan, and again cook over medium

continued

99

continued from page 99

heat, stirring constantly, until the mixture just comes to a boil and is very thick, about 2 minutes; remove the pan from the heat. Add the butter and vanilla extract, let sit for 2 minutes, and then stir until the butter is completely melted. Strain the mixture through a fine-mesh sieve into a bowl, cover the surface of the custard with plastic wrap or a piece of parchment paper, and refrigerate while preparing the crust.

To prepare the crust, roll the pâte brisée out on a well-floured board into a 10-inch circle. (See page 81 for information on working with pie dough.) Fit the dough into a 9-inch pie plate, fold the edges under, and flute (page 81). Bake until golden brown, 20 to 25 minutes. Let cool for 10 to 15 minutes. Using a pastry brush, paint the bottom and about 1/2 inch up the sides of the crust with the ganache (it adds a flavorful touch and also helps keep the crust from getting soggy). Chill the crust until the ganache is set, about 20 minutes.

Line the bottom of the crust with the banana slices, pour the chilled custard over the bananas, and refrigerate until well chilled, at least 3 hours.

Just before serving, whip the cream with the sugar and vanilla extract until it holds soft peaks, and spread it over the top of the pie.

Serve immediately, topped with Chocolate Sauce and garnished with shaved chocolate and mint sprigs.

Banana Cream Pie

CHOCOLATE CREAM PIE

Since chocolate is the star attraction in this pie, it's very important to use a high-quality one. Also be sure to use chopped bar chocolate and not chips, because the lecithin in the chips will keep them from melting smoothly into the pastry cream.

Follow the Banana Cream Pie master recipe, folding 6 ounces finely chopped bittersweet chocolate into the custard after straining it. Proceed as in the master recipe, omitting the bananas, if you prefer. Serve chilled, drizzled with Chocolate Sauce (page 62) and Caramel Sauce (page 58).

Serves 10

COCONUT CREAM PIE

If you want to give this variation an even more tropical twist, steep a few slices of ginger in the milk while it's heating up, and line the crust with slices of mango.

Follow the Banana Cream Pie master recipe, replacing 1 cup of the milk with coconut milk and adding 1 1/2 cups shredded sweetened coconut to the strained custard. Proceed as in the master recipe, omitting the bananas and sprinkling the pie with 1/2 cup toasted shredded sweetened coconut (page 8). Serve chilled, drizzled with Chocolate Sauce (page 62).

Serves 10

Lime Curd Pie With Brown Sugar Meringue

Once meringue is browned, it's already beginning to melt. If you are going to serve the whole pie at once, you have nothing to worry about. However, if you're preparing this pie for a smaller group of people and you want to enjoy the leftovers for a few days, top each slice with the meringue and brown it just before serving, as we do at the restaurant. Prepare just enough meringue to cover the number of slices you'll be serving, put it in a pastry bag, pipe it onto each individual slice, and then brown it with a propane torch.

Serves 10

Pâte Brisée for a single-crust pie (page 70)

3 ounces white chocolate, melted (page 8)

5 eggs, separated

1/2 cup fresh lime juice

Finely grated zest of 1 lime

3/4 cup sugar

1/2 cup cold unsalted butter, diced

1/4 cup coconut milk

1 cup loosely packed brown sugar

1 cup Berry Sauce (page 63), as accompaniment

1/2 cup shredded sweetened coconut, toasted (page 8), for garnish

Preheat a standard oven to 350° or a convection oven to 325°.

To prepare the crust, roll the pâte brisée out on a well-floured board into a 10-inch circle. (See page 81 for instructions on working with pie dough.) Fit the dough into a 9-inch pie plate, fold the edges under, and flute. Bake until golden brown, 15 to 20 minutes. Let cool completely.

Spread the white chocolate over the cooled crust and refrigerate until set, about 10 minutes.

Meanwhile, to prepare the lime curd, whisk together the egg yolks, lime juice and zest, and sugar in a metal bowl. Add the butter, set the bowl over a pan of simmering water, and cook, stirring often, until very thick, 6 to 8 minutes. Remove the pan from the heat and whisk in the

continued

103

continued from page 103

coconut milk. Pour the curd into the pie shell and refrigerate until well chilled, about 2 hours; keep refrigerated until ready to serve.

To prepare the meringue, place the egg whites in the bowl of a mixer fitted with the whip attachment and whip on high speed until frothy. While beating, add the brown sugar, about 1 tablespoon at a time, then continue beating until the sugar has completely dissolved and the whites are very shiny and hold a stiff peak, about 4 minutes. (Be sure to add the sugar slowly so it has time to dissolve; otherwise the egg whites will lose volume and be too soupy. Brown sugar tends to dissolve more slowly than white granulated sugar. To see if it has dissolved in the meringue, stop the mixer, remove a bit of the meringue, and rub it between two fingers; if you feel sugar granules, continue whipping the whites until the meringue is smooth.)

To serve, spread the meringue over the chilled pie. Using a propane torch (or under the broiler), carefully brown the meringue, about 2 minutes. (It will brown very fast, so if you're using the broiler, keep an eye on it so it doesn't burn.) Let cool for about 5 minutes before serving.

Serve immediately, with Berry Sauce and garnish with toasted coconut.

Variations

Lime Curd Pie

LEMON CURD TART

Lemon is the perfect substitute for lime!

Preheat a standard oven to 375° or a convection oven to 350°.

Prepare a single recipe of Nut Pâte Brisée (page 71), and press it into a 10-inch tart or flan pan with a removable bottom. (The easiest way to do this is to first press it into the sides of the pan, then finish with the bottom of the pan.) Bake until golden brown, about 20 minutes. Let cool completely.

Place 4 ounces chopped white chocolate and 1 tablespoon unsalted butter in a metal bowl set over a pan of simmering water (make sure the bottom of the bowl does not touch the water). When the chocolate has melted about halfway, remove the pan from the heat (leave the bowl on the pan), and let stand until completely melted; stir until smooth. Using a plastic spatula, spread the chocolate over the bottom of the prepared tart shell and refrigerate until set, about 10 minutes.

Prepare the curd as directed in the Lime Curd Pie master recipe, substituting the juice and finely grated zest of 1 lemon for the lime. Pour the curd into the prepared crust, and refrigerate until well chilled, about 2 hours.

Serve chilled with Berry Sauce (page 63) and softly whipped cream.

Serves 10

ORANGE-GINGER PIE WITH BROWN SUGAR MERINGUE

The ginger gives the filling a peppery bite, which tastes great with the sweet meringue.

Follow the Lime Curd Pie with Brown Sugar Meringue master recipe. When preparing the lime curd, substitute 1/2 cup freshly squeezed orange juice and the finely grated zest of 1 orange for the lime juice and zest, and add 1 tablespoon chopped fresh ginger along with the other ingredients. When the curd is thick, strain it through a fine-mesh sieve before pouring it into the crust. Proceed as directed in the master recipe.

Serve immediately with Berry Sauce (page 63). Omit the coconut garnish.

Serves 10

(master recipe)

Fresh Fruit tart

This is one of Melissa's family's favorite summertime desserts: a pâte sucrée crust filled with vanilla pastry cream topped with fresh raspberries they pick from their garden. Use any of your favorite summer berries in this tart. Perfectly ripe strawberries are wonderful, especially if you drizzle them with melted white and dark chocolate. Or make a pretty mixed berry tart and scatter blueberries over it; they add a splash of color and fill in the spaces between the strawberries.

Serves 12

Pâte Sucrée for a single tart shell (page 71)

1 1/2 cups Pastry Cream (page 54)

3 cups of your favorite summer berries

1 cup Berry Sauce (page 63), as accompaniment

1 1/2 cups whipped cream, as accompaniment

Preheat a standard oven to 400° or a convection oven to 375°.

To prepare the crust, roll the pâte sucrée out on a well-floured board into an 11-inch circle and fit it into a 10-inch flan or tart pan with a removable bottom. (See page 81 for information on working with dough.) Bake until golden brown, 20 to 25 minutes. Let cool completely.

Pour the pastry cream into the cooled crust. Starting on the outside and working to the center, arrange the berries over the tart, covering the entire surface.

Serve chilled with Berry Sauce and softly whipped cream.

Variation

Fresh Fruit tart

MASCARPONE FRESH FRUIT TART

Fresh peaches, berries, or apricots go well with this creamy filling. If you like, try a chocolate or even a nut crust instead.

Follow the Fresh Fruit Tart master recipe, substituting 1 1/2 cups mascarpone (page 9) sweetened with 2 tablespoons sugar for the pastry cream.

Serves 12

pictured on page 66

caramel-Pear tart with a Graham Shortbread crust

In each series of cooking classes that John and I teach, one of the recipes always seems to stand out and make an impression on our students. This is one of them. The combination of the graham flour in the crust and the creamy texture of the pears and caramel is sublime. Make sure you choose firm, slightly underripe pears, because ripe ones will disintegrate during the poaching process.

Serves 12

Poached Pears

5 cups white wine

1 cup sugar

Finely grated zest of 1 orange

1 cinnamon stick

1 (1-inch-thick) slice fresh ginger

5 or 6 firm pears, peeled, halved, and cored

Graham Shortbread Crust (page 75)

Caramel Filling

1 1/2 cups sugar

1/2 cup water

1 cup heavy whipping cream

1/4 cup pear brandy

1 egg

1/2 teaspoon ground nutmeg

1 1/2 cups whipped cream, as accompaniment

To poach the pears, combine the wine, sugar, orange zest, cinnamon stick, and ginger in a heavy saucepan over high heat. Bring to a boil, add the pears, lower the heat to medium, and poach until fork-tender, 8 to 10 minutes.

continued

continued from page 109

Cool the pears in the liquid and refrigerate until ready to use. (For the best flavor, refrigerate them in the liquid overnight, if possible.)

Preheat a standard oven to 375° or a convection oven to 350°.

To prepare the tart shell, press the dough into a well-greased 10-inch flan or tart pan with a removable bottom. (The easiest way to do this is to first press it into the sides of the pan, then finish with the bottom of the pan.) Bake just until set but not brown, about 10 minutes; let cool completely.

Lower the oven temperature to 350° (at this point, use a standard oven only).

Meanwhile, to prepare the caramel filling, place the sugar in a large sauté pan with sides or a heavy saucepan. Gently moisten the sugar with the water, being careful not to splash the water and sugar onto the sides of the pan. Cook the sugar mixture over high heat, without stirring, until you see any part of it turning brown, then swirl the pan to even out the color. Cook until golden brown, about 2 minutes longer. Carefully add the cream to the hot sugar, taking care to pour it in slowly because it will bubble up very violently. Add the brandy and cook, again without stirring, until the caramelized sugar has liquefied again and the mixture is very smooth and a deep golden brown. Remove the pan from the heat. Let cool until tepid, then whisk in the egg and nutmeg.

To assemble the tart, cut the poached pears into 1/4-inch-thick slices, reserving the poaching liquid for another use. Arrange the pear slices in concentric circles in the cooled tart shell, pour the caramel filling into the shell, and bake until the filling is bubbly, about 30 minutes. Let cool for about 20 minutes before serving.

Serve warm with softly whipped cream.

Variations

Caramel-Pear tart

CARAMEL-APPLE-NUT TART

This classic combination of apples, caramel, and nuts comes together more quickly than the master recipe, so if you want to serve an elegant dessert but you are pressed for time, it makes a great choice.

Follow the Caramel-Pear Tart master recipe, substituting 2 peeled, diced Granny Smith apples for the poached pears. (Do not poach the apples.) Arrange the apples in the tart shell, and distribute 1/2 cup chopped pecans, 1/2 cup chopped almonds, and 1/2 cup chopped hazelnuts over the apples. Pour the caramel filling over the apples and nuts, and bake as directed in the master recipe.

Serve warm with Mascarpone Ice Cream (page 210).

Serves 12

STRAWBERRY-CARAMEL TART

I really like to make this strawberry variation of the master recipe. When the berries cook with the caramel, they meld with its texture.

Follow the Caramel-Pear Tart master recipe, substituting Shortbread Crust (page 74) for the Graham Shortbread Crust (prebake the crust as directed in the master recipe) and 3 cups hulled, halved strawberries for the poached pears. Arrange the strawberries, cut side down, in concentric circles on the cooled tart shell. Pour the caramel filling over the strawberries, and bake as directed in the master recipe.

Serves 12

Italian Plum tart

Plums, that often overlooked fruit, make a wonderful focal point in this tart. Roasting the plums before baking them in the tart brings out their sugar and intensifies their flavor. Paired with the luscious almond pastry cream, it's a heavenly combination.

Serves 10

Pâte Sucrée for a single tart shell (page 71)

1/4 cup unsalted butter, melted

10 to 12 Italian plums, halved and pitted

2 tablespoons sugar

Almond Pastry Cream

2 cups half-and-half

2 eggs

2 egg yolks

1 cup sugar

1/3 cup flour

2 teaspoons pure vanilla extract

1/2 teaspoon almond extract

1 tablespoon dark rum

2/3 cup ground toasted almonds

1 1/2 cups whipped cream, as accompaniment

Preheat a standard oven to 400° or a convection oven to 375°.

To prepare the crust, roll the pâte sucrée out on a well-floured board into an 11-inch circle and fit it into a 10-inch flan or tart pan with a removable bottom. (See page 81 for instructions on working with tart dough.) Bake until golden brown, 20 to 25 minutes. Let cool.

Lower the oven temperature to 350° (for either type of oven).

Meanwhile, brush about half of the butter over a sheet pan. Place the plums, cut side down, on the pan, brush with the remaining butter, and sprinkle with the sugar. Bake just until the plums are soft and you see the skins lift slightly, 7 to 10 minutes; set aside.

To prepare the pastry cream, place the half-and-half in a saucepan over medium-high heat, and bring just to a boil. Meanwhile, whisk together the eggs, egg yolks, sugar, and flour in a large bowl. Slowly whisk 1 cup of the hot half-and-half into the egg mixture to temper it, or bring it up to the same temperature as the half-and-half. Whisk in the remaining half-and-half, pour the mixture back into the saucepan, and again cook over medium heat, stirring constantly, until very thick, 2 to 3 minutes; remove the pan from the heat. Add the vanilla extract, almond extract, rum, and almonds, and mix well. Let cool for about 5 minutes.

Pour the pastry cream into the tart shell. Using a palette knife or spatula, lift the plums off the pan and, starting at the edge of the crust and working your way to the center, arrange them in concentric circles on the pastry cream. Bake until the pastry cream is puffy, about 25 minutes. Let cool for 15 to 20 minutes before serving.

Serve warm, topped with softly whipped cream.

Variations

CHOCOLATE-CRUSTED PEACH-ALMOND TART

There's no need to precook the peaches as you do with the plums, since they are a softer fruit. If you like, use a plain pâte brisée instead of the chocolate, and if you can't find perfect peaches, try ripe apricot halves instead.

Follow the Italian Plum Tart master recipe, substituting Chocolate Pâte Brisée (page 70) for the Pâte Sucrée and 5 peeled, sliced peaches (page 10) for the roasted plums (be sure to skip the roasting step). Arrange the unbaked peach slices in concentric circles on the pastry cream, and then bake as directed in the master recipe.

Serve warm, drizzled with Caramel Sauce (page 58) and Chocolate Sauce (page 62).

Serves 10

STRAWBERRY-ALMOND TART

The fruit in this variation—halved strawberries—stands taller on the tart than the plums and peaches do, so gently nestle the strawberry halves into the pastry cream to allow them to cook properly.

Follow the Italian Plum Tart master recipe, substituting 3 cups hulled, halved fresh strawberries for the roasted plums (be sure to skip the roasting step). Nestle the unbaked strawberries in concentric circles in the pastry cream, and then bake as directed in the master recipe.

Serve warm, drizzled with Chocolate Sauce (page 62) and topped with softly whipped cream.

Serves 10

Italian Plum tart

(master recipe)
caramel-walnut tart

The cornmeal in the crust of this tart provides a wonderfully crisp texture that plays off the creamy, rich caramel, but any of the other crusts also pair well with this filling. For a more intense dessert, try the Chocolate Pâte Brisée (page 70). Or create a childhood fantasy dessert and pair it with the Graham Shortbread Crust (page 75), which tastes like a buttery graham cracker.

Serves 12

Caramel Filling

3/4 cup sugar

1/4 cup water

1 cup heavy whipping cream

1/4 cup honey

2 teaspoons pure vanilla extract

1/4 teaspoon salt

4 cups coarsely chopped toasted walnuts (page 10)

1/4 cup Tuaca liqueur

Cornmeal Crust (page 76)

1 quart Vanilla Bean Ice Cream (page 208),
    as accompaniment

1 cup Caramel-Apple Sauce (page 59), as accompaniment

Preheat the oven to 350°. Grease a 10-inch springform pan; set aside.

To prepare the caramel filling, place the sugar in a large sauté pan with sides or a heavy saucepan. Gently moisten the sugar with the water, being careful not to splash the water and sugar onto the sides of the pan. Cook the sugar mixture over high heat, without stirring, until you see any part of it turning brown, then swirl the pan to even out the color. Cook until golden brown, about 2 minutes longer. Carefully add the cream to the hot sugar, taking care to pour it in slowly because it will bubble up very violently, and cook, again without stirring, until the caramelized sugar has liquefied again and the mixture is very smooth and a deep golden brown, 2 to 3 minutes. (If you stir it now, the sugar will end up on your spoon and not in the sauce.) Remove the pan from the heat, add the honey, vanilla extract, salt, walnuts, and Tuaca, and mix well; set aside.

To assemble the tart, press about two-thirds of the dough into the bottom and about halfway up the sides of the prepared pan. Pour the caramel filling into the shell. On a well-floured board, roll the remaining dough out to a thickness of about 1/4 inch. Using a cookie cutter, cut shapes out of the dough, and then arrange them over the filling to cover. Bake until the filling is bubbly, about 45 minutes. Let cool for 15 to 20 minutes before serving.

To serve, run a knife around the sides of the pan to loosen the tart, then remove the outer ring.

Serve the tart topped with Vanilla Bean Ice Cream and drizzled with Caramel-Apple Sauce.

Variations

FIG-HAZELNUT-CARAMEL TART

The texture of the figs really plays off the rich caramel filling.

Follow the Caramel-Walnut Tart master recipe, substituting hazelnut liqueur for the Tuaca and 1 cup chopped toasted hazelnuts for the walnuts. Add 1 1/2 cups diced dried figs to the filling along with the nuts, and proceed as directed in the master recipe.

Serve warm or chilled with Vanilla Bean Ice Cream.

Serves 12

BOURBON-PECAN TART WITH A CHOCOLATE CRUST

The chocolate crust adds depth to this decadent tart.

Follow the Caramel-Walnut Tart master recipe, substituting Chocolate Pâte Brisée (page 70) for the Cornmeal Crust, bourbon for the Tuaca, and chopped pecans for the walnuts. Add 1/2 teaspoon ground cinnamon to the filling along with the nuts. Proceed as directed in the master recipe.

Serve warm or chilled with Mascarpone Ice Cream (page 210) or Chocolate Ice Cream (page 205).

Serves 12

caramel-walnut tart

(master recipe)

Lemon Cream tart

We tend to make a lot of lemon desserts at the Bistro in the winter. Customers are often surprised to find desserts served with a berry sauce at that time of year. At the height of berry season, we freeze the berries when they are at their best so we can have a little taste of summer.

Serves 12

Three-Nut Crust (page 76)

2 1/3 cups milk

5 egg yolks

1 cup sugar

5 tablespoons cornstarch

1/4 teaspoon salt

1/4 cup cold unsalted butter, diced

1/2 cup freshly squeezed lemon juice

1 cup Berry Sauce (page 63), as accompaniment

1 1/2 cups whipped cream, as accompaniment

Preheat a standard oven to 375° or a convection oven to 350°.

To prepare the tart shell, press the dough into a well-greased 10-inch flan or tart pan with a removable bottom. (The easiest way to do this is to first press it into the sides of the pan, then finish with the bottom of the pan.) Bake until golden brown, about 20 minutes; let cool completely.

To prepare the filling, place the milk in a saucepan over medium heat and bring just to a boil. Meanwhile, whisk together the egg yolks, sugar, cornstarch, and salt in a large bowl. Slowly whisk 1 to 1 1/2 cups of the hot milk into the egg mixture to temper it, or bring it up to the same temperature. Whisk in the remaining milk, pour the mixture back into the saucepan, and again cook over medium heat, stirring constantly, until the mixture comes to a boil and is very thick, about 2 minutes; remove the pan from the heat. Add the butter and lemon juice, let sit for 2 minutes, and then stir until the butter is completely melted. Strain the mixture through a fine-mesh sieve, and then pour it into the baked shell. Refrigerate until completely chilled, about 2 hours.

Serve chilled with Berry Sauce and softly whipped cream.

Variation

Lemon Cream tart

DREAMSICLE TART

This tart of Melissa's reminds me of the ice cream bar of the same name that I used to eat as a child.

Follow the Lemon Cream Tart master recipe, substituting 1/2 cup freshly squeezed orange juice and the zest of 1 orange for the lemon juice, and adding 2 teaspoons pure vanilla extract to the custard along with the orange. Proceed as directed in the master recipe.

Serve chilled with softly whipped cream and your favorite berries, if in season.

Serves 12

Orange-Spice Glazed Cookies (page 131)

cookies

Some cookie recipes can be traced back generations, and it's no wonder: In countries all over the globe, people have been enjoying these sweet, hand-held pastries for hundreds of years. Cookies have been a part of American cuisine at least since the early 1700s, thanks to the immigrants who brought along their traditional recipes and baking methods. The late 1900s brought cookie dough ice cream, a combination of two favorite American desserts and a testament to the enduring status cookies have as an American staple.

When you think of cookies, I bet what comes to mind is a favorite type that is near and dear to your heart, perhaps a recipe you have enjoyed since you were a kid. Most cookies are simple to prepare, making them perfect for that initiation into the kitchen. One taste of a hot, fresh cookie just out of the oven is all it takes for the allure of baking to take hold of you. Surrounded by wafting aromas and the comfortable feel of a warm kitchen, you find that the process of making cookies is almost as satisfying as that first bite. Baking cookies was the first experience in the kitchen for both my son and my daughter, as it was for me. My mom has always made the best peanut butter cookies, baking them for me when I was young and then teaching me her secret recipe when I was a bit older. (It's no longer a family secret; the recipe is in this book.) If your early memories are of store-bought cookies, it's never too late to create new memories—for yourself alone or for your family. You can find a cookie recipe for any mood or taste and easily add your own touches, too.

The recipes in this chapter represent the six basic types of cookies. Drop cookies, such as the Dark and White Chocolate Chunk Cookies, are formed by dropping the dough from a spoon onto a baking sheet. To prepare bar cookies, like the Bourbon Blonde Brownies and the Chocolate-Hazelnut-Caramel Bars, the dough is spooned into a shallow baking pan, baked, and then cut into squares. Molded cookies, such as Jenny's Great-Grandma's Gingersnaps, are shaped by rolling the dough by hand into balls or other shapes. The Meringue Cookies and Piped Butter Cookies fall under the category of pressed cookies, formed by pressing the dough through a pastry bag or cookie press. (You'll need a pastry bag and not a cookie press for both of these recipes; it's my tool of choice for any other kinds of pressed cookies, too.) The Vanilla Bean Shortbread Cookies are refrigerator cookies—known in an earlier era as icebox cookies—shaped by rolling dough into a log, chilling it until firm, and then slicing and baking. To make rolled cookies, you roll out the dough and cut it into shapes with cookie cutters; the Rolled Sugar Cookies are a classic example.

I tried to think of some pearls of cookie wisdom to share, but I couldn't come up with a neat list of tips that applied to the whole range of cookie types. Instead, I can offer one main piece of advice that will take you far in cookie baking, my mantra throughout this book: Do not overbake them. I promise this hint will make the difference between unremarkable cookies and ones that will create memories for yourself and those with whom you share the gift of tradition.

Piped Butter Cookies

I wanted to come up with a delicate cookie with a rich flavor that would lend itself to lots of variations, and I found that adding cream cheese to the dough gave just the right amount of richness. You can easily mix in many different flavors, such as citrus zest and extracts, to come up with your own renditions. I also wanted a cookie that could be formed using a pastry bag instead of a cookie press, which many people—including myself—do not own. Just pipe the dough into 1- or 2-inch rosettes and top with decorative sugar, and you'll have a very simple but elegant cookie.

Makes about 24 cookies

4 ounces cream cheese, at room temperature

1 1/2 cups unsalted butter, at room temperature

1 1/4 cups granulated sugar

2 eggs

1 teaspoon pure vanilla extract

3 1/4 cups flour

1/2 teaspoon salt

Decorative sugar, for sprinkling

Preheat the oven to 350°. Grease a sheet pan well and set aside.

Place the cream cheese, butter, and granulated sugar in the bowl of a mixer and beat on high speed, scraping down the sides of the bowl often, until light and fluffy, about 3 minutes. With the mixer on low speed, add the eggs and beat well. Add the vanilla extract, flour, and salt, and mix on low speed until all of the ingredients are incorporated. Increase the speed to medium and mix just until the dough is smooth. Place the dough in a pastry bag fitted with a large star tip.

On the prepared pan, pipe the dough into 1-inch rosettes or circles, then sprinkle with decorative sugar. Bake until golden brown, about 10 minutes. Let the cookies cool for about 5 minutes on the pan, then transfer to a rack or paper towels and let cool completely.

Variations

Piped Butter Cookies

PIPED CHOCOLATE COOKIES

These buttery rich cookies with silky centers of chocolate are much like the old-fashioned thumbprint cookies, but instead of a jam filling, the cookies are filled with ganache after they are baked. Of course, if you would like to make traditional thumbprint cookies, you can fill the indentations with jam before baking them. As always, don't be afraid to come up with your own variations of the master recipe.

Follow the Piped Butter Cookies master recipe, omitting the decorative sugar (I don't think they need the extra sugar when topped with ganache). Pipe the dough into 1-inch rosettes, then gently press your thumb into the center of each cookie to make an indentation (be careful not to break through the bottoms). Bake as directed in the master recipe.

While the cookies are cooling, place 3 ounces chopped bittersweet chocolate and 1 tablespoon butter in a metal bowl set over a pan of simmering water, making sure that the bottom of the bowl does not touch the water. When the chocolate has melted about halfway, remove the pan from the heat (leaving the bowl on the pan), and let the chocolate sit until completely melted; stir until smooth.

Place the chocolate in a parchment paper pastry bag (page 61) and cut a small hole in the tip. Fill the indentation in each cookie with chocolate. Let the chocolate cool until completely set before serving or storing.

Makes about 24 cookies

SPICED ALMOND STICKS

These long, elegant cookies can also be piped into rosettes. If you prefer, substitute pecans or even macadamia nuts for the almonds, or melt 4 ounces of bittersweet chocolate and drizzle it over the cooled cookies to give this variation another twist.

Follow the Piped Butter Cookies master recipe, substituting almond extract for the vanilla, decreasing the flour to 2 3/4 cups, and adding 1/2 cup very finely ground almonds, 1 teaspoon ground cinnamon, 1/2 teaspoon ground allspice, 1/2 teaspoon ground ginger, and 1/4 teaspoon ground cloves along with the flour. Place the dough in a pastry bag fitted with a large star tip (make sure it is wide enough that the almonds won't get stuck in the tip). On the prepared pan, pipe the dough into 1 1/2-inch-long sticks, sprinkle with decorative sugar, and bake as directed in the master recipe.

Makes about 24 cookies

Dark and White Chocolate Chunk Cookies

When I started working on this recipe, I wanted to create the ultimate chocolate chip cookie—a serious task, considering that they're just about the most famous cookies around! I started to play around with a pretty traditional recipe, but I just wasn't getting the combination of crispy on the outside and chewy on the inside that I was after. I ended up increasing the ratio of granulated sugar to brown sugar and using melted butter, and when the staff ate all 24 cookies in as many seconds, I knew I had my recipe.

Makes about 24 cookies

1 cup unsalted butter, melted

1 cup granulated sugar

1/2 cup firmly packed brown sugar

2 eggs

1 teaspoon pure vanilla extract

2 cups flour

1/2 teaspoon baking soda

Pinch of salt

1 cup chopped bittersweet chocolate

1 cup chopped white chocolate

3/4 cup chopped toasted pecans (page 10)

Preheat the oven to 350°. Grease a sheet pan well and set aside.

Place the butter and both sugars in the bowl of a mixer and beat on high speed, scraping down the sides of the bowl often, until smooth, about 3 minutes. With the mixer on low speed, add the eggs and vanilla extract, and beat well. Add the flour, baking soda, and salt, and mix on low speed until all of the ingredients are incorporated. Increase the speed to medium and mix just until the dough is smooth. Remove the bowl from the mixer and let the dough cool for a few minutes (it will be a bit warm because of the melted butter). Add the bittersweet and white chocolates and the pecans, and mix well by hand.

Place heaping tablespoonfuls of the dough on the prepared pan, making sure you give the cookies enough space to spread as they bake. Bake until light golden brown, about 10 minutes. Let the cookies cool on the pan for a few minutes, then transfer to a rack or paper towels and let cool completely—if you can wait that long.

Variations

Dark and White Chocolate Chunk Cookies

ALMOND AND WHITE CHOCOLATE COOKIES WITH LEMON

In many almond desserts, the almond component seems to overshadow the other flavors. These cookies, however, have a subtle almond flavor that complements the tang of the lemon zest—so be sure to use a gentle touch when adding the almond extract.

Follow the Dark and White Chocolate Chunk Cookies master recipe, adding 1/2 cup almond paste, 3/4 cup ground toasted almonds (page 10), and the finely grated zest of 1 lemon along with the sugar. Proceed as directed in the master recipe, substituting 1 teaspoon almond extract for the vanilla extract and 1 1/2 cups chopped white chocolate for the dark and white chocolate combination, and omitting the pecans. Bake as directed in the master recipe.

Makes about 24 cookies

OATMEAL COOKIES

Working on this recipe was my cookie purgatory. John's grandmother made the best oatmeal cookies around, so good that I could never make any that came close to hers. Being a chef and a cookbook author, I owed it to my standing in the family to develop a recipe that was at least as good, but I certainly didn't hold my breath for better. I baked about twenty variations of the master recipe to come up with this one. My solution was to decrease the eggs by one, cut the flour way down, and add the oatmeal along with raisins and dried cranberries. I was never so happy as when John told me these cookies were as good as Nana's oatmeal cookies. I literally danced around the kitchen!

Follow the Dark and White Chocolate Chunk Cookies master recipe, adding 1 egg instead of 2 and decreasing the flour to 3/4 cup. After removing the bowl from the mixer and letting the dough cool, add 2 cups old-fashioned oats, 1/2 cup raisins, and 1/2 cup dried cranberries. If you want to go all out, add 2 cups butterscotch chips. Mix well by hand. Bake as directed in the master recipe.

Makes about 24 cookies

Jenny's Great-Grandma's Gingersnaps

Jenny Morrison works as my assistant, and she also does the first round of editing of my books and helps me with the writing. She has become a friend over the last few years, so John and I invited her and her family on a beach trip we take each summer. She brought along a batch of these gingersnaps she made from her great-grandmother's recipe, and as soon as I tasted them, I knew they had to go in this book. Spicy and chewy, they are just how I like gingersnaps.

Makes about 30 cookies

3/4 cup unsalted butter, at room temperature

2 cups sugar

1/4 cup unsulfured molasses

1 egg

1 3/4 cups all-purpose flour

1/2 cup graham flour

Pinch of salt

2 teaspoons baking soda

1 teaspoon ground cinnamon

1 teaspoon ground cloves

1 teaspoon ground ginger

Preheat the oven to 350°. Grease a sheet pan well and set aside.

Place the butter and 1 cup of the sugar in the bowl of a mixer and beat on high speed, scraping down the sides of the bowl often, until light and fluffy, about 3 minutes. With the mixer on low speed, add the molasses and egg, and beat well. Add the flours, salt, baking soda, and spices, and mix on low speed until all of the ingredients are incorporated. Increase the speed to medium and mix just until the dough is smooth. Remove the bowl from the mixer.

Place the remaining 1 cup sugar on a large plate. Shape the dough into 1-inch balls, roll them in the sugar to coat, and place on the prepared pan, making sure you give the cookies enough space to spread as they bake. Bake until golden brown (they will be a bit darker than other drop cookies because the dough is dark to begin with), about 15 minutes. Let the cookies cool on the pan for a few minutes, then transfer to a rack or paper towels and let cool completely.

Variations

Jenny's Great-Grandma's Gingersnaps

APPLE-GINGERY GINGERSNAPS

I really like Jenny's great-grandma's gingersnap recipe and didn't want to alter it too much, but I thought that a tangy apple like Granny Smith would go great with the spices and molasses, so I tried it out. Diced very small and mixed into the dough, the apple gave just the right touch of texture and tang. Then, for just a bit more zip, I added chopped candied ginger and the zest of an orange, and ended up with a cookie that really satisfies.

Follow the Jenny's Great-Grandma's Gingersnaps master recipe. After removing the bowl from the mixer, add 1 peeled, diced Granny Smith apple, 1 tablespoon finely minced candied ginger, and the finely grated zest of 1 orange, and mix well by hand. Shape the dough, roll in sugar, and bake as directed in the master recipe.

Makes about 30 cookies

GINGERSNAP-MASCARPONE SANDWICHES

I thought the gingersnaps would be ideal for sandwich cookies, as a fun way to make a favorite cookie even more special. For this version I made the cookies a bit smaller and sandwiched them together with a simple creamy, slightly sweet filling of mascarpone cheese and sugar. If you want to play off the flavor of the ginger, cloves, and cinnamon in the cookies, mix in a drop or two of lemon or orange oil (available in higher-end cooking stores) to the filling.

Follow the Jenny's Great-Grandma's Gingersnaps master recipe, shaping the dough into smaller balls, about 1/2 inch in diameter. Roll in sugar and bake as directed in the master recipe, decreasing the baking time to 10 to 12 minutes. While the cookies are cooling, mix together 1 cup mascarpone cheese (page 9) with a dash of pure vanilla extract and 2 teaspoons powdered sugar. Spread about 1/2 teaspoon of the mascarpone mixture on the bottom of a cooled cookie and set another cookie on top to make a sandwich. Continue with the remaining cookies and filling.

Makes about 20 sandwich cookies

pictured on opposite page

(master recipe)

Rolled Sugar Cookies

My Aunt Judy made great sugar cookies when I was a child, and although I made fun of her Jell-O salad, I did love those cookies. They tasted great, thanks to lots of butter and a bit of cream of tartar that gave them a very distinctive tangy flavor. This cookie recipe is pretty darn close to Aunt Judy's, except that I use granulated sugar instead of the powdered sugar her recipe called for to make them a bit crisper.

Makes about 30 medium-sized cookies

1 1/4 cups unsalted butter, at room temperature

1 1/4 cups sugar

1 egg

1 teaspoon pure vanilla extract

1/2 teaspoon cream of tartar

3 cups flour

Pinch of salt

Decorative sugar or frosting (optional)

Preheat the oven to 350°. Grease a sheet pan well and set aside.

Place the butter and sugar in the bowl of a mixer and beat on high speed, scraping down the sides of the bowl often, until light and fluffy, about 3 minutes. With the mixer on low speed, add the egg and vanilla extract, and mix well.

Add the cream of tartar, flour, and salt, and mix on low speed until all of the ingredients are incorporated. Increase the speed to medium and mix until the dough is smooth.

Remove the dough from the mixer and form it into a ball. If it is too soft to handle, cover it with plastic wrap and refrigerate until it firms up a bit. On a well-floured board, roll the dough out to a thickness of about 1/4 inch. Cut into shapes with the cookie cutters of your choice. Place on the prepared pan and sprinkle with decorative sugar, if you like (or leave them plain and frost them after baking). Bake until golden brown, 10 to 12 minutes, depending on the size of the cookie cutters. Let the cookies cool for about 5 minutes on the pan, then transfer to a rack or paper towels and let cool completely. Frost and decorate the cookies after they have cooled, if desired.

Rolled Sugar Cookies

CHOCOLATE WINDOWPANE COOKIES

I roll these cookies much thinner than in the master recipe and sandwich them with a teaspoon or so of really good raspberry jam. The result is beautiful: powdered sugar–dusted cookies with jam peeking through.

Follow the Rolled Sugar Cookies master recipe, adding 1/2 cup sifted unsweetened cocoa powder along with the flour. On a well-floured board, roll the dough out to a thickness of about 1/8 inch. Cut out with the cookie cutter of your choice (use just one shape, since they will become sandwiches) and then, using a smaller cookie cutter, cut a "window" out of half of the cookies. Bake as directed in the master recipe, decreasing the baking time to 8 to 10 minutes.

When the cookies have cooled, dust the ones with the cutout windows with powdered sugar. Spread about 1/2 teaspoon raspberry jam in the center of each of the "windowless" cookies, then top each with a sugar-dusted "window" cookie.

Makes about 15 medium-sized cookies

ORANGE-SPICE GLAZED COOKIES

While working on this recipe, I aimed for cookies with a rich butter flavor, a very heady scent of spices, and a tangy, slightly sweet glaze. Baking the glaze for a few minutes gives it an almost crackly texture in your mouth.

Follow the Rolled Sugar Cookies master recipe, adding the finely grated zest of 1 orange, 1 teaspoon ground cinnamon, 1/2 teaspoon ground ginger, 1/2 teaspoon ground allspice, 1/2 teaspoon ground nutmeg, and 1/4 teaspoon ground cloves along with the flour. Roll out and cut the cookies and bake as directed in the master recipe.

While the cookies are baking, prepare the glaze by mixing together 1 cup powdered sugar, a dash of pure vanilla extract, and 2 tablespoons orange juice. When you remove the cookies from the oven, immediately brush each one with a good amount of the glaze, then place them back in the oven and bake until the glaze starts to crackle, 5 to 6 minutes. Let the cookies cool for about 5 minutes on the pan, then transfer to a rack or paper towels and let cool completely.

Makes about 30 cookies

pictured on page 118

(master recipe)
Mom's Peanut Butter Cookies

Over the years, comments I've made about my mom's cooking have appeared in some newspaper and magazine articles. Unfortunately, she has taken things the wrong way and now believes that I think she could never cook when I was growing up. When I asked my Dad for his baked bean recipe for my last book, it was the last straw! She will probably think that I put her recipe in this book to save my hide, but once again she is wrong—it is my favorite recipe for peanut butter cookies. Make sure that you use really good peanut butter, which will make a big difference in the final flavor.

Makes about 48 cookies

1 cup cold unsalted butter, diced

1 cup granulated sugar

1 cup firmly packed brown sugar

2 eggs

1 teaspoon pure vanilla extract

1 cup good-quality peanut butter (I like to use the crunchy variety for texture)

3 cups flour

2 teaspoon baking soda

1/2 teaspoon salt

Preheat the oven to 350°. Grease a sheet pan well and set aside.

Place the butter and both sugars in the bowl of a mixer and beat on high speed, scraping down the sides of the bowl often, until light and fluffy, about 3 minutes. With the mixer on low speed, add the eggs and vanilla extract, then add the peanut butter and mix well. Add the flour, baking soda, and salt, and mix on low speed until all of the ingredients are incorporated. Increase the speed to medium and mix just until the dough is smooth.

Using a tablespoon or a small ice cream scoop, form the dough into 1/2-inch balls and place on the prepared pan. Flatten them with a fork. Bake just until golden brown, about 10 minutes. Let the cookies cool for about 5 minutes on the pan, then transfer to a rack or paper towels and let cool completely.

Variation

Mom's Peanut Butter Cookies

PEANUT BUTTER EVERYTHING COOKIES

These chunky cookies have the full peanut butter flavor of the master recipe, plus everything else you can imagine: coconut, chocolate, oats, and even orange zest. The contrast of textures, from the chewy coconut to the soft melted chocolate, makes them some of my favorites.

Follow the Mom's Peanut Butter Cookies master recipe, decreasing the flour to 1 3/4 cups. After removing the bowl from the mixer, add 1 1/2 cups oatmeal, 1 cup chopped bittersweet chocolate, the finely grated zest of 1 orange, and 1 cup shredded sweetened coconut, and mix well by hand. Shape the dough and bake as directed in the master recipe.

Makes about 48 cookies

133

(master recipe)

Chocolate-Hazelnut-Caramel Bars

This recipe might look like a lengthy process, but each step is so simple that the bars come together pretty quickly. For a decadent dessert, cut the bars into larger squares and top them with homemade ice cream and caramel sauce.

Makes about 24 bars

Crust

2 cups flour

1/2 cup powdered sugar

Finely grated zest of 1 orange

1 teaspoon pure vanilla extract

Pinch of salt

1 cup cold unsalted butter, cut into pieces

Caramel Filling

2 1/2 cups sugar

1 cup water

1 1/4 cups heavy whipping cream

1/2 cup hazelnut liqueur

1 teaspoon pure vanilla extract

1/2 teaspoon ground nutmeg

2 cups ground toasted hazelnuts (page 10)

Ganache

12 ounces bittersweet chocolate, coarsely chopped

1 1/4 cups heavy whipping cream

1 tablespoon unsalted butter

Preheat the oven to 375°. Grease a 12 by 18-inch sheet pan well and set aside.

To prepare the crust, place the flour, powdered sugar, orange zest, vanilla extract, and salt in a food processor. With the machine running, slowly add the pieces of butter and process until the dough comes together into a smooth ball. Press the dough into the prepared pan. Bake just until the crust is set, about 10 minutes. (Don't let the crust get brown at all, or it will get too dark when you bake it with the filling.) Let cool for at least 15 minutes.

Lower the oven temperature to 350°.

To prepare the filling, place the sugar in a large sauté pan with sides or a heavy saucepan. Gently moisten the sugar with the water, being careful not to splash the water and sugar onto the sides of the pan. Cook the sugar mixture over high heat, without stirring, until you see any part of it turning brown, then swirl the pan to even out the color. Cook until golden brown, about 2 minutes longer. Carefully add the cream to the hot sugar, taking care to pour it in slowly because it will bubble up very violently. Add the hazelnut liqueur and cook until the caramelized sugar has liquefied again and the sauce is very smooth and a deep golden brown, about 5 minutes. Remove the pan from the heat, add the vanilla extract, nutmeg, and hazelnuts, and mix well. Pour the filling over the crust. Bake until the filling is set and is bubbly, about 30 minutes. Cool for 20 minutes. (For information on making caramel, see page 183.)

Meanwhile, to prepare the ganache, place the chocolate in a food processor. Place the cream and butter in a heavy saucepan over medium-high heat and bring just to a boil. Once the cream begins to boil, turn on the food processor, add the cream through the feed tube, and process until very smooth. Pour the ganache over the cooled bars and refrigerate for 2 hours. To serve, cut the bars into 2 by 2-inch squares.

Variation

Chocolate-Hazelnut-Caramel Bars

POACHED PEAR-PECAN BARS

This variation of the hazelnut bars is even more elegant and can easily be served as a more formal dessert. If you have the time, poach the pears ahead of time, let them cool in the liquid, and refrigerate overnight—it will really make a difference in their flavor. For another fruit variation that you can prepare more quickly, substitute 3 peeled, diced Granny Smith apples for the poached pears.

To poach the pears, peel and halve 3 firm seasonal pears. In a heavy saucepan over high heat, combine 3 cups white wine, 1 cup sugar, the finely grated zest of 1 orange, and 2 cinnamon sticks. Bring to a boil, add the pears, lower the heat to medium, and poach until fork-tender, 8 to 10 minutes. Cool the pears in the liquid and refrigerate until ready to use.

Follow the Chocolate-Hazelnut-Caramel Bars master recipe, substituting 1 1/2 cups ground toasted pecans (page 10) for the 2 cups hazelnuts. Drain and dice the pears and then add them to the caramel mixture along with the pecans. Proceed as directed in the master recipe.

Makes about 24 bars

(master recipe)

Meringue Cookies

Meringue cookies are very easy to prepare and take just 10 to 15 minutes to put together. Baking them, however, is a different story; it takes about 5 hours to bake and then finish drying the cookies in the oven, and it's even better to let them sit in the oven overnight. For a very simple dessert that is also very light, pipe the meringue into nest-like shapes and then fill the finished cookies with fresh berries and top with a bit of sweetened crème fraîche.

Makes about 30 cookies

6 egg whites

Pinch of cream of tartar

1/2 cup granulated sugar

1 teaspoon pure vanilla extract

1/2 cup powdered sugar

Preheat the oven to 325°. Line a sheet pan with parchment paper and set aside.

Place the egg whites and cream of tartar in the bowl of a mixer fitted with the whip attachment, and whip on high speed until frothy. While beating, add the sugar, about 1 tablespoon at a time, then add the vanilla extract and beat until the whites are very shiny and hold a stiff peak. (Be sure to add the sugar slowly so it has time to dissolve; otherwise the egg whites will lose volume and be too soupy.) Place the meringue in a pastry bag fitted with a medium star tip and pipe it onto the prepared pan in 1-inch rosettes. Bake until light golden brown, about 1 hour and 15 minutes. Turn off the heat and leave the cookies in the oven for at least 4 more hours or overnight if possible. The cookies should be very crisp. Sift the powdered sugar over the cookies.

Variations

Meringue Cookies

CHOCOLATE MERINGUE COOKIES

These cookies are crisp on the outside and have a rich chocolate flavor on the inside. For those of you looking for a dessert that is low in fat and still has great flavor, this is the one for you.

Follow the Meringue Cookies master recipe, gently folding 1/2 cup sifted unsweetened cocoa powder into the stiffly beaten egg whites. Proceed as directed in the master recipe.

Makes about 30 cookies

ALMOND-COCONUT MERINGUE COOKIES

This variation is somewhat like a macaroon but lighter, with just a bit of texture from the nuts and coconut.

Place 1/2 cup shredded sweetened coconut in a food processor and process until finely chopped; set aside.

Follow the Meringue Cookies master recipe, substituting 1 teaspoon almond extract for the vanilla extract. Gently fold 1/3 cup finely ground toasted almonds (page 10) and the coconut into the stiffly beaten egg whites. Place the mixture in a pastry bag fitted with a large star tip (so the nuts and coconut won't get caught in the tip). Pipe and bake as directed in the master recipe.

Makes about 30 cookies

(master recipe)

Chocolate Brownies

Everybody loves brownies, although we all seem to have a favorite type. I prefer dense, fudgy brownies like these over more cakelike ones, and if I can eat them warm, all the better. These are very simple brownies, with little besides chocolate plus some toasted nuts for garnish. I wanted a delicious but basic master recipe that I could build upon to create easy variations with more complex flavors and textures.

Makes about 16 brownies

5 ounces unsweetened chocolate, coarsely chopped

1/2 cup cold unsalted butter, diced

4 large eggs

1 1/2 cups sugar

1 teaspoon pure vanilla extract

1/4 cup flour

1 cup chopped toasted walnuts or pecans (page 10)

Pinch of salt

Preheat the oven to 350°. Line the bottom of a well-greased 9-inch round cake pan with parchment paper; set aside.

Place the chocolate and butter in a metal bowl set over a pan of simmering water, making sure that the bottom of the bowl does not touch the water. When the chocolate has melted about halfway, remove the pan from the heat (leaving the bowl on the pan), and let the chocolate sit until completely melted; stir until smooth. Set aside.

Place the eggs, sugar, and vanilla extract in the bowl of a mixer fitted with the whip attachment, and whip on high speed until the eggs are very light in color and fluffy, about 5 minutes. Add the melted chocolate, and mix on medium speed until well blended. Add the flour, nuts, and salt, and mix on low speed until all of the ingredients are incorporated. Increase the speed to medium and mix just until smooth. Pour the batter into the prepared pan and bake until a knife inserted in the brownies comes out covered with moist crumbs, 25 to 30 minutes (if there is any question, it's better to underbake rather than overbake them). Let cool for about 20 minutes, then cut the brownies into 16 wedges and serve.

Variations

Chocolate Brownies

DOUBLE CHOCOLATE–CREAM CHEESE BROWNIES

As their name suggests, these brownies definitely go beyond the simple ones in the master recipe. They have almost double the chocolate, with pockets of lush cream cheese batter swirled throughout.

Follow the Chocolate Brownies master recipe, substituting 4 ounces chopped bittersweet chocolate for the nuts. Pour half of the batter into the prepared pan. In a separate bowl, mix together 10 ounces room-temperature cream cheese, 1/3 cup sugar, 1/2 teaspoon pure vanilla extract, and 1 egg yolk. Using about half of the cream cheese mixture, spoon dollops over the chocolate batter, and then top with the remaining chocolate batter. Spoon dollops of the remaining cream cheese mixture over the top. Using a skewer, swirl the two batters together. Bake as directed in the master recipe.

Makes about 16 brownies

BROWNIE MOUSSE CAKE

This dessert takes a simple brownie recipe way beyond simple, making it perfect when you really want to impress your friends. Make sure you give your guests a light dinner before serving this hefty dessert.

Grease a 10-inch springform pan and wrap the outside with foil to prevent leaking; set aside. Follow the Chocolate Brownies master recipe, substituting toasted almonds for the walnuts or pecans. Pour the batter into the prepared pan, and bake as in the master recipe.

After the brownies have cooled, prepare the Chocolate Mousse master recipe (page 196), substituting almond liqueur for the orange liqueur. Pour the mousse over the cooled brownies and refrigerate until well chilled, about 2 hours. Run a knife around the sides of the pan to loosen the cake, then remove the outer ring.

Serve chilled with freshly whipped cream.

Serves 14

(master recipe)

Bourbon Blonde Brownies

Melissa often features these simple bars on the dessert menu. She makes a magnificent sundae out of them, topping the warm bars with vanilla ice cream, warm chocolate sauce, and chopped toasted nuts. And when she's feeling particularly decadent, she has the pantry cook split a banana, sprinkle it with sugar, and brown it with a propane torch to serve on the side.

Makes 24 bars

2 cups firmly packed brown sugar

1 2/3 cups unsalted butter

3 eggs

5 tablespoons bourbon

1 tablespoon pure vanilla extract

2 1/2 cups flour

1 tablespoon baking powder

1 teaspoon salt

1 2/3 cups chopped toasted pecans (page 10)

1 pound bittersweet chocolate, chopped

Preheat the oven to 350°. Grease a 9 by 13-inch pan; set aside.

Heat the brown sugar and butter in a saucepan over medium heat until melted, and mix well. Bring the mixture to a full boil, and boil for about 1 minute. Let cool completely (to speed up the process, you can refrigerate it). Transfer the mixture to the bowl of a mixer fitted with the paddle attachment. With the mixer on medium speed, add the eggs, one at a time, scraping down the sides of the bowl and beating well after each addition. Add the bourbon and vanilla extract, and mix well. Combine the flour, baking powder, and salt, and add to the batter, mixing well. Add the nuts and chocolate, and mix well. Pour the batter into the prepared pan and bake until a knife inserted in the batter comes out clean, 30 to 40 minutes. Let cool, then cut into 24 squares.

Variations

Bourbon Blonde Brownies

BISTRO CHOCOLATE-BOURBON BLONDE BROWNIE SUNDAES

Try this Bistro favorite with White Chocolate Chunk-Raspberry-Chocolate Ice Cream (page 206).

Bourbon Blonde Brownies

2 cups heavy whipping cream

2 tablespoons sugar

2 teaspoons pure vanilla extract

1 quart Vanilla Bean Ice Cream (page 208) or
    Mascarpone Ice Cream (page 210)

2 cups Chocolate Sauce (page 62), warmed

1 cup chopped toasted pecans (page 10)

Mint sprigs, for garnish

Prepare the Bourbon Blonde Brownies as directed in the master recipe.

Whip the cream with the sugar and vanilla extract until it holds soft peaks.

To make the sundaes, place 2 brownies on each plate. Top with a scoop of ice cream, drizzle with warm chocolate sauce, and then finish off with the whipped cream, toasted pecans, and a garnish of fresh mint.

Serves 12

TROPICAL RUM BROWNIES

Here is my own tropical spin on Melissa's master recipe.

Follow the Bourbon Blonde Brownies master recipe, substituting dark rum for the bourbon, and omitting the pecans and bittersweet chocolate. Mix 1 cup chopped toasted macadamia nuts (page 10), 1 cup shredded sweetened coconut, and 1 pound chopped white chocolate into the finished batter. Bake as directed in the master recipe.

Makes 24 bars

(master recipe)

vanilla Bean Shortbread cookies

These intensely vanilla-flavored cookies are great on their own, but they're also the perfect springboard for your own spin.

Makes about 20 cookies

2 cups flour

1 cup sugar

1/2 vanilla bean, split in half lengthwise

1/4 teaspoon pure vanilla extract

1/2 teaspoon salt

1 cup cold unsalted butter, diced

Place the flour and sugar in the bowl of a mixer fitted with the paddle attachment. Scrape the seeds from the inside of the vanilla bean into the flour mixture (discard the bean), and then add the vanilla extract and salt. With the mixer on low speed, slowly add the butter, a few pieces at a time, and mix just until the dough is smooth.

Spread a 20-inch-long piece of plastic wrap out on the counter. Place the dough on the plastic and form it into a 12-inch-long cylinder. Fold one side of the plastic over the dough, and then roll up the dough tightly in the excess plastic, rolling it on the counter to smooth it. Refrigerate the dough until well chilled, about 1 hour.

Preheat the oven to 350°. Grease a sheet pan well and set aside.

Using a serrated knife, cut the dough into 1/2-inch-thick slices and place on the prepared pan. Bake until golden brown, 12 to 15 minutes. Let the cookies cool for about 5 minutes on the pan, then transfer to a rack or paper towels and let cool completely.

Variations

Vanilla Bean Shortbread Cookies

PECAN-ESPRESSO SHORTBREAD COOKIES

Instead of baking this dough into cookies, try using it as a crust for a simple pastry cream-filled tart.

Follow the Vanilla Bean Shortbread Cookies master recipe, replacing 1/2 cup of the flour with 1/2 cup finely ground pecans and adding 3 tablespoons instant espresso powder along with the flour and sugar. Proceed as directed in the master recipe.

Makes about 20 cookies

CANDIED GINGER–COCONUT SHORTBREAD COOKIES

To give these cookies a pretty, showy look, drizzle melted white and dark chocolate over them after they've cooled.

Follow the Vanilla Bean Shortbread Cookies master recipe, adding 1/2 cup chopped shredded sweetened coconut and 2 tablespoons minced candied ginger along with the flour and sugar. Proceed as directed in the master recipe.

Makes about 20 cookies

(master recipe)

Almond-Anise Biscotti

After an elaborate and heavy dinner, sometimes a simple dessert of homemade biscotti, sliced fruit and cheese, and a glass of port or sherry is just the right conclusion. Biscotti can be made a day or two ahead and kept stored in an airtight container, so serving dessert will be a cinch.

Makes 24 biscotti

4 eggs

1 1/2 cups sugar

2 tablespoons anise seeds, lightly toasted (page xx)

4 teaspoons almond liqueur

1 tablespoon pure vanilla extract

3 1/2 cups flour

1 teaspoon baking soda

1/2 teaspoon salt

1 1/2 cups slivered toasted almonds (page 10)

Preheat the oven to 300°. Line a sheet pan with parchment paper; set aside.

Place the eggs and sugar in the bowl of a mixer fitted with the paddle attachment and beat on high speed, scraping down the sides of the bowl often, until smooth. Add the anise seeds, liqueur, and vanilla extract, and mix well. Combine the flour, baking soda, and salt, and add to the egg mixture. Mix on low speed until all of the ingredients are incorporated. Add the almonds, increase the mixer speed to medium, and mix until well blended (the dough will be very sticky). Transfer the dough to a well-floured board.

Divide the dough in half. Flour your hands well and form each half into a log about 3 inches wide and 12 inches long. (Don't worry about making them perfect; just make sure they are even.) Set the logs well apart on the prepared pan and bake for about 30 minutes. Test by gently pressing on one; if it springs back and is firm to the touch, it's done. Let cool on the pan until cool enough to handle, then transfer to a cutting board. Using a serrated knife, slice into 1-inch-thick cookies. Place the sliced cookies back on the sheet pan, standing them up so the cut sides aren't touching the pan, and leaving several inches between them so they can dry out in the oven. Bake until crisp and firm, about 30 minutes longer. Test by gently pinching the ends of a cookie; if it is soft, continue baking for 5 to 10 minutes (they will crisp up even more as they cool). Transfer to a rack or paper towels and let cool completely.

If you like, dip the bottoms of the cooled biscotti into melted chocolate (page 8).

Variations

WHITE CHOCOLATE–PISTACHIO BISCOTTI

You can substitute chopped dark chocolate for the white chocolate to add intensity.

Follow the Almond-Anise Biscotti master recipe, omitting the anise seeds, adding 1/2 cup chopped white chocolate along with the flour mixture, and substituting coarsely chopped pistachios for the almonds. Proceed as directed in the master recipe.

Makes 24 biscotti

ORANGE-HAZELNUT BISCOTTI

My favorite way to dress these up is to dip one end of each cooled cookie into melted white chocolate.

Follow the Almond-Anise Biscotti master recipe, adding the finely grated zest of 2 oranges to the eggs along with the sugar and substituting hazelnut liqueur for the almond liqueur. Proceed as directed in the master recipe, substituting chopped toasted hazelnuts (page 10) for the almonds.

Makes 24 biscotti

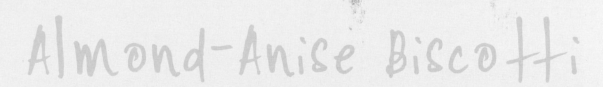

Almond-Anise Biscotti

Pecan Sticky Buns (page 157)

chapter four

Breakfast Sweets

When it comes to breakfast, nothing is better than a muffin or scone so fresh it's still steaming in the center when you break it open—especially if you were coaxed awake by its warm aroma mingled with the smell of coffee brewing. There's something so wonderful about this anticipation that it makes easing into the day an inviting idea. And if preparing breakfast rests on your shoulders and you have to get up earlier than everyone else does, at least you can be the first in line.

A really good breakfast bread or pastry can be the focal point of the whole meal. Just add some fresh fruit and excellent coffee, and the picture is complete. You'll find a recipe in this chapter for every type of breakfast or morning occasion, from a quick and easy Espresso Coffee Cake to Orange-Caramel Pull-Apart Bread that's special enough for a Sunday brunch. There's even Missy's Granola, which is full of flavor and very welcome on a busy weekday morning.

When choosing a recipe to prepare, be sure to consider the amount of time you have and how much effort you want to put into preparing it. For example, promising to serve a batch of cinnamon rolls hot from the oven at 8 o'clock in the morning might sound reasonable until you realize that you'll have to wake up before the birds to keep your word. If you're determined to make and serve cinnamon rolls—or any of the yeasted pastries that require several risings—before lunchtime, you can buy yourself at least an extra hour of sleep by making the dough the night before. After mixing it together, put the dough in a very large (at least triple the size of the dough) zip-top bag and let it go through the first rising in the refrigerator overnight.

In the morning, you'll only need to shape it and let it rise once more before baking, giving you time to read the newspaper and relax or, if you're expecting guests, straighten up the house, set the table, and slice some fruit.

On the other hand, it doesn't take long at all to make scones or muffins, and coffee cake is even faster yet. Putting them together takes just a few minutes. If you still would like to streamline the preparation and save time, you can measure out the dry ingredients the night before and have them ready and waiting. In the morning, add the wet ingredients, mix, and bake.

Although a breakfast bread or pastry fresh from the oven is the ultimate, most are just fine if you bake them the evening before. Just before serving, warm them in a low oven and they should taste and smell wonderful (but don't reheat them in a microwave oven, because they'll turn rubbery). Doughnuts are a definite exception. Since they are deep-fried, they're best eaten right away.

I love doughnuts so much that I have included recipes for both raised and cake varieties. The yeasted dough for the raised doughnuts requires two risings, so you do need to plan in advance if you want to make them. The cake doughnuts are much faster to prepare. It takes just 20 minutes to mix the dough and roll them out, so if you're really desperate, you can make them almost faster than you can drive to the nearest doughnut shop (and you don't have to worry about them cooling down on the way home). When you are ready to fry either type of doughnut, it's vital to have the temperature of the oil just right: 350° to 375°. If you don't have a thermometer handy, simply drop a cube of bread in the oil; if it turns brown in 30 to 40 seconds, the oil is the right temperature. Fry only as many doughnuts as will fit without overcrowding, and be sure to wait 2 to 3 minutes between batches to let the oil recoup, or come back up to temperature.

The last thing you want to do in the morning is run to the store for breakfast ingredients. Fortunately, these recipes are very versatile, so you can improvise with different combinations of spices, seasonal berries, nuts, and dried fruit. Once you taste really good breakfast pastries that you've made yourself, you'll never want to serve another packaged or store-bought muffin or pastry again.

Spice Cake Doughnuts

Every Christmas morning for the last ten years or so, I have made a batch of doughnuts. I have tried all kinds of doughnut recipes, and in this one I've finally achieved the doughnut of my dreams. I'm not sure why I am so enamored with doughnuts, but I love them hot from the fryer. Cake doughnuts are a bit denser than raised ones, but they're much faster to prepare. When frying the doughnuts, it's very important to have the oil hot enough. If it isn't, the doughnuts will soak up the fat and won't be very tasty, but oil at the right temperature will seal the outsides of the doughnuts, keeping them crisp and not greasy at all. Be sure to let the doughnuts cool just a bit before dredging them in sugar; otherwise the sugar will melt.

Makes about 24 doughnuts

3 1/2 cups flour

1 tablespoon plus 1 1/2 teaspoons baking powder

1 teaspoon ground cinnamon

1/2 teaspoon ground allspice

1/2 teaspoon ground ginger

Pinch of five-spice powder

1 teaspoon pure vanilla extract

1 cup milk

1/4 cup unsalted butter, at room temperature

1 cup granulated sugar

2 eggs

1 teaspoon salt

Vegetable oil, for deep-frying

2 cups granulated sugar or powdered sugar, for dredging

To prepare the dough, sift together the flour, baking powder, and spices; set aside. Add the vanilla extract to the milk; set aside.

Place the butter and the 1 cup granulated sugar in the bowl of a mixer fitted with the paddle attachment and beat on high speed, scraping down the sides of the bowl often, until light and fluffy, 3 to 4 minutes. With the mixer on medium speed, add the eggs, one at a time, scraping down the sides of the bowl and mixing well after each addition. Add half of the flour mixture and half of the milk, then mix on low speed until well blended. Scrape down the sides of the bowl, add the remaining flour mixture followed by the milk

continued

continued from page 149

and the salt, and mix well. Transfer the dough to a well-floured board and knead until smooth. Wrap the dough in plastic wrap and refrigerate for at least 1 hour or overnight.

Roll the chilled dough out onto a well-floured board to a thickness of about 1/2 inch. Cut with a doughnut cutter or a round cookie cutter (if you use a cookie cutter, use a smaller cutter to cut the centers out). Save the donut holes, or add them back to the scrap dough before you reroll it.

To fry the doughnuts, heat about 4 inches of vegetable oil in a large saucepan over high heat until it reaches 350°. (You can check the temperature with a candy thermometer, or place a piece of bread in the oil; if it turns brown in about 40 seconds, the oil should be at about 350°.) Meanwhile, line a sheet pan with paper towels, and have it ready by the fryer. When the oil is hot, add as many doughnuts as will fit without overcrowding, and cook on one side until golden brown, 2 to 3 minutes. Turn the doughnuts over and cook 2 to 3 minutes longer. Transfer to the paper towels to drain, and let cool for about 5 minutes. Continue cooking the remaining doughnuts and doughnut holes. The holes will cook a bit faster, so cook them separately. When the doughnuts have cooled (they should still be warm but not hot), dredge them in powdered or granulated sugar. Serve immediately; they are best eaten warm!

Variations

Spice Cake Doughnuts

CANDIED GINGER–ORANGE CAKE DOUGHNUTS

The candied ginger provides a surprise bite of spice, while the orange is a nice contrast to the heat and sweetness of the candied ginger.

Follow the Spice Cake Doughnuts master recipe, omitting the spices. Add the finely grated zest of 1 orange and 2 tablespoons finely minced candied ginger after the eggs are incorporated, and proceed as directed in the master recipe. If you like, dredge the doughnuts in vanilla sugar (page 11) instead of powdered or granulated sugar.

Makes about 24 doughnuts

CHOCOLATE-ESPRESSO DOUGHNUTS

Cake doughnuts already have a denser body than raised donuts, and adding chocolate makes them even denser. Because of the chocolate, these doughnuts do not rise as much as the spice doughnuts—but they're just as good!

Melt 3 ounces unsweetened chocolate in a metal bowl set over a pan of simmering water or melt in the microwave; set aside and keep warm.

Follow the Spice Cake Doughnuts master recipe, replacing 1/3 cup of the flour with unsweetened cocoa powder, omitting the allspice and ginger, and increasing the sugar to 1 1/2 cups. After the eggs are incorporated, add the melted chocolate and 1 heaping tablespoon instant espresso or coffee powder. Proceed as directed in the master recipe. Dredge the cooled doughnuts in powdered sugar. Serve warm.

Makes about 24 doughnuts

Raised Doughnuts

Raised doughnuts are some of my favorites, although after testing all of these recipes I think it might be a while before another doughnut crosses my lips. These are so nice and light—when you bite into them it's like biting into sweet air. I knew I had the right recipe for the book when two of my doughnut-loving staff started calling them Cappy Creams! The dough rises three different times, for at least an hour each time, so if you want to make these for breakfast, plan on getting up extremely early or starting the night before.

Makes about 24 doughnuts

1 1/4 cups milk

2 1/2 teaspoons active dry yeast

3/4 cup granulated sugar

4 cups flour

1/4 cup unsalted butter, at room temperature

1 egg

1 teaspoon pure vanilla extract

1/2 teaspoon salt

Vegetable oil, for deep-frying

1 1/2 cups sifted powdered sugar, for dredging

Heat the milk in a saucepan over medium heat until it reaches 100° to 110°, or until you can feel the heat with your fingertip. (Do not get the milk too hot or you will kill the yeast.) Pour the milk into a large bowl, add the yeast, about 1 tablespoon of the sugar, and about 1 1/2 cups of the flour, and mix well. Cover with plastic wrap, and let the dough rise in a warm place until doubled in volume, about 1 hour.

When the dough has risen, place the butter and the remaining sugar in the bowl of a mixer fitted with the paddle attachment and beat on high speed, scraping down the sides of the bowl occasionally, until light and fluffy, about 3 minutes. Add the egg and vanilla extract and mix well. Add the yeast mixture and mix on low speed until well blended. Add the remaining 2 1/2 cups flour and the salt, and mix until the dough comes together, about 2 minutes. Transfer the dough to a well-floured board and knead until very smooth and elastic. Place the dough in a large, well-greased bowl, cover with plastic wrap, and let rise until doubled in volume, 1 to 1 1/2 hours.

continued

153

continued from page 153

Roll the dough out onto a well-floured board to a thickness of about 1/2 inch. Cut with a doughnut cutter or a round cookie cutter (if you use a cookie cutter, use a smaller cutter to cut the centers out). Save the doughnut holes, or add them back to the scrap dough before you reroll it. Place the doughnuts and holes on a well-greased sheet pan, and let rise in a warm place for about 1 hour, or cover and refrigerate them overnight, and let rise in the morning.

To fry the doughnuts, heat about 4 inches of vegetable oil in a large saucepan over high heat until it reaches 350°. (You can check the temperature with a candy thermometer, or place a piece of bread in the oil; if it turns brown in about 40 seconds, the oil should be at about 350°.) Meanwhile, line a sheet pan with paper towels, and have it ready by the fryer. When the oil is hot, add as many doughnuts as will fit without overcrowding, and cook on one side until golden brown, 2 to 3 minutes. Turn the doughnuts over and cook about 2 minutes longer. Transfer to the paper towels to drain, and let cool for about 5 minutes. Continue cooking the remaining doughnuts and doughnut holes. The holes will cook a bit faster, so cook them separately. When the doughnuts have cooled (they should still be warm but not hot), dredge them in powdered sugar. Serve immediately.

Variations

Raised Doughnuts

RAISED DOUGHNUTS GLAZED WITH GANACHE

Most store-bought chocolate-glazed doughnuts are sickly sweet and have very little real chocolate flavor. Glazing these doughnuts in ganache gives them a rich and intense chocolate flavor—the way they should be.

Follow the Raised Doughnuts master recipe. Just before frying the doughnuts, prepare Ganache (page 47). Place the warm ganache in a shallow metal bowl. Fry the doughnuts and let cool for about 5 minutes. Hold each doughnut on the edges and dip one side in the warm ganache; set on a parchment paper–lined sheet pan and let cool until the ganache is set, about 10 minutes. Serve warm.

Makes about 24 doughnuts

LEMON DOUGHNUTS WITH VANILLA SUGAR

Preparing the vanilla sugar does require some forethought, but the simple addition really makes a big difference in the final flavor of the doughnuts.

Follow the Raised Doughnuts master recipe, adding the finely grated zest of 2 lemons to the milk before heating. Proceed as directed in the master recipe. Dredge the cooled doughnuts in 1 1/2 cups vanilla sugar (page 11). Serve warm.

Makes about 24 doughnuts

(master recipe)

Cinnamon Rolls

Melissa's family makes this recipe for Christmas morning and other special occasions. You can make the dough the night before and place it in the refrigerator overnight. The next morning, take the dough out, roll it up with the cinnamon and sugar, and let it rise for the last time. In no time you'll have fresh, hot cinnamon rolls for breakfast.

Makes 18 cinnamon rolls

2 cups plus 3 tablespoons milk

1 cup plus 6 tablespoons granulated sugar

2 teaspoons salt

1/4 cup unsalted butter

1 egg, lightly beaten

2 1/2 teaspoons active dry yeast

6 cups flour

1/4 cup unsalted butter, melted

4 teaspoons ground cinnamon

2 cups powdered sugar

Place 2 cups of the milk in a saucepan over medium heat and bring just to a boil. Combine 6 tablespoons of the sugar, the salt, and the butter in a large bowl, pour the hot milk over it, and let cool to 110° to 115°. In a small bowl, mix together the egg and yeast. Add to the cooled milk mixture, and mix well. Add the flour and mix until the dough is soft. Transfer the dough to a well-floured board and knead until very smooth and elastic, about 5 minutes. Place the dough in a large, well-greased bowl, cover with plastic wrap, and let rise until doubled in volume, about 1 hour.

Grease a 9 by 13-inch pan; set aside.

Punch the dough down, place on a well-floured board, and roll it out into a 10 by 14-inch rectangle and brush it with the melted butter. Combine the cinnamon and the remaining 1 cup sugar and sprinkle the mixture over the butter. Starting at one of the long sides, roll the dough up, and pinch the seam well to seal. Using a serrated knife, cut the dough into 2-inch-thick slices, and place them in the prepared pan. Cover with plastic wrap and let rise one more time, until doubled in volume, about 1 hour.

Meanwhile, preheat the oven to 350°.

When the rolls have risen, bake until golden brown, about 25 minutes. Let cool for about 5 minutes. While the rolls are cooling, combine the powdered sugar and the remaining 3 tablespoons milk to make a glaze. Drizzle the glaze over the cinnamon rolls, and serve warm.

Variations

Cinnamon Rolls

PECAN STICKY BUNS

These are so rich that you'll want to serve them as the focal point of a simple breakfast or brunch. All you'll need to add is some fresh fruit and really good yogurt.

Follow the Cinnamon Rolls master recipe. Just before slicing the dough into rolls, melt 1 cup unsalted butter in a saucepan over medium-high heat, add 3 1/2 cups brown sugar, and whisk until well blended. Add 1 cup light corn syrup and boil, whisking constantly, until the brown sugar has dissolved, about 1 minute. Pour the mixture into the prepared pan, and sprinkle with 2 cups chopped pecans. Cut the dough into 1-inch-thick slices, and place in the pan. Bake as directed in the master recipe.

After the baked rolls have cooled for 5 minutes, carefully flip the pan over onto a sheet pan to release the rolls. Let cool for 5 minutes longer before serving. Omit the glaze. Serve warm.

Makes 18 sticky buns

pictured on page 146

DRIED FRUIT CINNAMON ROLLS

Port-soaked dried fruit adds texture and distinctive flavor to an otherwise simple breakfast bread.

Combine 3/4 cup dried sour cherries and 3/4 cup dried cranberries with 2 cups ruby port in a saucepan over medium heat. Bring to a boil and cook until the fruit has absorbed almost all of the liquid, 5 to 6 minutes. Let cool completely, and then chop coarsely; set aside.

Follow the Cinnamon Rolls master recipe. After rolling the dough into a rectangle and sprinkling it with the cinnamon sugar, scatter the prepared fruit over the dough, and then top the fruit with 1 cup chopped toasted walnuts (page 10). Proceed as directed in the master recipe. Serve warm.

Makes 18 cinnamon rolls

(master recipe)

Hazelnut-Pear Scones

When Melissa has a few extra minutes at work, her favorite way to treat the staff is to bake scones. No matter what the flavor, they are always tender and buttery. The most important bit of advice for baking perfect scones is the same as for biscuits: don't overmix the dough. Once you learn the basic method, there's really no limit to the kinds of scones you can make. Be sure to take advantage of fresh fruit in the summer, any kind of toasted nut, and even bittersweet or white chocolate chips.

Makes 12 scones

3 cups flour

1/2 cup sugar

2 teaspoons baking powder

1/2 teaspoon salt

1/2 cup cold unsalted butter, diced

1/4 cup chopped toasted hazelnuts (page 10)

1 ripe pear, peeled, cored, and cut into small dice

1 cup heavy whipping cream

1 egg

2 tablespoons unsalted butter, melted

Preheat the oven to 375°. Line a sheet pan with parchment paper; set aside.

Place the flour, sugar, baking powder, and salt in a large bowl and mix well. Add the butter and, using your fingertips, blend until the mixture resembles a coarse meal. Add the hazelnuts and diced pear, and toss to combine. Mix together the cream and egg, add the mixture to the flour mixture, and stir until the dough just starts to come together (don't mix it completely, or the scones will be tough). Turn the dough out onto a well-floured board and form it into a ball. Cut the dough in half and form each half into a disk about 6 inches around and 1/2 inch thick. Cut each disk into 6 wedges. Place the scones on the prepared sheet pan, and brush with the melted butter. Bake until golden brown, 20 to 25 minutes. Let cool for about 5 minutes before serving. Serve warm.

Variations

Hazelnut-Pear Scones

ORANGE-ALMOND SCONES

As you know, we encourage you to take creative license with the recipes in this book. For this one, you can vary the spices or add a couple of tablespoons of minced candied ginger or 1 cup chopped dark or white chocolate.

Follow the Hazelnut-Pear Scones master recipe, adding the finely grated zest of 1 orange to the flour mixture, and substituting sliced toasted almonds (page 10) for the hazelnuts. Omit the pear.

ESPRESSO-CHOCOLATE SCONES

What a combination of ingredients to wake up to in the morning! You can use either dark or white chocolate, but why not go for it and use both?

Follow the Hazelnut-Pear Scones master recipe, adding 1 tablespoon instant espresso powder to the cream (let it sit for 5 minutes to dissolve) before combining it with the egg. Proceed as directed in the master recipe, substituting 1/2 cup chopped bittersweet chocolate for the nuts and omitting the pear.

SUMMER SCONES

These are meant to take advantage of whatever seasonal fruit looks the best at the market (or any combination of fruit if you can't pick a favorite). About 5 ounces of melted white chocolate drizzled over the top of the cooled scones makes a nice finishing touch.

Follow the Hazelnut-Pear Scones master recipe, adding the finely grated zest of 1 orange to the flour mixture. Add 1 cup of any of your favorite summer berries along with the nuts. Omit the pear.

PEACH-RASPBERRY SCONES

Peaches and raspberries are my favorite kinds of fruit, so when they are combined in Melissa's tender scones one bite will really make my day. I never fiddle with this recipe—it is just perfect.

Follow the Hazelnut-Pear Scones master recipe, omitting the nuts, and substituting 1/2 cup fresh raspberries and 1 small chopped fresh peach for the pear.

Cream Cheese Pinwheels

I think these are the most elegant of the breakfast pastries in this book, with such a pretty shape and layer upon delicate layer of crisp, buttery pastry. These are folded just like the paper pinwheels you probably made in kindergarten.

Makes 16 pinwheels

Puff Pastry (page 246)

6 ounces cream cheese

1/4 cup plus 2 tablespoons sugar

Dash of pure vanilla extract

1 egg yolk

Preheat a standard oven to 400° or a convection oven to 375°. Line a sheet pan with parchment paper; set aside.

Roll the puff pastry out on a well-floured board into a 14 by 14-inch square. Cut the square in half, then cut each half in half lengthwise to form 4 long pieces of dough. Cut each piece into 4 squares so that you have a total of 16 squares. Place one square on a work surface. Make a 1-inch diagonal cut from each corner toward the center of the square. Pick up one corner of the cut dough and fold it diagonally over toward the center of the square, and press it to seal. Working clockwise and skipping every other corner, fold the remaining corners to the center. Set the pinwheel on the prepared pan, and repeat with the remaining squares.

To prepare the filling, combine the cream cheese, 1/4 cup of the sugar, and the vanilla extract in a food processor and process until smooth. Scrape down the sides of the bowl, add the egg yolk, and process again until smooth.

Spoon about 1 tablespoon of the filling into the middle of each of the pinwheels. Sprinkle lightly with the remaining 2 tablespoons sugar, and bake until golden brown, about 20 minutes in a standard oven and 15 minutes in a convection oven. Let cool about 10 minutes before serving. Serve warm.

Variations

Cream Cheese Pinwheels

RASPBERRY-ALMOND CREAM CHEESE PINWHEELS

If you make your own jam, show it off in these lovely pastries. Although raspberry is my favorite, any flavor will also taste great.

Combine 1 cup sugar and 2/3 cup finely chopped toasted almonds (page 10), and spread the mixture out over a work surface. Follow the Cream Cheese Pinwheels master recipe, rolling the puff pastry out on the nut mixture instead of on a floured board. Proceed as directed in the master recipe, topping the filling on each pinwheel with about 1 tablespoon raspberry jam before baking.

Makes 16 pinwheels

APRICOT–CREAM CHEESE PINWHEELS

If you don't have nice, ripe apricots, you can substitute sliced fresh peaches or strawberries.

Peel and halve 8 ripe apricots (page 10); set aside. Follow the Cream Cheese Pinwheels master recipe, topping the filling on each pinwheel with an apricot half (cut side down) before baking.

Makes 16 pinwheels

Basic Muffins

Everyone needs a good, basic muffin recipe. This one can be altered to suit any style of breakfast, from a quick breakfast-on-the-run to an elegant brunch. Whatever the season or occasion, this recipe is just waiting for your imaginative touch.

Makes 12 muffins

1/2 cup unsalted butter, at room temperature

3/4 cup plus 2 tablespoons sugar

2 eggs

2 teaspoons pure vanilla extract

1/2 cup milk

2 cups flour

2 teaspoons baking powder

1/4 teaspoon salt

1/2 teaspoon ground nutmeg

Preheat the oven to 375°. Grease a 12-cup muffin tin; set aside.

Place the butter and 3/4 cup of the sugar in the bowl of a mixer fitted with the paddle attachment, and beat on high speed, scraping down the sides of the bowl often, until light and fluffy. Add the eggs, one at a time, again scraping down the sides of the bowl and mixing well after each addition. Add the vanilla extract and milk, and mix well (the mixture may look a bit broken, or separated, but don't worry). Combine the flour, baking powder, and salt in a large bowl. Using a large plastic spatula, gently fold the butter mixture into the flour mixture just until the batter comes together. (Do not overmix the batter, or the muffins will be tough.) Divide the batter among the muffin cups, filling each about three-fourths full. Combine the remaining 2 tablespoons sugar and the nutmeg, and sprinkle it over the tops. Bake until the muffins are golden brown and slowly spring back when touched lightly in the centers, 20 to 25 minutes. Let cool for about 5 minutes before removing from the cups. Serve warm.

Variations

Basic Muffins

Makes 12 muffins (all variations)

BLUEBERRY MUFFINS

This is our version of the classic muffin. I love summer mornings at the Bistro when Melissa gets blueberries as big as your fist and makes these muffins for the staff.

Follow the Basic Muffins master recipe, adding the finely grated zest of 1 lemon along with the eggs to the creamed butter and sugar. Toss 1 1/2 cups fresh blueberries with the flour mixture just before folding in the butter mixture. Bake as directed in the master recipe.

RASPBERRY–CREAM CHEESE MUFFINS

These are my favorite muffins in the book—the tangy creamy texture of the cream cheese and the sweet plump raspberries are a marriage made in muffin heaven. Although raspberries are my favorites, blackberries will also do nicely.

Follow the Basic Muffins master recipe, tossing 1 cup fresh raspberries and 1 ounce cream cheese, pinched off in small bits) with the flour mixture just before folding in the butter mixture. Bake as directed in the master recipe.

FRESH PEACH MUFFINS

Fresh peaches are perfect for so short a time that you should use them in as many recipes as pos-sible, but apricots make a fine substitute.

Follow the Basic Muffins master recipe, tossing 1 diced ripe peach with the flour mixture just before folding in the butter mixture. Bake as directed in the master recipe.

BANANA-NUT MUFFINS

I like to use toasted macadamia nuts in this recipe. To add even more flavor, fold 3/4 cup diced dried cherries into the batter.

Follow the Basic Muffins master recipe, adding 1 small, ripe mashed banana along with the eggs to the creamed butter mixture. Toss 1/2 cup chopped toasted walnuts (page 10) with the flour mixture just before folding in the butter mixture. Bake as directed in the master recipe.

LEMON MUFFINS

These muffins have a rich and tangy surprise in the centers.

Follow the Basic Muffins master recipe. After scooping the batter into the cups, place about 3/4 cup Lemon Curd (page 64) into a small pastry bag fitted with a small tip. Plunge the tip into the center of each muffin and fill with lemon curd. Smooth the batter over, sprinkle with sugar (omit the nutmeg), and bake as directed in the master recipe.

Pictured on opposite page

(master recipe)

Espresso Coffee Cake

The smell of this coffee cake wafting through the house will get your family up and moving on the laziest of Sunday mornings. The espresso makes this a coffee cake in every sense of the word.

Serves 12

Cake

1 1/2 cups unsalted butter, at room temperature

2 cups sugar

4 eggs

1 tablespoon pure vanilla extract

4 cups flour

2 teaspoons baking powder

1 teaspoon baking soda

1/2 teaspoon salt

2 cups sour cream

1/4 cup instant espresso powder

2 tablespoons hot water

Espresso Glaze

1 tablespoon instant espresso powder

2 teaspoons pure vanilla extract

2 cups powdered sugar

3 tablespoons milk

Preheat the oven to 350°. Grease a 9 by 13-inch pan; set aside.

To prepare the cake, place the butter and sugar in the bowl of a mixer fitted with the paddle attachment and beat on high speed, scraping down the sides of the bowl often, until light and fluffy, about 5 minutes. Add the eggs one at a time, mixing well after each addition, followed by the vanilla. Combine the flour, baking powder, baking soda, and salt. Add about half of the flour mixture to the butter mixture and mix well. Scrape down the sides of the bowl, add about half of the sour cream, and mix well. Add the remaining dry ingredients followed by the remaining sour cream, scraping down the sides of the bowl and mixing well after each addition. Combine the instant espresso powder and hot water in a medium bowl, add about a third of the batter, and mix well. Spread about half of the plain batter in the prepared pan. Top with the espresso batter, and then cover with the remaining plain batter. Bake until the cake slowly springs back when touched lightly in the center, about 45 minutes. Let cool for 5 minutes before glazing.

To prepare the glaze, dissolve the instant espresso powder in the vanilla extract. Place the powdered sugar in a bowl, add the espresso mixture and the milk, and mix well. (If it's too thick, add a bit more milk.) Pour the glaze over the cake and spread it out to the edges. Serve warm.

Variations

Espresso Coffee Cake

CARAMEL COFFEE CAKE

If you have read any of my other books you might know by now that I have a real love of caramel. Since it takes me a while to wake up in the morning, any time I can start my day with a piece of this coffee cake I am a much happier person. You can serve this coffee cake as the focal point of an entire breakfast.

Follow the Espresso Coffee Cake master recipe, substituting 1 cup Caramel Sauce (page 58) for the instant espresso powder and hot water mixture. Mix the sauce with a third of the plain batter, and proceed as directed in the master recipe, omitting the glaze and dusting the warm cake with powered sugar. Serve warm with softly whipped cream and drizzled with more Caramel Sauce, if you like.

Serves 12

continued

continued from page 167

APRICOT-ALMOND COFFEE CAKE

If the peaches you find at the market are riper than the apricots, by all means use them instead. Pecans or even macadamia nuts also make a good substitute for the almonds in this cake. You can make this cake the night before, and gently warm it in a low oven just before serving.

Follow the Espresso Coffee Cake master recipe, substituting 1 cup good-quality apricot preserves for the instant espresso powder and hot water mixture. Mix the preserves with a third of the plain batter, and proceed as directed in the master recipe. Just before baking, top the batter with 1 cup sliced almonds. Bake as directed in the master recipe, omitting the glaze and dusting the warm cake with powdered sugar.

Serves 12

FRESH FRUIT COFFEE CAKE

This cake is meant to show off seasonal fruit. When we go to the beach with groups of our friends in the summer, I like to buy whatever fresh fruit is offered at the stands along the way. Then, after we arrive at the beach house, I'll use the fruit when I bake this cake for breakfast.

Follow the Espresso Coffee Cake master recipe, substituting 2 cups fresh berries or diced fresh stone fruit (such as apricots or peaches) for the instant espresso powder and hot water mixture. Slightly mash the fruit, mix it with a third of the plain batter, and proceed as directed in the master recipe. Just before baking, top the batter with 2 cups Streusel Topping (page 78). Bake as directed in the master recipe, omitting the glaze and dusting the warm cake with powdered sugar.

Serves 12

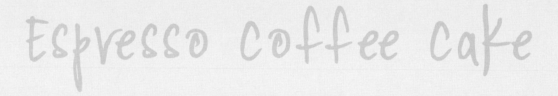

Espresso Coffee Cake

Zucchini Bread

Anyone with a garden has made zucchini bread. I like to serve it sliced and toasted, topped with a pat of butter. If you have any left the next day, use it to make an incredible version of French toast.

Makes 2 loaves

1 cup vegetable oil

2 cups sugar

3 eggs

2 teaspoons pure vanilla extract

2 cups shredded zucchini

1 (8-ounce) can crushed pineapple, drained

3 cups flour

1/2 teaspoon baking powder

2 teaspoons baking soda

1 teaspoon salt

3/4 teaspoon ground nutmeg

1 1/2 teaspoons ground cinnamon

1 cup chopped nuts

1 cup shredded sweetened coconut

Preheat the oven to 350°. Grease two 9 by 5-inch loaf pans; set aside.

Combine the oil, sugar, eggs, and vanilla extract in the bowl of a mixer fitted with the paddle attachment, and mix on medium speed until well blended, about 2 minutes. Add the zucchini and pineapple, and mix well. Add the flour, baking powder, baking soda, salt, and spices, and mix on low speed just until combined. Remove the bowl from the mixer, and fold in the nuts and coconut. Divide the batter between the 2 prepared pans, and bake until the bread slowly springs back when touched lightly in the center, about 1 hour. Let cool for about 15 minutes, then remove the bread from the pans. Serve warm or at room temperature.

Variations

Zucchini Bread

ZUCCHINI MUFFINS

This is a simple take on zucchini bread (who doesn't need another way to use the zucchini from their garden?). You can use grated carrots in the winter when your garden is finished for the season.

Prepare the batter as directed in the Zucchini Bread master recipe. Divide the batter among 24 well-greased muffin cups, filling them about three-fourths full. Bake until the muffins are golden brown and slowly spring back when touched lightly in the centers, 20 to 25 minutes. Let cool for 5 minutes before removing from the cups. Serve warm.

Makes about 24 muffins

CARROT BREAD

When zucchini isn't in season—or if you gave all of your garden's bounty to friends—try this carrot bread instead.

Follow the Zucchini Bread master recipe, substituting grated carrots for the zucchini.

Makes 2 loaves

orange-caramel Pull-Apart Bread

For some reason, this used to be known as monkey bread, but that name just doesn't give this elegant breakfast bread its due. When it's inverted on a plate, it's a tower of glistening, luscious orange caramel and buttery pastry.

Serves 12

Dough

1 1/4 cups milk

1/3 cup sugar

1 teaspoon salt

1/2 cup unsalted butter, diced

1 tablespoon active dry yeast

2 eggs

Finely grated zest and juice of 2 oranges

5 cups flour

Orange-Caramel Sauce

1/2 cup unsalted butter

3/4 cup firmly packed brown sugar

1/2 cup light corn syrup

Finely grated zest of 1 orange

1 cup sugar

1 teaspoon ground cinnamon

Finely grated zest of 1 orange

1/2 cup unsalted butter, melted

To prepare the dough, place the milk in a saucepan over medium heat and bring it just to a boil. Combine the sugar, salt, and butter in a large bowl, pour the hot milk over it, and let cool to 110° to 115°. Add the yeast, mix well, and let the mixture sit for about 10 minutes. Add the eggs and the orange zest and juice, and mix well. Add the flour and mix until combined. Transfer the dough to a well-floured board and knead until very smooth and elastic, about 10 minutes. Place the dough in a large, well-greased bowl, cover with plastic wrap, and let rise until doubled in volume, about 1 1/2 hours.

While the dough is rising, make the orange-caramel sauce. Melt the butter in a saucepan over medium-high heat, add the brown sugar, and whisk until well blended. Add the corn syrup and boil, whisking constantly, until the brown sugar has dissolved, about 1 minute. Stir in the orange zest. Pour the sauce into a well-greased Bundt pan or angel food cake pan; set aside.

continued

171

continued from page 171

Punch the dough down, place it on a well-floured board, and form it into a log about 18 inches long. Cut the log in half lengthwise, and then cut each half into 1-inch-thick slices to form about 36 pieces. Roll each piece into a ball.

Combine the 1 cup sugar, cinnamon, and orange zest. Dip each ball of dough in the melted butter, toss in the sugar mixture, and then place in the prepared pan. As you continue with the remaining balls of dough, layer them evenly in the pan. Cover with plastic wrap and let rise one more time, about 30 minutes (don't let them rise until doubled, or they'll spill out of the pan).

Meanwhile, preheat the oven to 350°.

When the bread has risen, bake until it is golden brown and sounds hollow when tapped, 50 minutes to 1 hour. Let cool for about 5 minutes, and then invert the pan onto a large plate to release the bread. Let cool for about 15 minutes before serving. Serve warm.

Missy's Granola

The key to making a flavorful, crunchy granola is to bake it slowly and stir it often so it won't overcook. It may not be as crisp as you want when you bring it out of the oven, but it will get crisper as it cools, so don't forget to stir it during this last stage.

Makes about 8 cups

1/3 cup chopped walnuts

1/3 cup chopped pecans

1/3 cup slivered almonds

2/3 cup hazelnuts

1/2 cup sesame seeds

1/2 cup bran

3 cups old-fashioned oats

1 cup shredded sweetened coconut

2 teaspoons ground cinnamon

1/2 cup unsalted butter

1/2 cup honey

1/4 cup lightly packed brown sugar

2 teaspoons pure vanilla extract

1/2 cup dried cherries

1/2 cup sliced dates

1/2 cup dried cranberries

Preheat the oven to 325°. Line a sheet pan with parchment paper; set aside.

In a large bowl, combine the nuts, sesame seeds, bran, oats, coconut, and cinnamon; set aside. Melt the butter in a small saucepan over medium heat, add the honey, brown sugar, and vanilla extract, and mix well. Pour over the nut mixture and toss well. Spread the granola in the prepared pan and bake, stirring every 10 minutes, until golden brown, about 30 minutes. Remove the pan from the oven, place the dried fruit on top of the granola (this will soften the dried fruit), and let cool completely.

The granola will keep in an airtight container for up to 2 weeks.

Espresso-Spice Crème Caramel (page 195)

chapter five

Puddings, custards, and Mousses

ustard is comfort food and, for many people, a reminder of childhood. Usually it's not very exotic, just a creamy, cool treat that can satisfy both the simple and the sophisticated palate. Generally speaking, it is a combination of eggs, milk, and sugar that is either cooked on the stove or baked. And although it might start with common ingredients, when finessed in the right way, those ingredients can be transformed into something very special. This chapter covers all the bases when it comes to custard.

A custard chapter would be incomplete without at least one pudding recipe. Pudding is the most basic dessert in this book, yet I consider it a stepping stone to its more sophisticated cousin, crème brûlée. Since we wrote this book for every skill level, we wanted to make sure there was a place for a novice to begin. Just as learning to play Chopsticks on the piano is the first step toward the goal of playing Beethoven, learning the basics of preparing pudding will teach you the basic skills you'll need to conquer more temperamental custards. But even if you're skilled in the kitchen, I think that you will be tempted to create the rich Caramel Pudding, the comforting Chocolate Pudding, or even the ultra-nostalgic Vanilla Pudding. Puddings are thickened with cornstarch and cooked on the stove, while custards are baked and thickened with egg yolks. As you cook pudding, stir it constantly so it won't burn. I recommend using a plastic spatula instead of a spoon; it reaches every bit of pudding in the pan, allowing you to stir it thoroughly and keep any part from overcooking.

Except for pudding, we serve all of the custards in this chapter at the Bistro. Crème brûlée is the most popular, with so many customers asking for it that Melissa almost always has one on the dessert menu. Over the years we've made crème brûlée in just about every flavor imaginable—including B-52 (a cocktail consisting of Kahlúa, Bailey's Irish Cream, and amaretto), orange, lemon, fresh berry, coconut, ginger-kaffir lime, and lavender—but traditional vanilla bean-infused crème brûlée is the perennial favorite. Melissa's bread pudding, another favorite at the Bistro, often pleasantly surprises customers. Unlike the ho-hum concoction that many people are familiar with, it is the ultimate bread pudding—more like a custard with a bit of bread than merely a vehicle for day-old bread.

Even before you bake them, crème brûlée, crème caramel, and bread pudding require some special attention. First, be sure to thoroughly whisk the eggs and sugar together; they should be very smooth. The most common stumbling block occurs during that seemingly simple yet crucial second step of combining the hot cream with the egg mixture. If you rush it, the eggs will scramble, so you must temper the egg mixture with the hot cream, slowly whisking in just enough to bring it up to the same temperature as the cream. Patience will really pay off here, with a perfectly textured custard.

Custard doesn't like to be rushed, so remember to bake it low and slow—at 300° for about an hour, if not longer. Also, to protect custard from any heat fluctuations in your oven, bake it in a water bath: Set the individual ramekins in a shallow pan, and then fill the pan about halfway with the hottest water you can get out of your tap. As with many of the recipes in this book, you should not overbake custard. And finally, before you chill it, first let it cool at room temperature for at least 20 minutes; otherwise, condensation can form on the top.

Mousse—French for foam or froth—steps beyond the few simple ingredients typical of custard. It can be sweet or savory, made with fruit, chocolate, shrimp, or crab, for example, but, of course, dessert is the focus here. Chocolate is my favorite flavor of mousse, and we've included recipes for both bittersweet and white chocolate versions.

Although the ingredients and steps involved in making mousse are just a bit more extensive than for custard, it isn't that much more challenging to prepare. Mousse begins with a sabayon base, a mixture of egg yolks, sugar, and liquor cooked over a water bath. Your patience is required only when you're on the next step: melting the chocolate. If you melt it too quickly, it can burn or seize up on you, so take the time to melt it slowly over a water bath. To fold the chocolate into the sabayon, use big, gentle strokes so you don't overwork the mixture. The froth in the mousse comes from the addition of whipped egg whites and cream, the final elements of preparation. When whipping the cream and the egg whites, make sure you don't overbeat either one—otherwise they will look like chunks of Styrofoam in the mousse. If you're making a fruit mousse—raspberry, for example—you will also need to add gelatin to give it body.

After you very gently fold in the whipped cream and egg whites, the mousse is finished and ready to chill.

Mousse can stand on its own and be served fairly unadorned, as in the master recipes, but part of its charm is that it can also be a component of more complicated desserts, such as the Chocolate Toffee Mousse Cake (page 253).

Whether it's a straightforward combination of three basic ingredients or a variation with the vibrant flavors of lemon zest and instant espresso powder, in this chapter you'll find a recipe for every palate and occasion. From a simple finish for a family dinner to an impressive conclusion for an elegant dinner party, these creamy desserts are sure to please everyone.

(master recipe)

Chocolate Pudding

Have you ever tasted homemade pudding? It's such a simple thing to prepare that I really don't know why anyone would buy the packaged stuff. This is Melissa's childhood recipe. When she got older, any time she and her mom started a diet together, they would make this pudding and eat it warm over bowls of cold vanilla ice cream as their last hurrah.

Serves 6

6 tablespoons unsweetened cocoa powder

1/2 cup sugar

3 tablespoons cornstarch

1/4 teaspoon salt

3 cups milk

4 egg yolks

3 ounces bittersweet chocolate, chopped

2 tablespoons unsalted butter

1 tablespoon pure vanilla extract

Combine the cocoa, sugar, cornstarch, and salt in a heavy saucepan. Add 1 cup of the milk and whisk until the dry ingredients are dissolved. Whisk in the egg yolks and the remaining 2 cups milk, then set the pan over medium heat and cook, stirring constantly with a plastic spatula, until the pudding begins to thicken and just comes to a boil. Remove from the heat, add the chocolate, butter, and vanilla extract, and let stand for 2 to 3 minutes before stirring, then stir until all of the chocolate has melted and the pudding is smooth. Pour into six 8-ounce serving dishes. Serve warm or refrigerate until well chilled, about 2 hours.

Variations

Chocolate Pudding

MOCHA PUDDING

Follow the Chocolate Pudding master recipe, adding 1 tablespoon instant espresso powder to the dry ingredients along with the cocoa powder.

Serves 6

CHOCOLATE AND WHITE CHOCOLATE CHUNK PUDDING

Follow the Chocolate Pudding master recipe. Place the warm pudding in a large bowl, set a piece of plastic wrap or parchment on the surface so that it doesn't form a skin, and refrigerate until well chilled, about 2 hours. Fold 4 ounces chopped white chocolate into the chilled pudding, then pour into six 8-ounce serving dishes.

Serve cold, topped with softly whipped cream.

Serves 6

Caramel Pudding

This is my favorite pudding. The caramel flavor comes through nicely, and even though the pudding is so very simple—just right for a family dinner—you can dress it up and serve it at a dinner party. For a more grown-up flavor, add 1/4 cup of your favorite liqueur to the egg yolks along with the half-and-half.

Serves 6

4 cups half-and-half

4 egg yolks

1/4 cup cornstarch

2 teaspoons pure vanilla extract

Pinch of salt

1 cup sugar

1 cup water

1/4 cup cold unsalted butter, diced

1 1/2 cups whipped cream, as accompaniment

Whisk together 2 cups of the half-and-half, the egg yolks, cornstarch, vanilla extract, and salt in a large bowl; set aside.

Place the sugar in a large sauté pan with sides or a heavy saucepan. Moisten the sugar with the water, being careful not to splash the water and sugar onto the sides of the pan. Cook the sugar mixture over high heat, without stirring, until you see any part of it turning brown, then swirl the pan to even out the color. Cook until golden brown, about 2 minutes longer. Carefully add the remaining 2 cups half-and-half to the hot sugar, taking care to pour it in slowly because it will bubble up violently. Cook, without stirring, until the caramelized sugar has liquefied again and the mixture is very smooth and a deep golden brown, 3 to 4 minutes. Remove the pan from the heat. (See page 183 for more information on making caramel.)

While whisking, slowly add 1 to 1 1/2 cups of the hot caramel to the egg yolk mixture to temper it, or bring it up to the same temperature. Add the remaining caramel, then pour the mixture back into the pan and cook over medium heat, stirring constantly with a plastic spatula, until the pudding begins to thicken and just comes to a boil, about 3 minutes. Immediately transfer the pudding to a mixing bowl, and whisk until smooth. Add the butter and let stand for 2 to 3 minutes before stirring, then stir until all of the butter has melted and the pudding is smooth. Pour into six 8-ounce serving dishes and refrigerate until well chilled, about 2 hours.

Serve cold with softly whipped cream.

Variation

Caramel Pudding

BLACK AND TAN

This combination of rich, fudgy ganache surrounding cool caramel pudding is probably nothing like the pudding you had as a kid.

Prepare 3 cups Ganache (page 47). Heat 1 1/2 cups of the ganache in a saucepan over low heat until very soft and pourable, divide it among six 8-ounce serving dishes, and refrigerate. Reserve the remaining ganache.

Prepare the Caramel Pudding as directed in the master recipe. Pour the warm pudding over the chilled ganache in each dish. Heat the remaining 1 1/2 cups ganache and pour it over the tops of the puddings. Refrigerate until well chilled, about 2 hours.

Serve cold, topped with softly whipped cream and shaved bittersweet chocolate (page 8).

Serves 6

Vanilla Pudding

Cold and silky smooth, with the simple but perfect flavor of vanilla, this is a dessert that both grownups and kids will love. It's a fun and easy recipe to teach to your children.

Serves 6

4 cups half-and-half

1 vanilla bean, split in half lengthwise

4 egg yolks

1/4 cup cornstarch

1/2 cup sugar

Pinch of salt

1/4 cup cold unsalted butter, diced

1 1/2 cups whipped cream, as accompaniment

Place the half-and-half and vanilla bean in a large saucepan over medium heat and bring just to a boil. Remove from the heat, cover with a lid, and let sit for about 20 minutes to steep; then scrape the seeds from the inside of the vanilla bean into the half-and-half (discard the bean). Reheat the half-and-half over medium heat until hot.

Meanwhile, whisk together the egg yolks, cornstarch, sugar, and salt in a large bowl until smooth. Slowly whisk 1 to 1 1/2 cups of the hot half-and-half into the egg yolk mixture to temper it, or bring it up to the same temperature. Add the remaining half-and-half, and whisk until smooth. Pour the mixture back into the pan and cook over medium heat, stirring often with a plastic spatula, until very thick, about 4 minutes. Transfer the pudding to a mixing bowl, and whisk until smooth. Add the butter and let stand for 2 to 3 minutes before stirring. Stir until all of the butter is melted and the pudding is smooth. Pour the pudding into six 8-ounce serving dishes and refrigerate until well chilled, about 2 hours.

Serve cold with softly whipped cream.

Caramelizing Sugar

Although caramelizing sugar is a simple procedure, I still find that people have a lot of questions about how to success-fully master the technique. These instructions should ensure that your caramel is always perfect.

1

2

3

4

1. Place the sugar in a heavy sauté pan or saucepan. Slowly add the water to moisten the sugar, but don't stir it, and be very care-ful to keep from splashing the water on the sides of the pan. (If the sugar-water gets on the sides of the pan, it will dry out as the sugar cooks and flake into the caramel, causing the caramel to crystallize. In other words, your beautifully caramelized sugar will look like alligator skin.) Set the pan over high heat.

2. Cook the sugar mixture over high heat, again without stirring.

3. Once you see any part of the sugar begin to turn brown, swirl the pan to even out the color.

4. Continue cooking over high heat until the caramel is a deep golden brown, about 2 more minutes. You may swirl the pan to even out the color, but I don't recommend using a spoon since it will stick on the caramel. Immediately remove the pan from the heat, or proceed with the recipe.

Chocolate Bread Pudding

Melissa makes the best bread pudding ever. Unlike a lot of bread puddings that must be covered in sauce to hide the dryness, hers has plenty of custard and is so creamy. Whenever she makes some at the restaurant, the kitchen staff always has to share at least one and sometimes two or even three when they come out of the oven. If you are using bread with a really thick crust, be sure to trim it all off so you'll have a tender bread pudding.

Serves 6

1 1/3 cups heavy whipping cream

1 1/3 cups whole milk

1 vanilla bean, split in half lengthwise

1/2 pound bittersweet chocolate, chopped

6 egg yolks

1/2 cup sugar

7 cups diced good-quality bread

1 cup Berry Sauce (page 63), as accompaniment

1 1/2 cups whipped cream, as accompaniment

Mint sprigs, for garnish

Preheat the oven to 300°.

Place the cream, milk, and vanilla bean in a heavy saucepan over medium heat and bring just to a boil. Remove the pan from the heat. Add the chocolate and let stand until the chocolate has melted, 4 to 5 minutes. Whisk until smooth.

Meanwhile, whisk together the egg yolks and sugar in a large bowl. Slowly whisk 1 to 1 1/2 cups of the hot chocolate mixture into the egg yolk mixture to temper it, or bring it up to the same temperature as the chocolate. Whisk in the remaining chocolate mixture, and then strain through a fine-mesh sieve. Scrape the seeds from the inside of the vanilla bean into the strained mixture (discard the bean).

Divide the bread among six 8-ounce ramekins. Pour the custard over the bread to completely cover it; let sit for about 5 minutes, occasionally pushing the bread down so it will soak up the custard. Place the ramekins in a shallow roasting pan, then fill the pan with enough hot water to reach about halfway up the sides of the ramekins. Carefully set the pan in the oven and bake just until set, about 1 hour. To test, press gently in the center of one of the puddings; if any custard comes up around the edges, cook them a bit longer. Remove the ramekins from the water bath; let cool for 15 minutes before serving.

Serve warm with Berry Sauce and softly whipped cream, garnished with mint sprigs.

Variations

Chocolate Bread Pudding

CHOCOLATE-RASPBERRY BREAD PUDDING

Berry sauce makes a fine accompaniment, but if you want to go all out, top this bread pudding warm from the oven with a scoop of Vanilla Bean Ice Cream (page 208).

Follow the Chocolate Bread Pudding master recipe, adding 1/4 cup raspberry liqueur to the custard after it has been strained. Just before pouring the custard over the bread, add 1/3 cup fresh raspberries to each custard cup. Proceed as in the master recipe.

Serve warm with Berry Sauce (page 63) and softly whipped cream, garnished with mint.

Serves 6

continued

continued from page 185

CHOCOLATE AND BRANDIED DRIED CHERRY BREAD PUDDING

Soaking the dried cherries—or any other dried fruit that you may choose to use—in brandy will soften the fruit and add even more flavor. If the cherries aren't soaked first, they might be a little dry and chewy in the pudding.

Soak 1 cup dried sour cherries in 1 cup brandy for at least 2 hours; set aside.

Follow the Chocolate Bread Pudding master recipe. Just before pouring the custard over the bread, distribute the soaked cherries and brandy among the ramekins. Proceed as in the master recipe.

Serve warm with Hard Sauce (page 190) and softly whipped cream.

Serves 6

HAZELNUT-WHITE CHOCOLATE BREAD PUDDING

If you aren't a fan of dark chocolate, this variation of the master recipe is for you. If you love both dark and white chocolate, distribute about 3/4 cup chopped bittersweet chocolate among the ramekins just before adding the custard to send it over the top.

Follow the Chocolate Bread Pudding master recipe, substituting chopped white chocolate for the bittersweet chocolate and adding 1/4 cup hazelnut liqueur to the custard after it has been strained. Before pouring the custard over the bread, divide 3/4 cup toasted ground hazelnuts (page 10) among the ramekins. Proceed as in the master recipe.

Serve warm with Caramel Sauce (page 58) and softly whipped cream, garnished with mint sprigs.

Serves 6

Chocolate Bread Pudding

Vanilla Bread Pudding

Melissa uses dense French country bread in her bread puddings. Many other types of bread also lend themselves to bread pudding. Try challah (a slightly sweet egg bread) or even day-old croissants for an extra-rich flavor. Remember that this is a custard, so treat it gently.

Serves 6

4 cups half-and-half

1 vanilla bean, split in half lengthwise

5 whole eggs

6 egg yolks

Pinch of salt

1 1/4 cups sugar

7 cups diced good-quality bread

1 cup Hard Sauce (page 190), as accompaniment

1 1/2 cups whipped cream, as accompaniment

Preheat the oven to 300°.

Place the half-and-half and vanilla bean in a saucepan over medium heat and bring just to a boil. Meanwhile, whisk together the eggs, egg yolks, salt, and sugar in a large bowl. Slowly whisk 1 to 1 1/2 cups of the hot half-and-half into the egg mixture to temper it, or bring it up to the same temperature. Whisk in the remaining half-and-half, and then strain through a fine-mesh sieve. Scrape the seeds from the inside of the vanilla bean into the custard (discard the bean), and mix well; set aside.

Divide the bread among six 8-ounce ramekins. Pour the custard over the bread to completely cover it; let sit for about 5 minutes, occasionally pushing the bread down so it will soak up the custard. Place the ramekins in a shallow roasting pan, then fill the pan with enough hot water to reach about halfway up the sides of the cups. Carefully set the pan in the oven and bake just until set, about 1 hour. To test, press gently in the center of one of the puddings; if any custard comes up in the center, cook them a bit longer. Remove the ramekins from the water bath; let cool for 15 minutes before serving.

Serve warm with Hard Sauce and softly whipped cream.

Variations   Vanilla Bread Pudding

Serves 6 (all variations)

LEMON-ALMOND BREAD PUDDING

If you have the time, steep the lemon zest in the half-and-half for 30 minutes before bringing it to a boil; the extra steeping time really makes the lemon flavor come through. Never add lemon juice to the half-and-half, though, because the lemon juice will curdle the cream.

Follow the Vanilla Bread Pudding master recipe, adding the finely grated zest of 2 lemons to the half-and-half along with the vanilla bean before heating. When the custard is finished, do not strain it; add 1 teaspoon almond extract and mix well. Just before pouring the custard over the bread, divide 1 1/2 cups toasted sliced almonds (page 10) among the ramekins. Proceed as in the master recipe.

Serve warm with Berry Sauce (page 63) and softly whipped cream. Omit the Hard Sauce.

APPLE BREAD PUDDING

Melissa makes this variation throughout the fall, switching to poached pears in the winter.

Peel and slice 2 large Granny Smith apples or other tart apples, and sauté them in 3 tablespoons unsalted butter and 2 tablespoons sugar until tender, about 4 minutes.

Transfer the apples to a mixing bowl and toss with 1 teaspoon ground cinnamon and 1/4 teaspoon ground nutmeg; set aside.

Follow the Vanilla Bread Pudding master recipe. After straining the finished custard, divide half of the bread among the 6 ramekins, then layer with half of the apples; repeat with the remaining bread and apples. Proceed as in the master recipe.

Serve warm with Caramel-Apple Sauce (page 59) and softly whipped cream. Omit the Hard Sauce.

SUMMER BREAD PUDDING

During the summer, we can't get enough of our fresh local berries. They are available for such a short time that Melissa uses them as much as possible, often in this colorful dessert.

Divide 3 cups of your favorite summer berries among the 6 ramekins; set aside.

Follow the Vanilla Bread Pudding master recipe, placing the bread over the berries in the ramekins. Proceed as in the master recipe.

Serve warm with Hard Sauce (page 190) and softly whipped cream.

pictured on opposite page

Hard Sauce

Hard Sauce is the traditional sauce served with bread pudding. It's potent, so remember that a little bit goes a long way.

Makes about 1 cup

1/2 cup unsalted butter, diced

1 cup powdered sugar

1 egg yolk

1/4 cup brandy, rum, or other liquor

Place the butter and powdered sugar in a metal bowl set over a pan of simmering water, and cook until the butter has melted. Whisk in the egg yolk and continue to cook until smooth and warm, about 2 minutes. Remove the bowl from the heat, add the brandy, and mix well.

Serve the sauce warm over baked bread puddings. The hard sauce will keep, refrigerated, for 1 week. Gently warm the sauce in a heavy saucepan over low heat, or in a microwave on low power.

Vanilla Crème Brûlée

As the "it" dessert of the moment, crème brûlée sells faster than any other dessert at the Bistro. Crème brûlée has an aura of being something that only a pastry chef would attempt. Actually, it's pretty easy to make at home, but there are a few things to remember when putting it together. Custard doesn't like to be rushed, so cook these nice and slow at just 300°. I know I say this time and time again, but it's worth repeating: If you have any question of doneness, always undercook rather than overcook.

Serves 6

4 cups heavy whipping cream

1 vanilla bean, split in half lengthwise

8 egg yolks

1 cup granulated sugar

Pinch of salt

1 cup superfine sugar (page 10)

Preheat the oven to 300°.

Place the cream and vanilla bean in a heavy saucepan over medium heat and bring just to a boil. Meanwhile, whisk together the egg yolks, granulated sugar, and salt in a large bowl. When the cream is hot, remove the vanilla bean and set aside. Slowly whisk 1 to 1 1/2 cups of the hot cream into the egg yolk mixture to temper it, or bring it up to the same temperature. Whisk in the remaining cream, and then strain through a fine-mesh sieve. Scrape the seeds from the inside of the vanilla bean into the custard (discard the bean), mix gently, and skim any foam from the surface.

Divide the custard among six 8-ounce ramekins. Set the ramekins in a shallow roasting pan, and fill the pan with enough hot water to reach about halfway up the sides of the ramekins. Carefully set the pan in the oven and bake just until set, about 1 hour. To tell if the custards are set, gently shake one; if it moves as one mass, it is done. Remove the ramekins from the water bath. Let cool until tepid, then refrigerate until well chilled, about 4 hours (overnight is even better if you have the time).

To serve, sprinkle each custard with a heaping tablespoon of superfine sugar. Using a propane torch (or the broiler), caramelize the sugar. Serve immediately.

Variations

Vanilla crème Brûlée

COCONUT CRÈME BRÛLÉE

When you're making this recipe, don't skimp and use low-fat coconut milk. You want all the flavor you can get, so this is not the time to save calories.

Follow the Vanilla Crème Brûlée master recipe, substituting 2 cups coconut milk for 2 cups of the cream. Proceed as in the master recipe.

If you don't have coconut milk, you can instead combine 4 cups heavy whipping cream and 1 1/2 cups toasted macaroon coconut (page 8) in a heavy saucepan over medium heat and bring the mixture just to a boil. Remove it from the heat, cover with a lid, and let steep for about 20 minutes. Strain the cream through a fine-mesh sieve, and again bring it just to a boil before adding it to the egg yolks and proceeding as in the master recipe.

Serves 6

LEMON-RASPBERRY CRÈME BRÛLÉE

I really like how the raspberries offset the creamy texture and rich flavor of the custard. But don't limit yourself to just raspberries, since all summer berries work in this recipe. If it isn't berry season, leave them out and serve this as a lemon crème brûlée.

Distribute 4 cups fresh raspberries among six 8-ounce ramekins; set aside.

Follow the directions for the Vanilla Crème Brûlée master recipe, adding the finely grated zest of 2 lemons to the cream along with the vanilla bean. Proceed as in the master recipe, pouring the custard over the raspberries just before baking.

Serves 6

Butterscotch Crème Brûlée

This is actually a variation of the Vanilla Crème Brûlée master recipe, but with an important extra step—making the butterscotch. If you like, you can add some chopped white chocolate or even some Irish Cream for a twist.

Serves 6

1/2 cup unsalted butter

1 cup firmly packed brown sugar

3 cups half-and-half

6 egg yolks

Pinch of salt

1 teaspoon pure vanilla extract

1 cup superfine sugar (page 10)

Preheat the oven to 300°.

Melt the butter in a saucepan over medium heat, then add the brown sugar and whisk until smooth. Let the mixture come to a boil and cook, stirring often, until it comes together and is smooth, about 3 minutes. Remove the pan from the heat and slowly whisk in the half-and-half; set aside.

Place the egg yolks in a large bowl. Slowly whisk 1 to 1 1/2 cups of the hot half-and-half mixture into the egg yolks to temper them, or bring them up to the same temperature. Whisk in the remaining half-and-half mixture, add the salt and vanilla, and whisk until smooth. Strain the custard through a fine-mesh sieve, skim any foam from the surface, and then divide it among six 8-ounce ramekins. Place the ramekins in a shallow roasting pan, and fill the pan with enough hot water to reach about halfway up the sides of the ramekins. Carefully set the pan in the oven and bake just until set, about 50 minutes. To tell if the custards are set, gently shake one; if it moves as one mass, it is done. Remove the ramekins from the water bath. Let cool until tepid, then refrigerate until well chilled, about 4 hours (overnight is even better if you have the time).

To serve, sprinkle each custard with a heaping tablespoon of superfine sugar. Using a propane torch (or the broiler), caramelize the sugar. Serve immediately.

(master recipe)

Crème Caramel

The custards in crème brûlée and crème caramel are pretty similar, except that in brûlée I use egg yolks and in crème caramel I use whole eggs. The whole eggs make a more stable custard that is easily removed from the ramekins, a key step in this dessert. As the baked custards chill, the caramel softens and turns into a golden sauce—so the longer you can let them chill, the more caramel sauce you'll be rewarded with.

Serves 6

1 1/2 cups sugar

1/2 cup water

2 1/2 cups half-and-half

1 vanilla bean, split in half lengthwise

5 eggs

1 1/2 cups whipped cream, as accompaniment

Mint sprigs, for garnish

Preheat the oven to 300°

To prepare the caramel, place 1 cup of the sugar in a large sauté pan with sides or a heavy saucepan. Gently moisten the sugar with the water, being careful not to splash the water and sugar onto the sides of the pan. Cook the sugar mixture over high heat, without stirring, until you see any part of it turning brown, then swirl the pan to even out the color. Cook until golden brown, about 2 minutes longer. Carefully divide the caramel among six 8-ounce ramekins; set aside. (See page 183 for more information on making caramel.)

Place the half-and-half and vanilla bean in a heavy saucepan over medium heat and bring just to a boil. Meanwhile, whisk together the eggs and the remaining 1/2 cup sugar in a large bowl. When the half-and-half is hot, remove the vanilla bean and set aside. Slowly whisk 1 to 1 1/2 cups of the half-and-half into the egg yolk mixture to temper it, or bring it up to the same temperature. Whisk in the remaining half-and-half. Scrape the seeds from the inside of the vanilla bean into the custard (discard the bean), mix gently, and then skim any foam from the surface.

Divide the custard among the ramekins. Set the ramekins in a shallow roasting pan, then fill the pan with enough hot water to reach about halfway up the sides of the ramekins. Carefully set the pan in the oven and bake just until set, 50 minutes to 1 hour. To tell if the custards are set, gently shake one; if it moves as one mass, it is done. Remove the ramekins from the water bath. Let cool until tepid, then refrigerate until well chilled, about 4 hours (overnight is even better).

To serve, carefully run a knife around each chilled custard and invert onto a plate. Serve immediately, topped with whipped cream and mint sprigs.

Variations

ESPRESSO-SPICE CRÈME CARAMEL

Traditional crème caramel has very simple but sophisticated flavors. This variation literally spices it up!

Follow the Crème Caramel master recipe. Just before heating the half-and-half, add 2 tablespoons instant espresso powder, 1 teaspoon ground cinnamon, 1/2 teaspoon ground ginger, and a pinch of ground cloves along with the vanilla bean. Proceed as in the master recipe.

Serve chilled, topped with chocolate-covered espresso beans instead of mint.

Serves 6

pictured on page 174

CHOCOLATE-ORANGE CRÈME CARAMEL

The chocolate changes the texture of this dessert from a light custard to an incredibly rich indulgence.

Follow the Crème Caramel master recipe. Just before heating the half-and-half, add the finely grated zest of 1 orange along with the vanilla bean. After removing the half-and-half from the heat, add 5 ounces chopped bittersweet chocolate; let stand for 2 minutes, and then stir until smooth. Proceed as in the master recipe.

Serve chilled, topped with whipped cream and shaved chocolate. Omit the mint sprigs.

Serves 6

Crème Caramel

(master recipe)
Chocolate Mousse

Chocolate mousse–what I think of as the grown-up and more elegant version of chocolate pudding–is wonderful on its own or simply topped with fresh berries. It is so versatile that you can use it to top a brownie torte or to fill cakes and pâte à choux. Don't worry if you don't have orange liqueur on hand–chocolate mousse lends itself to quite a few other flavors, such as coffee and nut liqueurs and Irish Cream. When cooking the egg mixture, watch it carefully or you may end up with orange-flavored scrambled eggs–so keep the water at a simmer and don't step away to answer the phone.

Serves 8

1 pound bittersweet chocolate, chopped

1/4 cup cold unsalted butter, diced

6 eggs, separated

1/2 cup sugar

Finely grated zest of 1 orange

1/2 cup orange liqueur

1/2 teaspoon pure vanilla extract

1 1/4 cups heavy whipping cream

1 1/2 cups whipped cream, as accompaniment

Shaved chocolate (page 8), for garnish

Place the chocolate and butter in a metal bowl set over a pan of simmering water (make sure the bottom of the bowl does not touch the water). When the chocolate has melted about halfway, remove the pan from the heat (leave the bowl on the pan), and let it stand until the chocolate and butter are completely melted; stir until smooth. Set the bowl aside in a warm (but not hot) place, so it will stay melted.

Set the pan of water back over the heat, add more water if needed, and bring it to a simmer. In another metal bowl, whisk together the egg yolks, sugar, orange zest, liqueur, and vanilla extract. Set the bowl over the pan of simmering water (again make sure that the bottom of the bowl does not touch the water) and cook, whisking constantly, until the mixture is very thick, like very softly whipped cream. (It's thick enough when you can see the bottom of the bowl as you whisk it.) Remove the bowl from the heat. Using a plastic spatula, gently fold in the warm chocolate; let cool for about 5 minutes.

While the chocolate mixture cools, place the cream in the bowl of a mixer fitted with the whip attachment and whip on high speed until it holds soft peaks. Gently fold the whipped cream into the chocolate mixture (it doesn't have to be perfectly combined); set aside.

Place the egg whites in the clean bowl of a mixer fitted with the whip attachment, and whip on high speed until they just hold soft peaks. Gently fold the whites into the chocolate mixture, mixing just until the mousse is smooth.

Divide the mixture among eight 8-ounce serving dishes (I like to use beautiful wineglasses), and refrigerate until chilled, about 2 hours.

About 15 minutes before serving, remove the mousse from the refrigerator. Serve cold, topped with softly whipped cream and garnished with shaved chocolate.

Variations

CHOCOLATE MOUSSE CAKE WITH A THREE-NUT CRUST

Try this cake with other crusts, too, such as the Chocolate Cookie Crumb Crust (page 77) or even one of the shortbread crusts (pages 74 and 75). It's important to give the cake plenty of time to chill before serving and to use a very hot knife to cut it—that way you'll have beautiful slices.

Prepare the Three-Nut Crust (page 76). Press it into a well-greased 10-inch springform pan; refrigerate for 30 minutes.

Follow the Chocolate Mousse master recipe, substituting 1/4 cup almond liqueur and 1/4 cup hazelnut liqueur for the orange liqueur. Pour the mousse into the prepared crust and refrigerate for at least 2 hours before serving.

To serve, run a knife around the sides of the pan to loosen the cake, then remove the outer ring. Serve chilled, garnished with softly whipped cream and mint sprigs. Omit the shaved chocolate.

Serves 14

MEXICAN MOCHA MOUSSE

I love to transform this mousse into beautiful and luscious parfaits. To do so, distribute 2 cups of warm Caramel Sauce (page 58) among 8 wineglasses, top with the mousse, and chill. Right before serving, top with softly whipped cream and the toasted almonds.

Follow the Chocolate Mousse master recipe, adding 2 tablespoons instant espresso powder and 1 teaspoon ground cinnamon to the melted chocolate and substituting coffee liqueur for the orange liqueur. Proceed as in the master recipe. Serve cold, topped with softly whipped cream, shaved chocolate, and 1/2 cup chopped toasted almonds.

Serves 8

Grilled Rum-Soaked Pineapple with Warm White Chocolate Mousse

Grilled pineapple, a fitting dessert for a barbecue, is even more memorable when paired with a silky white chocolate mousse. If you have a big group coming, prepare the mousse and place it in wineglasses to chill. After the dinner you can quickly grill the pineapple and serve it with the chilled mousse. When you have a small group and more time, make the mousse that evening and serve it warm.

Serves 8

Rum-Soaked Pineapple

1/3 cup dark rum

1 teaspoon ground cinnamon

1/2 teaspoon ground ginger

1/2 teaspoon ground nutmeg

1/2 teaspoon ground allspice

1 tablespoon unsalted butter, melted

1/4 cup loosely packed brown sugar

1 ripe pineapple, peeled, cored, and cut lengthwise into 16 spears

White Chocolate Mousse

6 ounces white chocolate, chopped

4 egg yolks

1/2 cup sugar

1/2 cup crème de cacao

1 cup heavy whipping cream

Ground cinnamon, for dusting

Mint sprigs, for garnish

To marinate the pineapple, combine the rum, cinnamon, ginger, nutmeg, allspice, butter, and brown sugar in a bowl, and mix well. Place the pineapple spears in a shallow pan, top with the marinade, and let sit at room temperature for at least 1 hour, or refrigerate overnight.

continued

continued from page 199

To prepare the mousse, place the white chocolate in a metal bowl set over a pan of simmering water (make sure the bottom of the bowl does not touch the water). When the chocolate has melted about halfway, remove the pan from the heat (leave the bowl on the pan), and let the chocolate stand until completely melted; stir until smooth. Set the bowl aside in a warm (but not hot) place, so the chocolate will stay melted.

Set the pan of water back over the heat, add more water if needed, and bring it to a simmer. In another metal bowl, whisk together the egg yolks, sugar, and crème de cacao. Set the bowl over the pan of simmering water (again make sure that the bottom of the bowl does not touch the water) and cook, whisking constantly, until the mixture is very thick, like very softly whipped cream. (It's thick enough if you can see the bottom of the bowl as you whisk it.) Remove the bowl from the heat. Using a plastic spatula, gently fold in the warm white chocolate; let cool for about 5 minutes.

While the white chocolate mixture cools, place the cream in the bowl of a mixer fitted with the whip attachment and whip on high speed until it holds soft peaks. Using a plastic spatula, gently fold the whipped cream into the chocolate mixture; set aside.

To grill the pineapple, place the pineapple spears on a very hot well-oiled grill and grill until brown, about 3 minutes per side.

To serve, place 2 warm pineapple spears on each plate and top with about 1/2 cup of the warm mousse. Serve immediately, dusted with a bit of cinnamon and garnished with mint sprigs.

Variation

Grilled Rum-Soaked Pineapple With Warm White Chocolate Mousse

DRUNKEN PEACHES WITH WHITE CHOCOLATE MOUSSE

If you like the idea of the white chocolate mousse paired with fruit, but you want to save yourself some time and don't want to worry about grilling at the last moment, this makes a nice option.

Omit the rum-soaked pineapple, and instead peel and slice 8 large peaches (page 11). Divide the peaches among 8 wineglasses and drizzle each with about 2 tablespoons good-quality bourbon; set aside.

Follow the White Chocolate Mousse master recipe, adding 1/4 teaspoon ground nutmeg and 1/4 teaspoon ground cinnamon to the egg yolks along with the sugar. Proceed as in the master recipe.

To serve, pour the warm mousse over the peaches and garnish with mint sprigs.

Serves 8

Rocky Road Ice Cream (page 206)

chapter six

Ice Creams, Sorbets, and Gelati

When I was growing up, my parents would drag my sister and me all over the state for Sunday drives, guided by a book called *Where to Find the Oregon in Oregon*. If Angie and I didn't whine and could keep from fighting too much, we were rewarded with ice cream when we reached our destination. Rarely were we denied the bribe, but not always due to perfect behavior. Since my parents wanted to stop for ice cream just as much as we did, they weren't about to let a little bickering in the back seat keep them from enjoying a scoop of their favorite flavor.

The love of ice cream is so universal, I wouldn't be surprised if it's the most popular dessert in the world. When I visited the former Soviet Union, people were nuts about it, and in France I was surprised to find that the ice cream shop seemed almost as common as the boulangerie. Versions of a sweet frozen dessert turn up all over the world, and it's no wonder. Ice cream has an old and far-reaching history. Lucky for us, ice cream made its way to Europe in the 1300s. At that point it was reserved for royalty, but by the 19th century, street vendors were offering it to the common folk. These days no one can seem to get enough, with billions of gallons sold each year in the United States.

Simply put, ice cream is a frozen sweetened, flavored dessert made primarily of dairy products. Of course, there's more to making a good-quality ice cream than that, but it's really not complicated at all. I prefer a French-style ice cream that has a cooked egg custard base, which is basically a crème anglaise blended with anything from chocolate to fresh seasonal berries. Many recipes for ice cream call for up to eight egg yolks and only heavy cream. If ice cream has too much fat, it can leave a coating on the roof of the mouth, which makes it hard for me to enjoy more than a spoonful or two. Since it's more fun to eat a whole bowl of ice cream, I prefer to use only a couple of egg yolks and a blend of two-thirds whole milk and one-third heavy cream. This combination helps emulsify the ice cream base and gives the ice cream the perfect amount of fat.

I also use a combination of milk and cream in my gelato recipes, with equal parts of each. Gelato, the Italian version of ice cream, is denser than the traditional ice cream available in the United States, mainly because less air is beaten into it during the freezing process. It is usually more intensely flavored, too, with a single ingredient as the focal point. In Italy, gelato is traditionally served a bit warmer than ice cream, which is another key to both its texture and its flavor.

The French frozen dessert known as sorbet inspired the Americanized version, sherbet, that we all remember eating out of little cups with wooden spoons when we were kids. Both sorbet and sherbet now go beyond that simple dessert from childhood, but basically sorbet is sweetened fruit juice or other liquid that has been frozen. Sherbet also contains milk, egg whites, and/or gelatin, which give it a creamier texture than its cousin, sorbet. Another tasty relative of sorbet, known as granité in France and granita in Italy, starts with the same basic ingredients. During the freezing process, however, it isn't stirred constantly, as sorbet is, which results in larger ice crystals and a coarser texture.

As with ice cream, too much alcohol and sugar can lower the freezing point and increase the time it takes to freeze sorbet. When I make sorbet, I like to add just a couple of tablespoons of cream to the base. This gives the sorbet a somewhat softer texture and makes it easier to scoop. Sorbet, like ice cream, is open to interpretation, and the flavorings you use can be as varied as puréed fruits, sweet wine, and even herbs. Just be sure to use fresh, seasonal ingredients for the most vibrant flavors.

Ice cream and sorbet are very easy to make and are very forgiving, too. In fact, as long as you keep from scrambling the custard base for ice cream and you make sure the ratio of sugar to liquid in sorbet is correct, you'll find that there's no such thing as messing up a batch—you've simply created a new flavor. When you try the master recipes and their variations, I hope you'll be inspired to improvise and try your own flavor combinations. Follow the simple guidelines, and let your imagination run wild.

These recipes were tested in an inexpensive ice cream maker that you can find in any kitchen store. Makers range in price from thirty or forty dollars to thousands of dollars for a commercial one. Unless you plan on transforming your kitchen into an ice cream "shoppe," a basic midrange ice cream maker will do just fine. When comparing models in your price range, be sure to look for a reputable brand, and then choose the one with the most power.

Chocolate Ice Cream

This chocolate ice cream is exquisite, especially if you use the best-quality chocolate you can find. I prefer to use a rich bittersweet chocolate, but if your tastes lean toward chocolate that's a bit less intense, by all means use that instead. At both ends of the spectrum, the variations show how versatile this recipe can be. Two are very adult, with the additions of coffee and liqueur, while the rocky road ice cream is a perennial kid-favorite flavor

Makes about 1 1/2 quarts

4 cups whole milk

2 cups heavy whipping cream

1 vanilla bean, split in half lengthwise

6 egg yolks

1 1/4 cups sugar

6 ounces good-quality chocolate, coarsely chopped

Place the milk, cream, and vanilla bean in a heavy saucepan over medium heat and bring just to a boil. Meanwhile, whisk together the egg yolks and sugar in a large bowl. Slowly whisk 1 to 1 1/2 cups of the hot milk mixture into the egg yolk mixture to temper it, or bring it up to the same temperature. Pour the mixture back into the saucepan and again cook over medium heat, stirring constantly, until it has thickened slightly and just barely coats the back of a spoon, 5 to 7 minutes; remove the pan from the heat. (Ideally you do not want the mixture to come to a boil, but

if it does, keep it from overcooking by immediately removing it from the heat, adding a single ice cube, and stirring; it should be thick and cooked enough.) Scrape the seeds from the inside of the vanilla bean into the mixture (discard the bean), then add the chocolate and stir until completely melted. Refrigerate until it cools to at least 40°, about 2 hours.

To freeze the ice cream, follow the manufacturer's directions for your ice cream maker. Transfer the ice cream to a covered container and place it in the freezer until completely frozen.

Variations Chocolate Ice Cream

Makes about 1 1/2 quarts (all variations)

WHITE CHOCOLATE CHUNK–RASPBERRY-CHOCOLATE ICE CREAM

If you don't have raspberry liqueur, try a contrasting flavor like an orange liqueur, or use crème de cacao to intensify the chocolate flavor.

Follow the Chocolate Ice Cream master recipe. While the ice cream base is chilling, toss 1 pint fresh raspberries with 1/3 cup raspberry liqueur; set aside. Begin freezing the ice cream. When the ice cream is very thick yet still soft (after about 20 minutes, depending on your ice cream maker), add the berries and liqueur and 3/4 cup chopped white chocolate. Continue freezing to a soft consistency. Transfer the ice cream to a covered container and place it in the freezer until completely frozen.

MEXICAN MOCHA ICE CREAM

I got the idea for this flavor combination from the Mexican bar chocolate you can buy in Mexican grocery stores.

Follow the Chocolate Ice Cream master recipe, adding 2 heaping tablespoons each of instant espresso powder and ground cinnamon to the milk and cream along with the vanilla bean. Cook the mixture over low heat instead of medium (to give the cinnamon enough time to steep) until it just comes to a boil, then proceed as in the master recipe. Begin freezing the ice cream. When the ice cream is very thick, but still soft (after about 20 minutes, depending on your ice cream maker), add 1 cup chopped toasted almonds (page 10). Continue freezing to a soft consistency. Transfer the ice cream to a covered container and place it in the freezer until completely frozen.

ROCKY ROAD ICE CREAM

I loved this flavor when I was a kid, but the kind I ate back then never had the secret ingredient in this version: homemade marshmallows. You can use packaged marshmallows if you prefer, but they won't compare.

Follow the Chocolate Ice Cream master recipe. Begin freezing the ice cream. When the ice cream is very thick yet still soft (after about 20 minutes, depending on your ice cream maker), add 1 cup chopped toasted pecans (page 10), 1 cup Mini-Marshmallows (page 207), and 3 ounces finely chopped good-quality chocolate. Continue freezing to a soft consistency. Transfer the ice cream to a covered container and place it in the freezer until completely frozen.

pictured on page 202

Mini-Marshmallows

As with just about everything, homemade is always best—and that definitely includes marshmallows. These are so creamy they melt in your mouth (nothing like the packaged kind that contain things I don't even want to think about). They are easy to prepare, a perfect thing to make with your kids on a Saturday afternoon.

Makes 6 cups

1 1/4 cups granulated sugar

1 tablespoon plus 1 teaspoon light corn syrup

2/3 cup water

1 tablespoon plus 1 teaspoon unflavored gelatin

2 teaspoons pure vanilla extract

1 1/2 cups sifted powdered sugar, for coating

Grease an 8 by 8-inch pan, line the bottom with parchment paper, grease the parchment paper, and set aside.

Place the granulated sugar, corn syrup, and 1/3 cup of the water in a saucepan over high heat, and cook, without stirring, until it registers 260° on a candy thermometer or reaches the hard-ball stage.

Place the gelatin and the remaining 1/3 cup water in the bowl of a mixer fitted with the whip attachment and start the mixer on low speed. Carefully add the hot syrup, then increase the speed to high, and whip until very thick and fluffy, about 5 minutes. Add the vanilla extract and mix well. Pour the marshmallow mixture into the prepared pan, spread it out with a plastic spatula, and let cool completely. Cover with plastic wrap, making sure the plastic doesn't touch the marshmallow mixture. Let stand at room temperature for at least 12 hours. Remove it from the pan and, using a sharp knife, cut it into small dice. Toss the cut marshmallows in the powdered sugar to coat (discard any excess sugar). The marshmallows will keep in an airtight container for up to 2 days.

(master recipe)

Vanilla Bean Ice Cream

When it's made right, I think vanilla is the most perfect flavor of ice cream, even when it's up against all the other amazing flavor combinations that are available. It also makes an ideal springboard for showcasing seasonal fruit, such as fresh peaches or raspberries. If I come across a really good vanilla ice cream—with a perfumy but not overpowering vanilla aroma and a rich but not too cloying texture—it truly makes my day!

Makes about 1 1/2 quarts

4 cups whole milk

2 cups heavy whipping cream

1 vanilla bean, split in half lengthwise

6 egg yolks

1 1/4 cups sugar

Place the milk, cream, and vanilla bean in a heavy saucepan over medium heat and bring just to a boil. Meanwhile, whisk together the egg yolks and sugar in a large bowl. Slowly whisk the hot milk mixture into the egg yolk mixture to temper it, or bring it up to the same temperature. Pour the mixture back into the saucepan and again cook over medium heat, stirring constantly, until it has thickened slightly and just barely coats the back of a spoon, 5 to 7 minutes; remove the pan from the heat. (Ideally you do not want the mixture to come to a boil, but if it does, keep it from overcooking by immediately removing it from the heat, adding a single ice cube, and stirring; it should be thick and cooked enough.) Scrape the seeds from the inside of the vanilla bean into the mixture (discard the bean), and mix well. Refrigerate until it cools to at least 40°, about 2 hours.

To freeze the ice cream, follow the manufacturer's directions for your ice cream maker. Transfer the ice cream to a covered container and place it in the freezer until completely frozen.

Variations Vanilla Bean Ice Cream

Makes about 1 1/2 quarts (all variations)

FRESH PEACH ICE CREAM

This is the ultimate summer ice cream. Don't even attempt it if you can't find nice ripe fruit—you'll do the ice cream a disservice, and you'll be disappointed.

Follow the Vanilla Bean Ice Cream master recipe. While the ice cream base is chilling, peel 3 peaches and cut into large dice (page 10). Toss the peaches with 1/4 cup sugar and 1/3 cup bourbon; set aside. Begin freezing the ice cream. When the ice cream is very thick, but still soft (after about 20 minutes, depending on your ice cream maker), add the peaches and bourbon. Continue freezing to a soft consistency. Transfer the ice cream to a covered container and place it in the freezer until completely frozen.

RASPBERRY-LEMON ICE CREAM

Raspberries and lemon go so well together. When combined with the vanilla ice cream, they are perfectly matched.

Follow the Vanilla Bean Ice Cream master recipe, adding the finely grated zest of 2 lemons to the milk and cream along with the vanilla bean. Cook the mixture over low heat instead of medium (to give the lemon zest enough time to steep) until it just comes to a boil. Proceed as in the master recipe, straining the mixture through a fine-mesh sieve before refrigerating it. While the ice cream base is chilling, toss 1 pint fresh raspberries with 1/4 cup raspberry liqueur and the juice of 1 lemon; set aside. Begin freezing the ice cream. When the ice cream is very thick, but still soft (after about 20 minutes, depending on your ice cream maker), add the raspberries, liqueur, and juice. Continue freezing to a soft consistency. Transfer the ice cream to a covered container and place it in the freezer until completely frozen.

FRESH MINT ICE CREAM

To make mint chocolate chip ice cream, add 1/2 cup finely shaved chocolate (page 8) to the finished ice cream just before transferring it to the freezer.

Follow the Vanilla Bean Ice Cream master recipe, adding 1 cup fresh mint leaves to the milk and cream along with the vanilla bean. Cook the mixture over low heat instead of medium (to give the mint enough time to steep) until it just comes to a boil. Proceed as in the master recipe, straining the mixture through a fine-mesh sieve before refrigerating it. Freeze to a soft consistency. Transfer the ice cream to a covered container and place it in the freezer until completely frozen.

(master recipe)

Mascarpone Ice Cream

When John and I were in Avignon, we came across a tiny ice cream shop that served some of the best ice cream we've ever had. Their tiramisu flavor was unforgettable, and as soon as we returned home I had to try my hand at creating my own version, which begins with this mascarpone ice cream. Mascarpone, a creamy, slightly sweet triple-cream cheese, gives the ice cream an incredibly rich texture and density, making it a good base for the addition of other flavors.

Makes about 1 1/2 quarts

4 cups whole milk

1 vanilla bean, split in half lengthwise

6 egg yolks

1 1/4 cups sugar

2 cups mascarpone cheese (page 9)

Place the milk and vanilla bean in a heavy saucepan over medium heat and bring just to a boil. Meanwhile, whisk together the egg yolks and sugar in a large bowl. Slowly whisk the hot milk mixture into the egg yolk mixture to temper it, or bring it up to the same temperature as the milk. Pour the mixture back into the saucepan and again cook over medium heat, stirring constantly, until it has thickened slightly and just barely coats the back of a spoon, 5 to 7 minutes; remove the pan from the heat. (Ideally you do not want the mixture to come to a boil, but if it does, keep it from overcooking by immediately removing it from the heat, adding a single ice cube, and stirring; it should be thick and cooked enough.) Scrape the seeds from the inside of the vanilla bean into the mixture (discard the bean), then add the mascarpone cheese and mix well. Refrigerate until it cools to at least 40°, about 2 hours.

To freeze the ice cream, follow the manufacturer's directions for your ice cream maker. Transfer the ice cream to a covered container and place it in the freezer until completely frozen.

Mascarpone Ice Cream

Makes about 1 1/2 quarts (all variations)

TIRAMISU ICE CREAM

Here's my rendition of my favorite ice cream from Avignon.

Follow the Mascarpone Ice Cream master recipe, adding 1 tablespoon instant espresso powder to the ice cream base after it has chilled. Begin freezing the ice cream. When the ice cream is very thick, but still soft (after about 20 minutes, depending on your ice cream maker), add 1/4 cup coffee liqueur and 1/3 cup shaved good-quality bittersweet chocolate. Continue freezing to a soft consistency. Transfer the ice cream to a covered container and place it in the freezer until completely frozen.

WHITE CHOCOLATE–HAZELNUT ICE CREAM

If you want to substitute another type of nut for the hazelnuts, try chopped toasted macadamia nuts. They make a great match with the white chocolate.

Follow the Mascarpone Ice Cream master recipe, adding 5 ounces chopped white chocolate to the hot milk mixture; stir until melted. Proceed as directed in the master recipe, and begin freezing the ice cream. When the ice cream is very thick, but still soft (after about 20 minutes, depending on your ice cream maker), add 1/4 cup hazelnut liqueur and 1 cup chopped toasted hazelnuts (page 10). Continue freezing to a soft consistency. Transfer the ice cream to a covered container and place it in the freezer until completely frozen.

STRAWBERRY-MASCARPONE ICE CREAM

If you're lucky enough to have a garden with fraises des bois—those tiny, jewel-like strawberries—or can find them in a farmer's market, use them whole in place of sliced strawberries. The difference they'll make is amazing.

Follow the Mascarpone Ice Cream master recipe. While the ice cream base is chilling, toss 2 cups cleaned and halved small strawberries with 1/4 cup Grand Marnier; set aside. Begin freezing the ice cream. When the ice cream is very thick, but still soft (after about 20 minutes, depending on your ice cream maker), add the strawberries and liqueur and 1 tablespoon finely chopped orange zest. Continue freezing to a soft consistency. Transfer the ice cream to a covered container and place it in the freezer until completely frozen.

continued

continued from page 211

PROFITEROLES

This very simple recipe is one of my family's perennial favorites, in part because of the countless combinations of ice creams and sauces you can use. The crisp yet tender pâte à choux also adds to the allure. Pâte à choux is the base for eclairs, those wonderful treats filled with pastry cream and smothered in chocolate. But that's only the beginning of how you can transform this versatile pastry. You can bake it and then fill the pastries with ice cream, drizzle them with warm caramel sauce, and listen to your guests rave. To give the Profiteroles extra crunch, try topping them with chopped toasted nuts.

Pâte à Choux

1 cup milk

1/2 cup cold unsalted butter, diced

1 cup flour

Pinch of salt

5 to 6 eggs

1 1/2 quarts Strawberry-Mascarpone Ice Cream (page 211)

2 cups Chocolate Sauce (page 62)

2 cups whipped cream

To make the pâte à choux, preheat the oven to 375°. Grease a sheet pan; set aside. Place the milk and butter in a saucepan over high heat and cook until the butter has melted and the milk comes to a boil. Add the flour and salt, and mix with a wooden spoon until the dough comes together. Decrease the heat to low and cook, stirring often, for about 2 minutes to dry the dough.

Transfer the dough to a mixer fitted with the paddle attachment. With the mixer on high speed, add 5 of the eggs, one at a time, mixing well after each addition. The dough should have some shine, and when the paddle is pulled up, the dough should hold a stiff peak. If the dough is too stiff to hold a peak, add the last egg and mix well.

Place the dough in a pastry bag fitted with a medium star tip, and pipe it on the prepared pan into about thirty-six 1 1/2-inch rosettes. Bake for 20 minutes, then lower the oven temperature to 350° and bake for another 20 minutes. Lower the temperature to 200° and bake until the rosettes are crisp and dry (so they won't deflate after you remove them from the oven), about 30 minutes longer. (If you remove them too soon, they might sink down and become soggy, so if you have the time, you can leave them in the oven after you turn it off so they can dry out even more.) Let cool completely on the pan.

To serve, split each rosette in half and fill the bottom half with a scoop of ice cream, topping with the remaining half. Place 3 profiteroles on each plate, drizzle with the Chocolate Sauce, and then top with whipped cream. Serve immediately.

Serves 12

pictured on opposite page

(master recipe)

Espresso Coupe

A coupe—the French version of an ice cream sundae—gets its name from the type of dish this dessert is served in, a wide, shallow glass similar to an ice cream dish. This dessert is another one that's easy to modify, just by changing the type of ice cream or sauce you use. As long as you make sure your espresso is nice and cold, these come together in a flash.

Serves 6

1 quart Mascarpone Ice Cream (page 210)

6 shots espresso or 1 cup extra-strong coffee, chilled

1 cup Chocolate Sauce (page 62)

1 cup whipped cream, as accompaniment

18 chocolate-covered espresso beans, for garnish

Scoop the ice cream into 6 tall glasses, pour the chilled espresso over the ice cream, and drizzle with Chocolate Sauce. Top each coupe with whipped cream and garnish with 3 espresso beans. Serve immediately.

Variation

Espresso Coupe

CARAMELIZED BANANA COUPE

Cut 3 bananas in half lengthwise, leaving the peel on. Sprinkle each half with about 1 tablespoon superfine sugar (page 10). Using a propane torch (or the broiler), caramelize the sugar. Remove the peel before placing each banana half in a tall glass. Scoop 1 pint Vanilla Bean Ice Cream (page 208) into the glasses, and drizzle with the Chocolate Sauce. Omit the espresso and the espresso beans. Top each coupe with whipped cream and shaved chocolate (page 8). Serve immediately.

Serves 6

coconut Sorbet

I like that this sorbet is refreshing and slightly rich at the same time. Unlike many sorbets, which solidify so much that you practically need a jackhammer to dish up a bowl, this one has a touch of cream that gives it a smooth, scoopable texture. In the winter, when tropical fruit is in season, try any of the variations to bring a spicy Asian meal (or even something heavier like osso buco) to a simple, satisfying conclusion.

Makes about 1 quart

4 cups coconut milk

1 3/4 cups sugar

1/4 cup heavy whipping cream

Place the coconut milk and sugar in a heavy saucepan over medium heat and bring to a boil. Boil for about 3 minutes, or until the sugar has dissolved, then remove the pan from the heat. Add the cream and mix well. Refrigerate until it cools to at least 40°, about 2 hours.

To freeze the sorbet, follow the manufacturer's directions for your ice cream maker. Transfer the sorbet to a covered container and place in the freezer until completely frozen.

Variations

coconut Sorbet

TROPICAL GINGER SORBET

If you can't find ripe pineapple, use diced ripe mango.

Follow the Coconut Sorbet master recipe, adding 3 (1-inch-thick) slices fresh ginger to the coconut milk mixture. Cook the mixture over low heat instead of medium (to give the ginger enough time to steep) for about 15 minutes. Strain the mixture through a fine-mesh sieve, add the cream, and proceed as in the master recipe. While the sorbet base is chilling, toss 1 cup small diced ripe pineapple with 1/4 cup dark rum; set aside. Begin freezing the sorbet. When the sorbet is very thick, but still soft (about 20 minutes, depending on your ice cream maker), add the pineapple and rum. Continue freezing to a soft consistency. Transfer the sorbet to a covered container and place it in the freezer until completely frozen.

Makes about 1 quart

continued on page 217

continued from page 215

SPICE ICE CREAM SANDWICHES
WITH COCONUT SORBET

Everyone remembers eating ice cream sandwiches as a child. These, however, made from piped almond spice cookies and homemade coconut sorbet, are a bit fancier than those cardboard cookies surrounding bad vanilla ice cream. Peanut Butter Everything Cookies (page 133) also make excellent ice cream sandwiches when filled with your favorite ice cream. If you prefer, you can roll the ice cream sandwiches in toasted nuts or even grated chocolate. But don't stop there—let your imagination go and dream up other combinations and embellishments. If you are a traditionalist, try using the dough for Chocolate Windowpane Cookies (page 131), rolled and cut and sandwiched with Vanilla Bean Ice Cream (page 208). One taste and you'll know exactly what those childhood treats should have tasted like.

1 batch uncooked dough for Spiced Almond Sticks (page 123)

1 quart Coconut Sorbet (page 215)

2 cups shredded unsweetened coconut, toasted (page 8)

Preheat the oven to 350°. Grease a sheet pan well; set aside.

Pipe the cookie dough onto the prepared pan into about sixteen 3-inch circles, and bake until golden brown, about 12 minutes. Let the cookies cool for about 5 minutes on the pan, then transfer to a rack or paper towels and let cool completely.

To form the sandwiches, place a large scoop of sorbet on the bottom side of a cooled cookie, top with another cookie, and then roll the exposed sorbet in the coconut. Wrap the sandwich in plastic wrap and place it in the freezer. Continue with the remaining cookies and sorbet. Freeze the sandwiches for at least 1 hour before serving.

Serves 8

pictured on opposite page

COCONUT-LIME-RUM SORBET

The rum adds a rich element to the master recipe, while lime adds the perfect amount of tanginess.

Follow the Coconut Sorbet master recipe, adding the finely grated zest and juice of 1 lime to the coconut milk mixture. Proceed as in the master recipe, adding 1/4 cup dark rum along with the cream.

Makes about 1 quart

(master recipe)

chocolate Sorbet

I wanted to make a frozen treat with an intense chocolate flavor, but I didn't want it to be creamy, like ice cream. The tiny bit of cream in this sorbet helps soften the texture, but the focus is definitely on the chocolate.

Makes about 1 1/2 quarts

4 cups water

2 cups sugar

1 cup unsweetened cocoa powder

1 teaspoon pure vanilla extract

1/4 cup heavy whipping cream

1/4 cup crème de cacao

Place the water, sugar, cocoa powder, and vanilla extract in a heavy saucepan over high heat and bring to a boil. Boil for about 5 minutes, or until the sugar has dissolved, then remove the pan from the heat. Add the cream and crème de cacao, and mix well. Refrigerate until it cools to at least 40°, about 2 hours.

To freeze the sorbet, follow the manufacturer's directions for your ice cream maker. Transfer the sorbet to a covered container and place in the freezer until completely frozen.

Variations

Chocolate Sorbet

MOCHA SORBET

If you are a real coffee aficionado, use this sorbet in the Espresso Coupe (page 214).

Follow the Chocolate Sorbet master recipe, substituting very strong, freshly brewed coffee for the water and coffee liqueur for the crème de cacao. Proceed as in the master recipe.

Makes about 1 1/2 quarts

CHOCOLATE-MINT SORBET

Any kind of mint will do this sorbet justice—as long as it's very fresh.

Follow the Chocolate Sorbet master recipe, adding 1 cup fresh mint leaves to the cocoa powder mixture. Bring to a boil over low heat instead of high (to give the mint enough time to steep), then simmer for about 8 minutes. Proceed as in the master recipe, straining the mixture through a fine-mesh sieve before refrigerating it.

Makes about 1 1/2 quarts

(master recipe)

Hazelnut Gelato

Hazelnut is a classic gelato flavor, but you can use other toasted nuts if hazelnuts are not your favorite or if you are aller-gic to them (like my dad is). If you do substitute another type of nut, be sure to use a liqueur that will complement the nuts.

Makes about 2 quarts

3 cups whole milk

3 cups heavy whipping cream

1 vanilla bean, split in half lengthwise

2 cups ground toasted hazelnuts (page 10)

1/2 cup hazelnut liqueur

5 egg yolks

1 1/4 cups sugar

Combine the milk, cream, vanilla bean, hazelnuts, and liqueur in a large bowl; cover and let steep in the refriger-ator for at least 24 hours.

Place the milk mixture in a heavy saucepan over low heat, and bring just to a boil. Remove the pan from the heat, cover, and let it steep for 1 hour. Set the saucepan over low heat, and again bring the mixture just to a boil. Mean-while, whisk together the egg yolks and sugar in a large bowl. Slowly whisk the hot milk mixture into the egg yolk mixture to temper it, or bring it up to the same tempera-ture. Pour the mixture back into the saucepan, whisk until

smooth, and cook over medium-low heat, stirring con-stantly with a plastic spatula until it has thickened and coats the back of a spoon, 5 to 7 minutes. Scrape the seeds from the inside of the vanilla bean into the mixture (discard the bean). Strain the mixture through a fine-mesh sieve. Refrigerate for at least 2 hours, or until well chilled (it should be at least 40° or colder).

To freeze the gelato, follow the manufacturer's directions for your ice cream maker. Transfer the gelato to a covered container and place in the freezer until completely frozen.

Variations

Hazelnut Gelato

FRESH BERRY GELATO

This gelato is infused with the flavor of summer. The berries (or diced fresh fruit) steeped in the cream and milk give a flavor that's deeper than traditional ice cream.

Follow the Hazelnut Gelato master recipe, omitting the nuts and hazelnut liqueur. Add 4 cups fresh berries and 1/2 cup of your favorite liqueur along with the vanilla bean to the milk and cream mixture before letting it steep in the refrigerator. Proceed as directed in the master recipe.

Makes about 2 quarts

VANILLA GELATO

This gelato is just great all by itself, but you can also use it as a starting point for a flavor combination of your own.

Follow the Hazelnut Gelato master recipe, omitting the nuts and hazelnut liqueur. (If you like, you can add 1/2 cup bourbon along with the vanilla bean to the milk and cream mixture before letting it steep in the refrigerator.) Proceed as directed in the master recipe.

Makes about 2 quarts

Lemon Gelato

The key to a good gelato is in the flavoring of the base. In this recipe, I start the process 24 hours before I even begin cooking the base. If you experiment with this recipe, be sure to give the flavoring ingredient plenty of time to infuse the cream.

Makes about 2 quarts

3 cups whole milk

3 cups heavy whipping cream

1 vanilla bean, split in half lengthwise

Finely grated zest of 3 lemons

5 egg yolks

1 1/4 cups sugar

Combine the milk, cream, vanilla bean, and lemon zest in a large bowl; cover and let steep in the refrigerator for at least 24 hours.

Place the milk mixture in a heavy saucepan over low heat, and bring it just to a boil. Meanwhile, whisk together the egg yolks and sugar in a large bowl. Slowly whisk the hot milk mixture into the egg yolk mixture to temper it, or bring it up to the same temperature. Pour the mixture back into the saucepan, whisk until smooth, and cook over medium-low heat, stirring constantly with a plastic spatula until it has thickened and coats the back of a spoon, 5 to 7 minutes. Strain the mixture through a fine-mesh sieve. Scrape the seeds from the inside of the vanilla bean into the mixture (discard the bean). Refrigerate until it cools to at least 40°, about 2 hours.

To freeze the gelato, follow the manufacturer's directions for your ice cream maker. Transfer the gelato to a covered container and place in the freezer until completely frozen.

Variations

Lemon Gelato

ROSE PETAL AND SHAVED WHITE CHOCOLATE GELATO

The very best place to find organic rose petals is in your own garden, so you can know for sure that they haven't been sprayed.

Follow the Lemon Gelato master recipe, substituting 4 cups organic rose petals for the lemon zest and straining the mixture through a fine-mesh sieve before refrigerating it. Begin freezing the gelato. When the gelato is very thick, but still soft (after about 20 minutes, depending on your ice cream maker), add 1 1/2 cups grated white chocolate. Continue freezing to a soft consistency. Transfer the gelato to a covered container and place it in the freezer until completely frozen.

Makes about 2 quarts

ORANGE-CINNAMON GELATO

Cinnamon is the star flavor in this gelato. Be sure to taste the milk mixture after steeping the cinnamon in it. If the cinnamon flavor isn't pronounced, let it steep 30 minutes longer, or until the flavor has nicely developed.

Follow the Lemon Gelato master recipe, adding 4 cinnamon sticks along with the vanilla bean to the milk mixture and substituting the grated zest of 3 oranges for the lemon zest. Proceed as directed in the master recipe.

Makes about 2 quarts

Griddle Cones

These cones are crispy and sweet—not unlike traditional sugar cones. Sometimes I like to make them even more special by brushing the insides with melted bittersweet chocolate.

Makes 6 cones

2 eggs

1/2 cup sugar

1/4 cup unsalted butter, melted

2 1/2 tablespoons milk

1/2 teaspoon pure vanilla extract

1/3 cup plus 1 tablespoon flour

Pinch of salt

Vegetable oil, for the griddle

Whisk together the eggs and sugar in a mixing bowl. Add the butter, milk, and vanilla, and mix well. Add the flour and salt, and whisk until the batter is smooth. (It should be fairly thin, about the consistency of a crepe batter.)

Lightly rub a large griddle or an 8-inch nonstick sauté pan with a few drops of vegetable oil, and heat it over medium heat until hot. Ladle about 1/4 cup of batter onto the griddle and, using the back of the ladle or a palette knife, spread it out into a 5- or 6-inch circle (the thinner the better). Cook until golden brown, 3 to 4 minutes, and then gently flip it over and cook until light brown, about 3 minutes. Remove it from the griddle and, working very quickly, start at the edge and roll it into a cone. Squeeze the tip of the cone to seal it (so the ice cream doesn't drip all over your shoes). Transfer to a rack and let cool completely. Continue with the remaining batter, brushing the pan each time with oil.

Fill the cooled cones with scoops of ice cream (but don't press too hard—the cones are delicate and break easily).

1a

1b

2

3a

3b

4

5a

5b

6

Making Griddle Cones

Making these cones may take a bit longer than opening a package, but they look and taste better and are definitely worth the effort.

1. Lightly rub a large griddle or an 8-inch nonstick sauté pan with a few drops of vegetable oil, and heat it over medium heat until hot. Ladle about 1/4 cup or 2 ounces of the batter into the pan.

2. Using a palette knife, gently spread the batter into a circle about 6 inches across. Spread the batter as thin as possible without making any holes.

3. Cook until golden brown, 3 to 4 minutes, and then gently turn it over.

4. Continue cooking on the other side until golden brown, 2 to 3 minutes longer, and then remove it from the pan.

5. Let cool for a few seconds (if you wait too long it will be too stiff), and then gently roll it into a cone.

6. Press the tip of the cone down to seal it. Transfer the cone to a rack or a parchment-lined sheet pan and let cool completely. Use immediately, because they won't keep.

Chocolate Turtle Torte (page 231)

chapter seven

Desserts for Special Occasions

on't be intimidated by the name of this chapter—these recipes aren't necessarily for when Julia Child comes to your house for dinner. On the other hand, they aren't for those spur-of-the-moment dessert cravings either. We call this chapter "Desserts for Special Occasions" because the recipes require more time and attention than most of the others in this book. You'll want to save these desserts for those times when a special effort is warranted.

Several of the recipes are Bistro favorites. We change our dinner menu every month, but Melissa creates an entirely new array of desserts at least once a week. Some desserts, like the Chocolate Silk, Coconut Cream Cake, and Melissa's German Chocolate Cake (my favorite birthday cake and the dessert that earned her the job), are so

popular with customers that they make regular appearances on the dessert menu. Due to *extremely* high demand, the Chocolate Turtle Torte, which Mark created when we first opened the Bistro, never leaves the menu. Inspired by turtle candies, it's an eye-catching torte composed of layers of caramel and pecans, chocolate mousse, and ganache. Even in the restaurant's commercial kitchen, it takes Melissa two days to prepare all of its elements and put it together.

Almost every week we receive requests for each of these recipes. Until now, we've never had anything formally written out, instead giving customers the recipes written in chef's shorthand and not with the home cook in mind. We've sent many people on their way with a photocopy of the well-worn typewritten recipe we use at the Bistro for the turtle tortes. I've often wondered how they've turned out; with obscure instructions that make perfect sense to a professional chef, the recipe presented further challenges because it yields four tortes. Melissa's Coconut Cream Cake has been the one guarded secret, but after so many requests she finally relented and agreed to share it. This chapter gave us a good excuse to get organized and write the recipes out to satisfy those requests.

Some of the other recipes in this chapter have never been on the Bistro menu, and I wrote them especially for this section of the book. I had a great time dreaming them up, and I found inspiration from all angles. Taking a bite of a delicious palmier, that classic French pastry, while I was in Paris, I started to imagine how I could put my own spin on it. I came up with a very Northwest incarnation, rolling the flaky puff pastry in sugar and ground toasted hazelnuts.

The Caramel-Apple Egg Rolls came about when I was trying to figure out how to make use of some lumpia wrappers (larger egg roll wrappers) that I had on hand. I first considered using them in place of puff pastry in the Rasberry–Almond Praline Napoleons (I've always loved napoleons, and I knew I had to create a napoleon recipe for the book). Instead, inspired by their Asian roots, I filled the wrapper with a caramel-apple mixture, rolled them up, deep-fried them, and paired them with ice cream. Because most people don't equate egg rolls with dessert, the egg rolls make a fun twist on this common Asian food. They are the quickest dessert to put together in this chapter, but they do require deep-frying, which is something that most of us don't want to take on at home on a regular basis.

Although these desserts take some time, they are worth the extra effort. And whether it's spending an afternoon making puff pastry or just whisking up a batch of pastry cream, making the individual components can be just as satisfying as receiving the kudos you're bound to be given as the pastry chef. No matter what the occasions—small celebrations or grand affairs—I hope you will share these recipes with family and friends for years to come.

chocolate turtle torte

Our chef, Mark Dowers, brought this fantastic dessert to the Bistro when we first opened. It has four main elements: a pâte brisée crust, a caramel-nut filling, chocolate mousse, and chocolate ganache. Melissa prepares the recipe over the course of two days. First she makes the crust and the filling and lets them cool overnight. The next morning she makes the mousse, spreads it over the filling, and then chills it for at least 3 hour. Then she tops that with the ganache, and chills the whole thing for at least another hour before it's ready for our customers. So whenever you want to serve this torte for a dinner party, plan on starting to prepare it at least the night before. It's possible to make it all in one day, of course, but you and the cake might suffer!

Serves 16

Crust

1 3/4 cups flour

2 tablespoons sugar

1/2 cup cold unsalted butter, diced

1 egg beaten with 3 tablespoons water

Praline Filling

1 1/2 cups sugar

1/2 cup water

3/4 cup cold unsalted butter, diced

3/4 cup half-and-half

1/3 cup honey

1 1/2 cups coarsely chopped pecans

Mousse

1 pound bittersweet chocolate, chopped

1/2 cup cold unsalted butter, diced

6 eggs, separated

1 cup sugar

1/4 cup coffee liqueur

Pinch of salt

3/4 cup heavy whipping cream

Ganache (page 47)

1 cup Caramel Sauce (page 58), as accompaniment

1 1/2 cups whipped cream, as accompaniment

continued

continued from page 231

Grease a 10-inch springform pan; set aside.

To prepare the crust, place the flour and sugar in the bowl of a food processor and pulse to mix. Add the butter and pulse until the butter is coarsely blended. With the machine running, add the egg mixture and mix just until the dough forms a ball on top of the blades. Roll the dough out on a well-floured board into a 12-inch circle, press it into the bottom and up the sides of the prepared springform pan, and refrigerate until ready to use.

To prepare the filling, place the sugar in a large sauté pan with sides or a heavy saucepan. Gently moisten the sugar with the water, being careful not to splash the water and sugar onto the sides of the pan. Cook the sugar mixture over high heat, without stirring, until you see any part of it turning brown, then swirl the pan to even out the color. Cook until golden brown, about 2 minutes longer. Lower the heat to medium-low, and add the butter. Carefully add the half-and-half to the hot sugar, taking care to pour it in slowly because it will bubble up very violently, and cook, without stirring, until the caramelized sugar has liquefied again and the sauce is very smooth and a deep golden brown, about 15 minutes. Remove the pan from the heat, add the honey and pecans, and mix well. Let cool completely.

Preheat the oven to 350°.

Pour the cooled filling into the prepared crust, and fold the sides of the crust over the top of the filling. Bake until the crust is golden brown and the caramel is bubbling, 30 to 35 minutes. Let cool completely.

To prepare the mousse, place the chocolate and butter in a metal bowl set over a pan of simmering water (make sure the bottom of the bowl does not touch the water). When the chocolate has melted about halfway, remove the pan from the heat (leave the bowl on the pan), and let stand until the chocolate and butter are completely melted; stir until smooth. Set the bowl aside in a warm (but not hot) place, so the mixture will stay melted.

Set the pan of water back over the heat, add more water if needed, and bring it to a simmer. In another metal bowl, whisk together the egg yolks, sugar, and liqueur. Set the bowl over the pan of simmering water (again make sure that the bottom of the bowl does not touch the water), and cook, whisking constantly, until the mixture is very thick, like very softly whipped cream. (It's thick enough if you can see the bottom of the bowl as you whisk it.) Remove the bowl from the heat. Using a plastic spatula, gently fold in the warm chocolate.

Place the egg whites and salt in the bowl of a mixer fitted with the whip attachment, and whip on high speed until they just hold a soft peak. Gently fold the whites into the chocolate mixture, mixing just until the mousse is smooth.

Place the cream in the bowl of a mixer fitted with the whip attachment, and whip on high speed until it holds stiff peaks. Gently fold the whipped cream into the chocolate mixture.

Pour the mousse over the cooled filling. Refrigerate for at least 3 hours or overnight.

Warm the ganache in a metal bowl set over a pan of simmering water or in a glass or ceramic bowl in the microwave until soft and pourable. Pour it over the cooled mousse and refrigerate for at least 1 hour before serving.

To serve, run a knife around the sides of the pan to loosen the cake, then remove the outer ring. Cut the torte with a very hot knife and serve with caramel sauce and softly whipped cream.

pictured on page 228

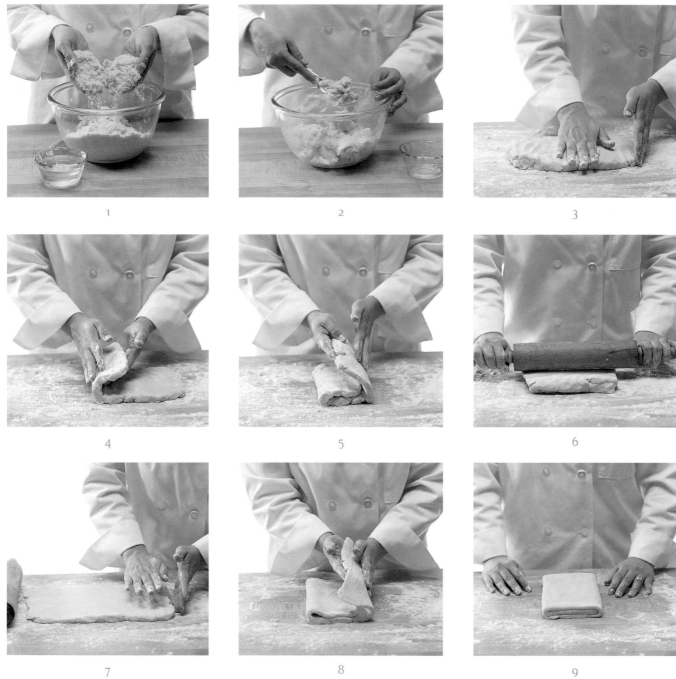

1

2

3

4

5

6

7

8

9

Making Puff Pastry

The traditional method of making puff pastry is the ultimate way to prepare it. However, most of us don't have the time to spend on that lengthy process. Here is a method, known as the "blitz" method, that cuts the preparation time considerably.

1. Place the flour, salt, and butter in a mixing bowl. Mix with your fingertips until it is well blended and resembles a coarse meal.

2. Add the cold water and mix with a large dinner fork just until the mixture begins to come together and is well moistened. (As with pie dough, wetter is better than dry.)

3. Turn the dough out onto a well-floured board. Using your hands, form it into a 4 by 12-inch rectangle.

4. Fold over about a third of the dough.

5. Fold over the remaining third of the dough.

6. Turn the dough 90 degrees and roll it into about a 6 by 14-inch rectangle.

7. Using your hands, square the corners of the dough.

8. Again fold over about a third of the dough, and then fold over the remaining third. Again turn the dough 90 degrees, and repeat the rolling, folding, and turning process 2 more times.

9. Wrap the dough in plastic wrap and refrigerate for at least 2 hours. Use as directed in the recipe.

coconut cream cake

We had to include this recipe in the book because so many Bistro customers requested it. Like all of Melissa's cake, it's gigantic. Whenever people see this coconut concoction floating through the dining room on a plate, they all want a piece. Once the cake layers are surrounded by the pastry cream filling, they start to soften, and the boundaries between cake and filling start to blend into one delicious creamy concoction covered by frosting and toasted coconut.

Serves 16

Cake

1 cup cold unsalted butter, diced

2 cups sugar

4 eggs

2 teaspoons pure vanilla extract

3/4 teaspoon salt

1 tablespoon baking powder

3 cups sifted cake flour

1 1/4 cups coconut milk

Cream Filling

Coconut Pastry Cream (page 55)

1 cup heavy whipping cream

Quick Buttercream (page 52)

1 1/2 cups shredded sweetened coconut, toasted (page 8)

1 cup Chocolate Sauce (page 62), as accompaniment

Preheat the oven to 350°. Grease two 9-inch cake pans and line the bottoms with parchment paper; set aside.

To prepare the cake, place the butter and sugar in the bowl of a mixer fitted with the paddle attachment and beat on high speed, scraping down the sides of the bowl often, until light and fluffy, about 5 minutes. With the mixer on low speed, add the eggs, one at a time, scraping down the sides of the bowl and mixing well after each addition. Add the vanilla extract and mix well, again scraping down the sides of the bowl. Combine the salt and baking powder with the flour. Add about half of the dry ingredients to the batter, beat on low speed until well blended, and then add about half of the coconut milk and beat well. Add the remaining dry ingredients followed by the remaining coconut milk, beating well after each addition.

continued on page 238

continued from page 236

Divide the batter between the prepared pans and bake until the cake springs back when touched lightly in the center, 25 to 30 minutes. Let cool for about 10 minutes, then remove the cakes from the pans and let cool completely.

To prepare the filling, place the pastry cream in a large bowl; set aside. In the bowl of a mixer fitted with the whip attachment, whip the cream on high speed just until it holds soft peaks. Using a plastic spatula, fold the whipped cream into the pastry cream until smooth.

To assemble the cake, split the layers of the cooled cake. Fill the layers with the cream filling, and frost the cake with the buttercream. (See page 19 for instructions on splitting, filling, and frosting the cake.) Sprinkle the toasted coconut over the top and sides of the cake.

Serve on a pool of Chocolate Sauce.

German Chocolate Cake

All of Melissa's cakes are extraordinary and this one is no exception! Four layers of rich, moist cake are filled with a gooey coconut-pecan caramel and then swathed with ganache frosting.

Serves 14

Cake

4 ounces bittersweet chocolate, chopped

1/2 cup boiling water

1 cup cold unsalted butter, diced

2 cups sugar

4 eggs, separated

2 teaspoons pure vanilla extract

1/2 teaspoon salt

1 teaspoon baking soda

2 1/4 cups flour

1 cup buttermilk

Gooey Pecan Filling

3 cups shredded sweetened coconut

2 cups chopped pecans

1 (10-ounce) can evaporated milk

1 1/2 cups sugar

4 egg yolks

1/2 cup unsalted butter

2 teaspoons pure vanilla extract

Ganache (page 47), cooled to room temperature

Preheat the oven to 350°. Grease two 9-inch cake pans and line the bottoms with parchment paper; set aside.

To prepare the cake, combine the chocolate and boiling water in a small bowl, and let sit for 2 minutes. Stir until the chocolate has completely melted; let cool for about 5 minutes.

Meanwhile, place the butter and sugar in the bowl of a mixer fitted with the paddle attachment and beat on high speed, scraping down the sides of the bowl often, until light and fluffy, about 5 minutes. With the mixer on low speed, add the egg yolks, one at a time, scraping down the sides of the bowl and mixing well after each addition. Add the vanilla extract and mix well. With the mixer on low speed, slowly add the chocolate mixture (be careful not to splatter), and mix well, again scraping down the sides of the bowl. Combine the salt and baking soda with the flour.

continued

239

continued from page 239

Add about a third of the dry ingredients to the batter, beat on low speed until well blended, then add about a third of the buttermilk, and beat well. Continue alternating the remaining dry ingredients and buttermilk, scraping down the sides of the bowl and beating well after each addition.

In a clean bowl of a mixer fitted with the whip attachment, whip the egg whites on high speed until they hold soft peaks. Using a plastic spatula, gently fold the whites into the batter. Divide the batter between the prepared pans and bake until the cake springs back when touched lightly in the center, 30 to 35 minutes. Let cool for about 10 minutes, then remove the cakes from the pans and let cool completely.

To prepare the filling, place the coconut and pecans in a large bowl; set aside. Combine the evaporated milk, sugar, egg yolks, and butter in a saucepan over medium-high heat and cook, whisking constantly so the eggs won't scorch, until the mixture just comes to a boil. Remove the pan from the heat, immediately pour the mixture over the coconut and pecans, add the vanilla extract, and mix well. Cover and refrigerate until well chilled, at least 2 hours.

Place the cooled ganache in the bowl of a mixer fitted with the paddle attachment and beat on medium-high speed until it begins to thicken and lighten in color, 3 to 4 minutes. To assemble the cake, split the layers of the cooled cake, and fill the layers with the pecan filling, reserving 3/4 cup. Frost the sides of the cake with the whipped ganache, reserving 3/4 cup. See page 19 for instructions on splitting, filling, and frosting the cake layers.

Place the reserved ganache in a pastry bag fitted with a star tip, and pipe a border around the top of the cake. Spread the reserved filling over the top and to the ganache border. Chill the cake for at least 1 hour before serving.

Chocolate Silk

This is another recipe that our chef, Mark Dowers, created during the pre-Melissa years at the Bistro; it's been a standard on our dessert menu since then. As the name implies, the tart's mousse filling is cool and silky on your palate. It is very easy to modify–simply use a different liqueur or scatter a pint of fresh summer berries over the prepared crust before covering it with the mousse.

Serves 14

Chocolate-Pecan Crust

1 cup chocolate cookie crumbs

3/4 cup firmly packed brown sugar

1 3/4 cups ground pecans

Pinch of ground cinnamon

Pinch of ground nutmeg

1/2 cup cold unsalted butter, diced

Mousse

1 pound bittersweet chocolate, chopped

1/2 cup unsalted butter, softened

1 cup sugar

7 eggs

1 teaspoon pure vanilla extract

1/2 cup brandy or hazelnut liqueur

1/2 cup heavy whipping cream

Topping

8 ounces hazelnut-flavored chocolate or bittersweet chocolate

2 cups heavy whipping cream

1 cup Chocolate Sauce (page 62), as accompaniment

1 1/2 cups whipped cream, as accompaniment

Fresh seasonal berries, as accompaniment (optional)

Preheat the oven to 350°. Grease a 10-inch springform pan; set aside.

To prepare the crust, combine the cookie crumbs, brown sugar, pecans, cinnamon, nutmeg, and butter in a food processor and process until well blended. Press into the bottom and all the way up the sides of the prepared pan. Bake until set, about 10 minutes, and let cool completely.

continued

continued from page 241

To prepare the mousse, place the chocolate in a metal bowl set over a pan of simmering water (make sure the bottom of the bowl does not touch the water). When the chocolate has melted about halfway, remove the pan from the heat (leave the bowl on the pan), and let stand until completely melted; stir until smooth. Set the bowl aside in a warm (but not hot) place, so the chocolate will stay melted.

Meanwhile, place the butter and sugar in the bowl of a mixer fitted with the paddle attachment and beat on high speed, scraping down the sides of the bowl often, until light and fluffy, about 5 minutes. Add the eggs, one at a time, scraping down the sides of the bowl and beating well after each addition. Add the chocolate, mix well, and then add the vanilla extract, brandy, and cream, and mix until smooth. Pour the mousse into the prepared crust and refrigerate for at least 1 hour.

To prepare the topping, melt the chocolate in a metal bowl set over a pan of simmering water as you did for the mousse, and keep warm.

Meanwhile, place the cream in the bowl of a mixer fitted with the whip attachment and beat on medium-high speed just until it begins to thicken, about 3 minutes. With the mixer on medium speed, slowly add the melted chocolate and beat just until blended. Pour over the mousse and refrigerate until well chilled, about 2 hours.

To serve, cut the tart with a very hot knife. Serve with Chocolate Sauce, softly whipped cream, and fresh berries when in season.

Espresso-orange Soufflés

I've been fascinated by soufflés ever since I starting cooking in high school. When I was the chef at Fullers restaurant in Seattle, soufflés were a regular menu item, so I made hundreds of them–and my interest waned. I rediscovered them on a trip to France, rekindling my affection for this elegant dish.

Serves 4

2 tablespoons butter

1 cup sugar

2/3 cup half-and-half

3 tablespoons instant espresso powder

Finely grated zest of 1 orange

3 egg yolks

2 teaspoons cornstarch

1/4 cup coffee liqueur

5 egg whites

1 cup Chocolate Sauce (page 62), as accompaniment

Preheat the oven to 425°. Generously butter four 8-ounce ramekins, using about 1/2 tablespoon for each, and dust them with 1/4 cup of the sugar; set aside.

Place the half-and-half, espresso powder, and orange zest in a heavy saucepan over medium heat and bring just to a boil. Meanwhile, whisk together the egg yolks, cornstarch, liqueur, and 1/2 cup of the sugar in a large bowl. Slowly whisk 1 to 1 1/2 cups of the hot half-and-half into the egg mixture to temper it. Whisk in the remaining half-and-half, pour the mixture back into the saucepan, and again cook over medium heat, stirring constantly with a plastic spatula, until very thick, 3 to 4 minutes. Transfer the mixture to a large bowl and set aside, or cover and refrigerate until ready to use.

Place the egg whites in the bowl of a mixer fitted with the whip attachment and whip on high speed until very foamy. With the mixer on high speed, slowly add 2 tablespoons of the sugar to the egg whites and whip just until the whites hold soft peaks. Using a plastic spatula, gently fold the egg whites into the espresso mixture just until combined. Divide the soufflé batter among the ramekins, sprinkle with the remaining 2 tablespoons sugar, and bake until the soufflés have risen about 1 inch above the rims of the ramekins, 12 to 15 minutes.

Serve immediately, drizzled with warm Chocolate Sauce.

(master recipe)

Caramel-Apple Egg Rolls

The similarities between this dessert and traditional egg rolls stops at the wrappers. Here, golden-brown layers of crispy phyllo-like pastry surround a warm apple filling. These egg rolls are very easy to prepare; so as long as you are making a batch, double it and freeze the extras. For a classy dessert at a moment's notice, simply take them out of the freezer and let stand for 15 to 20 minutes, deep-fry them, and serve with your favorite ice cream or with caramel sauce.

Makes 12 egg rolls

Apple Filling

3 Granny Smith apples, peeled, cored, and cut into small dice

2/3 cup sugar

1/3 cup bourbon

2 tablespoons unsalted butter

1 teaspoon pure vanilla extract

1 teaspoon ground cinnamon

1/2 teaspoon ground allspice

1/2 teaspoon ground nutmeg

Pinch of ground cloves

1 heaping tablespoon finely diced candied ginger

12 lumpia wrappers (available at Asian markets)

1 egg, beaten with 1 tablespoon cold water

Vegetable oil, for deep-frying

2/3 cup powdered sugar

1 quart Vanilla Bean Ice Cream (page 208) or 1 cup
    Caramel Sauce (page 58), as accompaniment

To prepare the filling, toss the apples with about 1 tablespoon of the sugar and set aside. Place the remaining sugar in a large sauté pan over high heat and cook, without stirring, until the sugar starts to caramelize and turns golden brown, 3 to 4 minutes (it happens fast, so don't leave the stove). Add the apples and toss to coat with the sugar. Remove the pan from the heat, add the bourbon, and then place it back over the heat. (The bourbon can flame up, so be very careful.) Bring the bourbon to a boil, add the butter, vanilla extract, cinnamon, allspice, nutmeg, and cloves, and cook over high heat until the apples are tender, about 4 minutes. Transfer the mixture to a large bowl and let cool until tepid. Add the candied ginger and mix well.

To prepare the egg rolls, place 1 lumpia wrapper on a flat surface, with a corner pointing toward you (as you look down on it, the wrapper should be a diamond shape). Place a heaping tablespoon of the filling on the wrapper about 1/2 inch from the corner closest to you, and then fold the corner over the filling. Fold the side corners over the filling, then roll to the opposite corner to form a cylinder. Brush the edge of the wrapper with the beaten egg to seal. Continue with the remaining wrappers and filling.

Heat about 4 inches of vegetable oil in a large saucepan over high heat until it reaches 350°. (You can check the temperature with a candy thermometer, or place a piece of bread in the oil; if it turns brown in about 40 seconds, the oil should be at about 350°.) Add as many egg rolls as will fit without overcrowding, and fry until golden brown, 1 to 2 minutes. Drain on paper towels. Let cool for 3 to 4 minutes, then dust with powdered sugar. Continue with the remaining egg rolls.

Serve warm or at room temperature with Vanilla Bean Ice Cream or Caramel Sauce.

Variation

Caramel-Apple Egg Rolls

PEAR-CHOCOLATE EGG ROLLS

Follow the Caramel-Apple Egg Rolls master recipe, substituting pears for the apples and bourbon or Tuaca liqueur for the bourbon, and omitting the spices. When the filling has cooled, fold in 5 ounces chopped bittersweet chocolate. Proceed as directed in the master recipe.

Serve warm or at room temperature with Vanilla Bean Ice Cream (page 208).

Makes 12 egg rolls

Hazelnut Palmiers

Traditional palmiers are layers and layers of crisp pastry surrounded by caramelized sugar. My version includes caramelized hazelnuts, which add more depth than just the sugar alone. You can also use just about any other nut and can even add ground spices, such as cinnamon and ginger, to the sugar-nut mixture. Although this tasty pastry can be served on its own, I like to serve it as an accompaniment to lighter desserts, such as sorbet or fresh fruit. It travels well, making it a perfect dessert for an elegant picnic. The step-by-step photos on pages 248 and 249 clearly illustrate how to shape these buttery treats.

Makes about 30 cookies

Puff Pastry

2 1/4 cups flour

1 cup cold unsalted butter, diced

1/2 teaspoon salt

3/4 cup cold water

1/2 cup toasted hazelnuts (page 10)

1 cup sugar

To make the pastry, place the flour, butter, and salt in a large bowl. Using your fingertips, mix the butter with the flour until it resembles a coarse meal. Add the water and mix with a fork just until it comes together.

Transfer the dough to a well-floured board and form it into a rough rectangle. Fold one-third of the dough toward the center. Fold the other third over toward the center. Turn the dough 90 degrees. Sprinkle it with flour and roll

it out into a 6 by 14-inch rectangle. Fold the dough in thirds again. Turn it 90 degrees, sprinkle with flour, and roll it out again. Repeat the process 2 more times.

Cover the dough with plastic wrap and refrigerate until well chilled, at least 1 hour. Remove the chilled dough from the refrigerator and let it sit at room temperature for 10 to 20 minutes.

Place the hazelnuts and about 1/2 cup of the sugar in a food processor and process until finely ground. Sprinkle the hazelnut mixture over a flat work surface. Roll the pastry out over the hazelnut mixture into a 9 by 13-inch rectangle, adding more sugar if necessary so the pastry does not stick to the board or your rolling pin. Place the pastry rectangle on the board with a short end toward you. Fold the pastry in half vertically (lengthwise) to mark the center, and then unfold. Starting from the right side, roll up the pastry until it reaches the center mark. Next, roll up the left side of the pastry until it reaches the center mark, so the two spirals meet in the center. Tightly wrap the pastry in plastic wrap. Refrigerate for 1 hour until the pastry is firm, to help make slicing the dough easier.

Preheat the oven to 375°.

Using a serrated knife, cut the chilled pastry into 1/2-inch-thick cookies. Transfer the cookies to a sheet pan lined with parchment paper, loosening the spirals just a bit so the pastry has room to puff. Place the pan on the bottom rack of the oven and bake until the sugar on the bottom of the cookies begins to caramelize, 10 to 13 minutes. Remove the pan from the oven, turn the cookies over, and continue baking until the sugar on the other side has caramelized and the cookies are golden brown, about 10 minutes longer. Transfer to a rack and let cool for about 10 minutes before serving, or let cool completely and store in an airtight container until ready to serve.

Making Palmiers

I hope these how-to photos inspire you to make these delicious cookies that have such an elegant shape. They're really not as complicated to form as the directions may sound.

1. Remove the chilled dough from the refrigerator and let it sit at room temperature for 10 to 20 minutes. Dust the board and the dough with a generous amount of the sugar and nut mixture.

2. Roll the dough into about a 9 by 13-inch rectangle.

3. Place the short end closest to you, fold the dough in half to mark the center, and then unfold it.

4. Starting on the right side, roll the dough in to meet the center mark.

5. Roll the left side of the dough in to meet the center mark.

6. Wrap the dough in plastic and chill in the refrigerator until firm, about 1 hour.

7. Remove the chilled dough from the refrigerator. Using a very sharp knife, cut the dough into 1/2-inch-thick slices.

8. Place the slices on a sheet pan lined with parchment paper. Open each cookie slightly.

9. Bake 10 to 13, until the sugar on the bottom of the cookies begins to caramelize. Remove the pan from the oven, turn the cookies over, and continue baking until the sugar on the other side has caramelized and the cookies are golden brown, about 10 minutes longer.

7

8

9

Raspberry-Almond Praline Napoleons

When I was the chef at Fullers restaurant in Seattle, my pastry chef, Jim, made the most amazing napoleons. In this recipe, I wanted to emulate his multilayered confection. Once you try this dessert, you won't regret all the time and attention you gave to it. If you make all of the components in advance, the napoleons are a snap to put together.

Makes 12 napoleons

Almond Praline

2/3 cup sliced toasted almonds (page 10)

1 cup sugar

1/3 cup water

Almond-Praline Pastry Cream

1 1/2 cups half-and-half

1/2 vanilla bean, split in half lengthwise

1/2 teaspoon almond extract

3 tablespoons almond liqueur

4 egg yolks

1/3 cup sugar

1 1/2 tablespoons cornstarch

Pinch of salt

Puff Pastry (page 246)

1 cup heavy whipping cream

1 tablespoon sugar

1/2 teaspoon pure vanilla extract

About 3 1/2 cups fresh raspberries

1 cup Berry Sauce (page 63), as accompaniment

To make the praline, place the toasted almonds in a single layer on a well-greased sheet pan; set aside.

Place the sugar in a large sauté pan with sides or a heavy saucepan. Gently moisten the sugar with the water, being careful not to splash the water and sugar onto the sides of the pan. Cook the sugar mixture over high heat, without stirring, until you see any part of it turning brown, then swirl the pan to even out the color. Cook until golden brown, about 2 minutes longer. Pour the caramelized sugar over the toasted almonds. Let cool completely.

continued on page 252

continued from page 250

Break the cooled praline into pieces or grind it finely in a food processor. (The praline will keep in an airtight container for 2 days.)

To prepare the pastry cream, place the half-and-half and the vanilla bean in a heavy saucepan over medium heat and bring just to a boil. Meanwhile, whisk together the almond extract, liqueur, egg yolks, sugar, cornstarch, and salt in a large bowl. Slowly whisk 1 to 1 1/2 cups of the hot half-and-half into the egg yolk mixture to temper it, or bring it up to the same temperature. Whisk in the remaining half-and-half, pour the mixture back into the saucepan, and again cook over medium heat, stirring constantly with a plastic spatula, until very thick, about 2 minutes (it's thick enough when you start to see the bottom of the pan as you stir). Remove the pan from the heat and strain the pastry cream through a fine-mesh sieve into a large bowl. Scrape the seeds from the inside of the vanilla bean into the strained pastry cream (discard the bean). Cover and refrigerate until well chilled, about 2 hours. Just before serving, fold in the ground almond praline.

Preheat the oven to 400°. Grease a sheet pan well and set aside.

While the pastry cream is cooling, roll the puff pastry out on a well-floured board into a 12 by 14-inch rectangle. Cut the pastry lengthwise into 6 equal strips, then cut each strip in half to form 12 rectangles. Place on the prepared pan and bake until golden brown and puffed, about 20 minutes. Gently set another clean sheet pan on top of the pastry (this keeps the pastry from puffing up too much), and bake 10 minutes longer. Transfer the pastries to a rack and let cool completely.

To assemble the napoleons, in the bowl of a mixer fitted with the whip attachment, whip the cream with the sugar and vanilla extract on high speed until it holds soft peaks. Split the cooled pastries in half horizontally. Place each bottom half on a serving plate. Divide the pastry cream among the 12 bottom halves, then top with the raspberries, whipped cream, and the top halves of the pastry. Serve immediately, drizzled with Berry Sauce.

chocolate toffee Mousse cake

If you're feeling industrious and want to make the mother of all birthday cakes, try this compilation of four different recipes. When friends and family of the Bistro celebrate milestone birthdays, Melissa makes an industrial-size version. For a few moments at least, it helps distract the birthday boy or girl from feeling his or her age.

Serves 14

Pecan Butter Toffee

2 1/4 cups sugar

1/2 cup heavy whipping cream

1/4 cup light corn syrup

1/4 teaspoon cream of tartar

1 1/4 cups cold unsalted butter, diced

1 teaspoon salt

1 1/4 cups pecan pieces, toasted (page 10)

2 teaspoons pure vanilla extract

8 ounces bittersweet chocolate, melted (page 8)

Old-Fashioned Chocolate Cake (page 16), cooled and split into 4 layers

Chocolate Mousse Filling (page 57)

Ganache (page 47)

To make the toffee, lightly grease a sheet pan; set aside.

Place the sugar, cream, corn syrup, and cream of tartar in a heavy saucepan, and mix well. Bring the mixture to a boil over high heat and cook, stirring often, for about 3 minutes. Add the butter and salt, and continue cooking until it registers 238° on a candy thermometer or reaches the softball stage. Remove the pan from the heat, add the pecans and vanilla extract, and mix well. Pour the toffee into the prepared pan and let cool completely.

Break the cooled toffee into rough pieces. Using a pastry brush, paint the back of the toffee pieces with the melted chocolate. Place on a sheet of parchment paper to cool. (The toffee will keep in an airtight container for up to 3 days.)

Preheat the oven to 350°.

continued on page 255

continued from page 253

To assemble the cake, coarsely chop enough of the toffee to make 2 cups; break the remaining toffee into larger pieces and reserve for garnish. Place one layer of the cake on a large plate and top with about a third of the chocolate mousse, spreading it out to the edges. Sprinkle about a third of the chopped toffee over the mousse, and top with another layer of cake. Repeat with the remaining mousse, toffee, and cake, leaving the final layer of cake plain.

Wrap the cake with plastic wrap and refrigerate.

Make the ganache and let cool until thick enough to spread easily. Use it to frost the cake.

Spike the remaining pieces of toffee (that you haven't eaten) on top of the cake.

index

Almonds
-anise biscotti, 144-45
-apricot coffee cake, 168
-coconut meringue cookies, 137
genoise, 27
Italian buttercream, 49
-lemon bread pudding, 188
-orange scones, 159
paste, 6
-peach tart, chocolate-crusted, 113
-praline pastry cream, 250, 252
praline-raspberry napoleons, 250, 252
-raspberry cream cheese pinwheels, 162
sticks, spiced, 123
-strawberry tart, 113
three-nut crust, 76
toasting, 10
and white chocolate cookies with lemon, 126
Angel food cakes, 30
chocolate, 31
coconut, 31
hazelnut, 31
orange, 31
Apples. See also Cider
bread pudding, 188
-caramel egg rolls, 244-45
-caramel-nut tart, 111
crisp, 84
-gingery gingersnaps, 128
pie, 88
pie, maple-bourbon, 89
-rhubarb pie, 98
-sour cream pie, 89
Apricots
-almond coffee cake, 168
cream cheese pinwheels, 162
peeling, 10

Baking powder, 6-7
Baking soda, 6-7
Bananas
coupe, caramelized, 214
cream pie, 99-100
-nut muffins, 164
Berries. See also individual berries
cheesecake, 38
cobbler, 82-83
crisp, 84
gelato, 221
and lemon pound cake, 33
pie, 86
sauce, 63
summer bread pudding, 188
tart, 106
Biscotti
almond-anise, 144-45
orange-hazelnut, 145
white chocolate-pistachio, 145
Black and tan, 181
Blackberries. See Berries
Blueberries. See also Berries
-citrus pie, 87
muffins, 164
Bourbon
blonde brownies, 140
blonde brownie sundaes, chocolate, 141
drunken peaches with white chocolate
mousse, 201
-maple apple pie, 89
-pecan tart with chocolate crust, 115
Brandy
chocolate and brandied dried cherry bread
pudding, 186
hard sauce, 190
Bread. See also Bread puddings
carrot, 170
orange-caramel pull-apart, 171-72
zucchini, 169

Bread puddings
apple, 188
chocolate, 184-85
chocolate and brandied dried cherry, 186
chocolate-raspberry, 185
with hard sauce, 190
hazelnut-white chocolate, 186
lemon-almond, 188
summer, 188
vanilla, 187
Brownies
bourbon blonde, 140
chocolate, 138
double chocolate-cream cheese, 139
mousse cake, 139
sundaes, chocolate-bourbon blonde, 141
tropical rum, 141
Brown sugar buttercream, 53
Buns, pecan sticky, 157
Butter, 7
Buttercream, 48
almond, 49
brown sugar, 53
espresso-shaved chocolate, 53
ginger, 49
lemon, 49
making, 51
mint, 53
quick, 52
white chocolate quick, 53
Buttermilk, 7
Butterscotch crème brûlée, 193

Cakes. See also Angel food cakes;
Cheesecakes; Coffee cakes;
Gingerbread; Pound cakes
almond genoise, 27
brownie mousse, 139
carrot, 40
chocolate, old-fashioned, 16

chocolate buttermilk, 17
chocolate genoise, 27
chocolate mousse, with three-nut crust, 197
chocolate-raspberry, individual, 23
chocolate toffee mousse, 253, 255
chocolate turtle torte, 231–33
citrus-scented, 25
coconut cream, 236, 238
dark and white chocolate-hazelnut, 22
flourless chocolate, 20
flourless dried cherry-chocolate, 22
genoise, 26
German chocolate, 239–40
poppyseed, 25
splitting, filling, and frosting, 19
tips for, 14–15
yellow butter, 24
zucchini, 41
Caramel
  -apple egg rolls, 244–45
  -apple-nut tart, 111
  -apple sauce, 59
  black and tan, 181
  -chocolate-hazelnut bars, 134–35
  coffee cake, 167
  -fig-hazelnut tart, 115
  -orange pull-apart bread, 171–72
  -orange sauce, 171–72
  -pear tart with graham shortbread crust,
    109–10
  pudding, 180–81
  sauce, 58
  -strawberry tart, 111
  -walnut tart, 114–15
Caramelizing, 183
Carrots
  bread, 170
  cake, 40
Cheesecakes
  berry, 38
  chocolate, 39
  mocha-orange, individual, 39

sour cream, 37–38
testing for doneness, 37
Cherries, dried
  brandied, and chocolate bread pudding, 186
  -chocolate cake, flourless, 22
  -chocolate pound cake, 33
  cranberry pie with dried fruit and hazel-
    nuts, 95
  dried fruit cinnamon rolls, 157
  -pear pie, 91
Cherries, fresh
  cobbler, 83
Chocolate. See also White chocolate
  angel food cake, 31
  bittersweet, 7
  black and tan, 181
  bourbon blonde brownies, 140
  -bourbon blonde brownie sundaes, 141
  and brandied dried cherry bread
    pudding, 186
  bread pudding, 184–85
  brownie mousse cake, 139
  brownies, 138
  buttermilk cake, 17
  cake, flourless, 20
  cake, flourless dried cherry-, 22
  cake, German, 239–40
  cake, old-fashioned, 16
  caramelized banana coupe, 214
  cheesecake, 39
  -cherry pound cake, 33
  chip ice cream, mint, 209
  chips, 7
  cookie crumb crust, 77
  cookies, piped, 122
  -cream cheese brownies, double, 139
  cream cheese frosting, 46
  cream pie, 101
  crust, bourbon-pecan tart with, 115
  -crusted peach-almond tart, 113
  dark and white chocolate-hazelnut cake, 22
  espresso coupe, 214

  -espresso doughnuts, 152
  -espresso scones, 159
  ganache, 47
  garnishes, 29
  genoise, 27
  -hazelnut-caramel bars, 134–35
  ice cream, 205
  melting, 8
  meringue cookies, 137
  Mexican mocha ice cream, 206
  Mexican mocha mousse, 197
  -mint sorbet, 219
  mocha pudding, 179
  mocha sorbet, 219
  mousse, 196–97
  mousse cake with three-nut crust, 197
  mousse filling, 57
  -orange crème caramel, 195
  -orange sour cream frosting, 45
  pastry cream, 55
  pâte brisée, 70
  peanut butter everything cookies, 133
  -pear egg rolls, 245
  -pecan crust, 241
  profiteroles, 212
  pudding, 178
  -raspberry bread pudding, 185
  -raspberry cakes, individual, 23
  rocky road ice cream, 206
  sauce, 62
  semisweet, 7
  shaved, and espresso buttercream, 53
  shaving, 8
  shortbread crust, 75
  silk, 241–42
  sorbet, 218
  sour cream frosting, 44
  tiramisu ice cream, 211
  toffee mousse cake, 253, 255
  turtle torte, 231–33
  unsweetened or baking, 7
  whipped cream frosting, 43

Chocolate., *continued*
    and white chocolate chunk cookies, 125
    and white chocolate chunk pudding, 179
    -white chocolate chunk-raspberry
        ice cream, 206
    windowpane cookies, 131
Cider
    caramel-apple sauce, 59
Cinnamon rolls, 156
Cinnamon rolls, dried fruit, 157
Citrus-scented cake, 25
Cobblers
    berry, 82–83
    biscuit topping for, 82
    cherry, 83
    peach-Tuaca, 83
Cocoa powder, 7
Coconut
    -almond meringue cookies, 137
    angel food cake, 31
    -candied ginger shortbread cookies, 143
    cream cake, 236, 238
    cream pie, 101
    crème brûlée, 192
    German chocolate cake, 239–40
    -lime-rum sorbet, 217
    pastry cream, 55
    sorbet, 215
    toasting, 8
    tropical ginger sorbet, 215
Coffee cakes
    apricot-almond, 168
    caramel, 167
    espresso, 166–67
    fruit, 168
Cones, griddle, 224, 227
Cookies. *See also* Biscotti; Brownies;
    Gingersnaps
    almond and white chocolate, with
        lemon, 126
    almond-coconut meringue, 137
    candied ginger-coconut shortbread, 143

chocolate-hazelnut-caramel bars, 134–35
chocolate meringue, 137
chocolate windowpane, 131
dark and white chocolate chunk, 125
meringue, 136
oatmeal, 126
orange-spice glazed, 131
peanut butter, mom's, 132
peanut butter everything, 133
pecan-espresso shortbread, 143
piped butter, 121
piped chocolate, 122
poached pear-pecan bars, 135
rolled sugar, 130
spiced almond sticks, 123
types of, 120
vanilla bean shortbread, 142
Cornmeal crust, 76
Corn syrup, 8
Coupe
    caramelized banana, 214
    espresso, 214
Cranberries, dried
    dried fruit cinnamon rolls, 157
    oatmeal cookies, 126
Cranberries, fresh
    -orange-nut pie, 94
    -pear pie, 91
    pie with dried fruit and hazelnuts, 95
Cream, 8
Cream cheese
    apricot pinwheels, 162
    berry cheesecake, 38
    chocolate cheesecake, 39
    -double chocolate brownies, 139
    frosting, 46
    frosting, chocolate, 46
    individual mocha-orange cheesecakes, 39
    pinwheels, 161
    raspberry-almond pinwheels, 162
    raspberry muffins, 164
    sour cream cheesecake, 37–38

Cream of tartar, 8
Crème brûlée
    butterscotch, 193
    coconut, 192
    lemon-raspberry, 192
    vanilla, 191
Crème caramel, 194–95
    chocolate-orange, 195
    espresso-spice, 195
Crème fraîche, 79
Crisps
    classic topping for, 84
    fruit, 84
    fruit, individual, 85
    oatmeal-nut, 85
Crusts. *See also* Pâte brisée; Pâte sucrée;
    Pie dough
    baking times, 68
    Cappy's, 72
    chocolate cookie crumb, 77
    chocolate-pecan, 241
    chocolate shortbread, 75
    cornmeal, 76
    crumb, 77
    graham shortbread, 75
    making, 68
    orange-pecan shortbread, 75
    shortbread, 74
    three-nut, 76
Custards, tips for, 175–76

Doughnuts
    candied ginger-orange cake, 152
    chocolate-espresso, 152
    frying, 148
    lemon, with vanilla sugar, 155
    raised, 153–54
    raised, glazed with ganache, 155
    spice cake, 149–50
Dreamsicle tart, 117
Drunken peaches with white chocolate
    mousse, 201

E Egg rolls
    caramel-apple, 244–45
    pear-chocolate, 245
Eggs, 8–9
Equipment, 4–6
Espresso
    -chocolate doughnuts, 152
    -chocolate scones, 159
    coffee cake, 166–67
    coupe, 214
    individual mocha-orange cheesecakes, 39
    Mexican mocha ice cream, 206
    Mexican mocha mousse, 197
    mocha pudding, 179
    mocha sorbet, 219
    mocha sour cream frosting, 45
    -orange soufflés, 243
    -pecan shortbread cookies, 143
    -shaved chocolate buttercream, 53
    -spice crème caramel, 195
    tiramisu ice cream, 211

F Fig-hazelnut-caramel tart, 115
Fillings
    chocolate mousse, 57
    white chocolate mousse, 56
Flour, 9
Flowers, sugared, 65
Frostings. *See also* Buttercream
    chocolate cream cheese, 46
    chocolate sour cream, 44
    chocolate whipped cream, 43
    cream cheese, 46
    ganache, 47
    mocha sour cream, 45
    orange-chocolate sour cream, 45
    orange whipped cream, 43
    whipped cream, 42
Fruit, dried
    cinnamon rolls, 157
    cranberry pie with hazelnuts and, 95
    granola, Missy's, 173

Fruit, fresh. *See also individual fruits*
    coffee cake, 168
    crisp, 84
    crisps, individual, 85
    mascarpone tart, 107
    summer scones, 159
    tart, 106

G Ganache, 47
Garnishes, chocolate, 29
Gelato
    berry, 221
    hazelnut, 220
    lemon, 222
    orange-cinnamon, 223
    rose petal and shaved white chocolate, 223
    tips for, 203–4
    vanilla, 221
Genoise, 26
    almond, 27
    chocolate, 27
German chocolate cake, 239–40
Ginger. *See also* Gingerbread; Gingersnaps
    buying, 9
    candied, 9
    -coconut shortbread cookies, candied, 143
    Italian buttercream, 49
    -orange cake doughnuts, candied, 152
    -orange pie with brown sugar meringue, 105
    sorbet, tropical, 215
Gingerbread, 35
    gingery pecan, 36
    pear-lemon, with pear-wine syrup, 36
Gingersnaps
    apple-gingery, 128
    Jenny's great-grandma's, 127
    -mascarpone sandwiches, 128
Glaze, lemon, 32
Graham cracker crumb crust, 77
Graham shortbread crust, 75
Granola, Missy's, 173
Griddle cones, 224, 227

H Hard sauce, 190
Hazelnuts
    angel food cake, 31
    -chocolate-caramel bars, 134–35
    cranberry pie with dried fruit and, 95
    -dark and white chocolate cake, 22
    -fig-caramel tart, 115
    gelato, 220
    -orange biscotti, 145
    palmiers, 246–47
    -pear scones, 158
    three-nut crust, 76
    toasting, 10
    -white chocolate bread pudding, 186
    -white chocolate ice cream, 211

I Ice cream
    caramelized banana coupe, 214
    chocolate, 205
    chocolate–bourbon blonde brownie sundaes, 141
    espresso coupe, 214
    in griddle cones, 224, 227
    mascarpone, 210
    Mexican mocha, 206
    mint, 209
    mint chocolate chip, 209
    peach, 209
    raspberry-lemon, 209
    rocky road, 206
    strawberry-mascarpone, 211
    tips for, 203–4
    tiramisu, 211
    vanilla bean, 208
    white chocolate chunk–raspberry-chocolate, 206
    white chocolate–hazelnut, 211
Italian buttercream, 48
Italian plum tart, 112–13

Lemon
  -almond bread pudding, 188
  and berry pound cake, 33
  citrus-scented cake, 25
  cream tart, 116
  curd, 64
  curd tart, 105
  doughnuts with vanilla sugar, 155
  gelato, 222
  glaze, 32
  Italian buttercream, 49
  muffins, 164
  -pear gingerbread with pear-wine syrup, 36
  pound cake, 32
  -raspberry crème brûlée, 192
  -raspberry ice cream, 209
Lime
  -coconut-rum sorbet, 217
  curd pie with brown sugar meringue,
      103-4

Macadamia nuts
  tropical rum brownies, 141
Maple-bourbon apple pie, 89
Marshmallows
  mini-, 207
  rocky road ice cream, 206
Mascarpone, 9
  espresso coupe, 214
  fruit tart, 107
  -gingersnap sandwiches, 128
  ice cream, 210
  -strawberry ice cream, 211
  tiramisu ice cream, 211
  white chocolate-hazelnut ice cream, 211
Meringue cookies, 136
Mexican mocha ice cream, 206
Mexican mocha mousse, 197
Milk, 9
Mint
  buttercream, 53
  chocolate chip ice cream, 209

-chocolate sorbet, 219
ice cream, 209
Molasses, 9-10
Mousse
  cake, brownie, 139
  cake, chocolate, with three-nut crust, 197
  cake, chocolate toffee, 253, 255
  chocolate, 196-97
  chocolate silk, 241-42
  filling, chocolate, 57
  filling, white chocolate, 56
  Mexican mocha, 197
  tips for, 176-77
  white chocolate, 199-200
Muffins
  banana-nut, 164
  basic, 163
  blueberry, 164
  lemon, 164
  peach, 164
  raspberry cream cheese, 164
  zucchini, 170

Napoleons, raspberry–almond praline, 250, 252
Nuts. See also individual nuts
  -banana muffins, 164
  -caramel-apple tart, 111
  granola, Missy's, 173
  pâte brisée, 71
  storing, 10
  three-nut crust, 76
  toasting, 10

Oats/oatmeal
  cookies, 126
  -nut crisp, 85
  streusel topping, 78
Orange
  -almond scones, 159
  angel food cake, 31
  blueberry-citrus pie, 87
  –candied ginger cake doughnuts, 152

-caramel pull-apart bread, 171-72
-caramel sauce, 171-72
-chocolate crème caramel, 195
-chocolate sour cream frosting, 45
-cinnamon gelato, 223
citrus-scented cake, 25
-cranberry-nut pie, 94
curd, 64
dreamsicle tart, 117
-espresso soufflés, 243
-ginger pie with brown sugar meringue, 105
-hazelnut biscotti, 145
-mocha cheesecakes, individual, 39
-pecan shortbread crust, 75
-spice glazed cookies, 131
whipped cream frosting, 43

Palmiers
  hazelnut, 246-47
  making, 249
Pastry bag, parchment paper, 61
Pastry cream, 54
  almond-praline, 250, 252
  chocolate, 55
  coconut, 55
Pâte à choux, 212
Pâte brisée, 70
  chocolate, 70
  nut, 71
Pâte sucrée, 71
Peaches
  -almond tart, chocolate-crusted, 113
  drunken, with white chocolate mousse, 201
  ice cream, 209
  muffins, 164
  peeling, 10
  -raspberry pie, 87
  -raspberry scones, 159
  -Tuaca cobbler, 83
Peanut butter
  cookies, mom's, 132
  everything cookies, 133

Pears
  -caramel tart with graham shortbread crust, 109–10
  -chocolate egg rolls, 245
  -cranberry pie, 91
  -dried cherry pie, 91
  -hazelnut scones, 158
  -lemon gingerbread with pear-wine syrup, 36
  -pecan bars, poached, 135
  pie, 90
Pecans
  bourbon blonde brownies, 140
  -bourbon tart with chocolate crust, 115
  butter toffee, 253
  -chocolate crust, 241
  chocolate silk, 241–42
  chocolate toffee mousse cake, 253, 255
  chocolate turtle torte, 231–33
  cranberry-orange-nut pie, 94
  -espresso shortbread cookies, 143
  German chocolate cake, 239–40
  gingerbread, gingery, 36
  oatmeal-nut crisp, 85
  -orange shortbread crust, 75
  -poached pear bars, 135
  rocky road ice cream, 206
  sticky buns, 157
  three-nut crust, 76
  toasting, 10
Pie dough. See also Crusts
  making, 73
  rolling, 81, 93
Pies. See also Crusts; Pie dough
  apple, 88
  apple-sour cream, 89
  banana cream, 99–100
  berry, 86
  blueberry-citrus, 87
  chocolate cream, 101
  coconut cream, 101
  cranberry, with dried fruit and hazelnuts, 95
  cranberry-orange-nut, 94

lime curd, with brown sugar meringue, 103–4
  maple-bourbon apple, 89
  orange-ginger, with brown sugar meringue, 105
  peach-raspberry, 87
  pear, 90
  pear-cranberry, 91
  pear-dried cherry, 91
  rhubarb-apple, 98
  rhubarb-raspberry, 98
  strawberry-rhubarb, 96, 98
Pineapple
  grilled rum-soaked, with warm white chocolate mousse, 199–200
  tropical ginger sorbet, 215, 217
Pinwheels
  apricot-cream cheese, 162
  cream cheese, 161
  raspberry-almond cream cheese, 162
Pistachio–white chocolate biscotti, 145
Plum tart, Italian, 112–13
Poppyseed cake, 25
Pound cakes
  berry and lemon, 33
  chocolate-cherry, 33
  lemon, 32
Profiteroles, 212
Puddings. See also Bread puddings
  black and tan, 181
  caramel, 180–81
  chocolate, 178
  chocolate and white chocolate, 179
  mocha, 179
  tips for, 175–76
  vanilla, 182
Puff pastry, 235, 246
  hazelnut palmiers, 246–47
  raspberry–almond praline napoleons, 250, 252

Raisins
  oatmeal cookies, 126
Raspberries. See also Berries
  -almond cream cheese pinwheels, 162
  –almond praline napoleons, 250, 252
  -chocolate bread pudding, 185
  -chocolate cakes, individual, 23
  cream cheese muffins, 164
  -lemon crème brûlée, 192
  -lemon ice cream, 209
  -peach pie, 87
  -peach scones, 159
  -rhubarb pie, 98
  –white chocolate chunk-chocolate ice cream, 206
Red wine syrup, 78
Rhubarb
  -apple pie, 98
  -raspberry pie, 98
  -strawberry pie, 96, 98
Rocky road ice cream, 206
Rolls
  cinnamon, 156
  dried fruit cinnamon, 157
Rose petal and shaved white chocolate gelato, 223
Rum
  brownies, tropical, 141
  -coconut-lime sorbet, 217
  hard sauce, 190
  -soaked pineapple, grilled, with warm white chocolate mousse, 199–200
  tropical ginger sorbet, 215

Sauces
  berry, 63
  caramel, 58
  caramel-apple, 59
  chocolate, 62
  hard, 190
  orange-caramel, 171–72

Scones
    espresso-chocolate, 159
    hazelnut-pear, 158
    orange-almond, 159
    peach-raspberry, 159
    summer, 159
Shortbread cookies
    candied ginger-coconut, 143
    pecan-espresso, 143
    vanilla bean, 142
Shortbread crust, 74
    chocolate, 75
    graham, 75
    orange-pecan, 75
Sorbet
    chocolate, 218
    chocolate-mint, 219
    coconut, 215
    coconut, spice ice cream sandwiches with,
        217
    coconut-lime-rum, 217
    mocha, 219
    tips for, 203-4
    tropical ginger, 215
Soufflés, espresso-orange, 243
Sour cream
    -apple pie, 89
    cheesecake, 37-38
    frosting, chocolate, 44
    frosting, mocha, 45
    frosting, orange-chocolate, 45
Spices, 10
Sticky buns, pecan, 157
Strawberries. See also Berries
    -almond tart, 113
    -caramel tart, 111
    -mascarpone ice cream, 211
    -rhubarb pie, 96, 98
Streusel topping, 78
Sugar, 10
    caramelizing, 183
    vanilla, 11

Summer bread pudding, 188
Summer scones, 159
Sundaes
    caramelized banana coupe, 214
    chocolate-bourbon blonde brownie, 141
    espresso coupe, 214
Syrup, red wine, 78

Tarts. See also Crusts
    bourbon-pecan, with chocolate crust, 115
    caramel-apple-nut, 111
    caramel-pear, with graham shortbread
        crust, 109-10
    caramel-walnut, 114-15
    chocolate-crusted peach-almond, 113
    chocolate silk, 241-42
    dreamsicle, 117
    fig-hazelnut-caramel, 115
    fruit, 106
    Italian plum, 112-13
    lemon cream, 116
    lemon curd, 105
    mascarpone fruit, 107
    strawberry-almond, 113
    strawberry-caramel, 111
Tiramisu ice cream, 211
Toffee
    mousse cake, chocolate, 253, 255
    pecan butter, 253
Tropical ginger sorbet, 215, 217
Tropical rum brownies, 141

Vanilla, 11
    bread pudding, 187
    crème brûlée, 191
    gelato, 221
    ice cream, 208
    Italian buttercream, 48
    pudding, 182
    quick buttercream, 52
    shortbread cookies, 142
    sugar, 11

Walnuts
    -caramel tart, 114-15
    cranberry-orange-nut pie, 94
    toasting, 10
Whipped cream frosting, 42
    chocolate, 43
    orange, 43
White chocolate, 8
    and almond cookies with lemon, 126
    chunk and chocolate pudding, 179
    chunk-raspberry-chocolate ice cream, 206
    and dark chocolate chunk cookies, 125
    and dark chocolate-hazelnut cake, 22
    -hazelnut bread pudding, 186
    -hazelnut ice cream, 211
    mousse, 199-200
    mousse filling, 56
    -pistachio biscotti, 145
    quick buttercream, 53
    shaved, and rose petal gelato, 223
    tropical rum brownies, 141
Wine syrup, red, 78

Yellow butter cake, 24

Zest, 6, 11
Zucchini
    bread, 169
    cake, 41
    muffins, 170